BINAH VOLUME 3

Jewish Intellectual History in the Middle Ages

The BINAH Series is a publication of
THE INTERNATIONAL CENTER FOR
UNIVERSITY TEACHING
OF JEWISH CIVILIZATION, Jerusalem

Academic Chairman	Nehemia Levtzion
Chairman, Governing Council	Moshe Davis
Associate Editor	Priscilla Fishman
BINAH Series	

co-published with

THE OPEN UNIVERSITY OF ISRAEL,
Tel Aviv

President	Menahem E. Yaari

BINAH VOLUME 3

Jewish Intellectual History in the Middle Ages

Edited by
JOSEPH DAN

BINAH: Studies in Jewish History,
Thought, and Culture

PRAEGER

Westport, Connecticut
London

Library of Congress Cataloging-in-Publication Data

Jewish intellectual history in the Middle Ages / edited by Joseph Dan.
    p. cm.—(Binah ; v. 3)
    Articles translated from Hebrew.
    Includes bibliographical references.
    ISBN 0–275–94777–7 (alk. paper hc).—ISBN 0–275–94778–5 (pb)
    1. Judaism—History—Medieval and early modern period, 425–1789.
  2. Jews—Intellectual life. I. Dan, Joseph. II. Series.
    BM180.J38   1994
    296.3—dc20   93–50086

British Library Cataloguing in Publication Data is available

Library of Congress Catalog Card Number: 93–50086
ISBN: 0–275–94777–7 (hb)
        0–275–94778–5 (pb)

First published in 1994

Praeger Publishers, 88 Post Road West, Westport, CT 06881
An imprint of the Greenwood Publishing Group, Inc.

Printed in the United States of America

The paper used in this book complies with the Permanent
Paper Standard issued by the National Information Standards
Organization (Z39.48–1984).

10 9 8 7 6 5 4 3 2 1

The revitalization of the Hebrew language and culture during this century has led to a florescence of Jewish scholarly activity in Israel, in the United States, and in academic centers throughout the world.

Over the years, Israel's institutions of higher learning have produced a sizable corpus of scholarly monographs in Hebrew. These works have appeared in academic journals, but because of the linguistic barrier, this exciting material has largely been inaccessible to the educated reader in other countries.

The BINAH Series has been developed to bridge this gap. Its focus on Jewish history, thought, and culture seeks to make available to a broad, interested public the fruits of these scholarly studies in Jewish civilization.

To
IRVING AND BERTHA NEUMAN

for their love of learning
and devotion to scholars

A man of understanding who hears
a wise saying commends it and
adds to it.

Ecclesiasticus 21, 16

CONTENTS

INTRODUCTION

The studies in Jewish thought presented in this collection, originally written and published in Hebrew, have been adapted into English in an attempt to bridge the language gap between the English-speaking student of Jewish civilization and the large group of scholars who write and publish in Hebrew.

When European scholars in the early nineteenth century laid the foundations for the scientific, philological approach to Jewish history and culture, the language used for this modern, scholarly, systematic study was German. Later in the last century, a growing number of Jewish scholars began to publish their studies in Hebrew and in English, establishing new centers for Jewish scholarship in England, the United States, and Eretz Israel. The mass emigration of Jews from Europe to America and Israel encouraged this process in the twentieth century and, after the Holocaust, Israel and the United States emerged as the largest centers of Jewish scholarship.

When the Hebrew University of Jerusalem was founded in 1925, it incorporated the Institute of Jewish Studies that had been established the previous year to serve as a center of scholarship in Jewish civilization. This institute grew rapidly, and in the last sixty years some of the most prominent scholars in Jewish Studies have taught therein. Graduates of the Hebrew University played a major role in the establishment of the other universities in Israel—in Tel Aviv, Ramat Gan, Haifa, and Beersheva.

Today, Israel has become the major center of Jewish scholarship and publications in the academic world. At the same time, Jewish Civilization Studies have assumed a growing role in the life of the vast Jewish community in the United States. In the last generation, the importance of these studies has been recognized within the general academic world, and courses in Hebrew and in Jewish civilization are being taught in hundreds of institutions of higher learning in North America and throughout the world.

Thus, two great communities of scholars studying and teaching Jewish civilization emerged, one publishing mainly in Hebrew, and one publishing mainly in English—not to mention the developing scholarship in other areas of the world and in other languages. While the scholars are familiar with each other's languages, their students often are not. An ongoing effort to translate scholarly books and articles from Hebrew to English and other languages has become necessary. The collection presented here is one detail in this large picture.

The BINAH series is designed especially for the undergraduate student in a university, who is taking a general "Introduction to Judaism" course or studying a more specialized area of Jewish civilization. The articles are all adapted from scholarly journals and have not previously been available in English. They are not parts or chapters of books, but present a thesis in its entirety, as intended by the author.

The term "adapted" should be explained. The articles presented in this collection were published in first-rate scholarly journals; they were written by scholars, for scholars, and they often lack explanations of important terms, names, and dates which were assumed to be well known to the readers of the original Hebrew version. On the other hand, the authors often include, especially in the notes, detailed discussions of related scholarly problems that were not directly connected with the main thesis of the article. A straight translation of these papers would present the undergraduate student with so much detail and discussion that the effort of assimilating its contents would be disproportionate to such a student's needs. It was, therefore, decided to present the articles in an adapted form, adding explanations and clarifications where necessary in the body of the paper, and omitting notes and references to side issues. It should be emphasized that each article was carefully read either by the author or, in the case of scholars who are no longer with us, by an expert in the field, to ensure that the adaptation was accurate and true to the content of the original Hebrew text.

While the first two volumes of BINAH focused broadly on Studies in Jewish History and Studies in Jewish Thought, this third book in the series attempts to narrow somewhat the scope of the articles included, and to concentrate on a specific field—in this case, Jewish Intellectual History in the Middle Ages, between the ninth and the sixteenth centuries. The same approach directs the selection of material for the fourth volume, which will be devoted to Jewish Intellectual History in

Late Antiquity. It is hoped that this concentration will be helpful to users of the volumes.

Yet, the purpose of this series is definitely not to produce another set of textbooks or collections of articles on specific subjects; enough of these are published every year. BINAH is dedicated to the presentation of current and classical Hebrew scholarship selected from Hebrew journals and *festschrifts*; the quality of each individual paper is the decisive factor for its inclusion, rather than the search for a comprehensive presentation of a subject. In the present volume only two classical papers are included—those by I. Baer on Rashi and his times, and by José María Millás Vallicrosa on the scientific works of Spanish Jews. The other nine articles represent current research in Hebrew, all published in the last few years. The articles included in this volume merely hint at the wealth of scholarly studies published in Hebrew and should serve to indicate the important potential available for the teaching of Jewish civilization on the undergraduate level.

A further note concerning the selection of the articles is in order. Among the many considerations guiding us, the way a paper presents its subject is a cardinal one. It is very difficult to translate or adapt a paper dealing with a detail, even a very important one; and there is very little hope that such a study will be found helpful in an undergraduate classroom. Rather, we chose papers that present a wider field, portray a particular phenomenon against the background of its period—pointing to its roots and indicating its impact on future cultural, historical, and social developments. We sincerely hope that the best of such articles will find their way into the BINAH series.

1

ROBERT BONFIL

Cultural and Religious Traditions in Ninth-Century French Jewry

The main sources for the understanding of Jewish culture in medieval Europe are, of course, in Hebrew. We have very little information from non-Jewish writers concerning cultural and religious developments within Judaism, especially in the early centuries of that period. One of the relatively rare, meaningful, and reliable descriptions of Jewish religious thought in the works of a Christian theologian appears in the testimony concerning the Jewish faith written by Agobard of Lyons within the framework of a fierce attack against Jews and Judaism. This complex and important document is analyzed in detail in this study.

Anyone seeking to sketch the cultural profile of the Jews of Christian Europe in the Dark Ages, that is, the period up to the eleventh century, is frustrated by the dearth of documentary material available—scraps of information, most of it engraved on stone tablets, a few charters of protection which raise more questions than they answer, dim traces of the sale and purchase of plots of land, remnants of tales imbued with the splendor of ancient times that fire the imagination, and, above all, stereotype allusions to Jewish figures made by Christians whose intentions were not wholly innocent. This darkness is suddenly illuminated, however, by an outburst of literary activity in southern Italy in the ninth century, and in the north and center of that country in the tenth century. From then on, the trickle of information gradually grows to a stream, and it is precisely this sudden "wealth" which

This article was first published in *Studies in Jewish Mysticism, Philosophy and Ethical Literature*, presented to Isaiah Tishby on his 75th birthday, ed. J. Dan and J. Hacker (Jerusalem: The Magnes Press, 1986). The translation/adaptation is by Yael Guiladi.

throws into relief the extreme poverty of the information existing about pre-tenth century times. This very contrast acts as a stimulus to go back to the work done by earlier scholars and re-sift through the scant remains of that period; perhaps we will discover, on the edge of the road paved by pioneers, something they did not perceive.

In this article we will take another look at some of the slanderous remarks made by Agobard, archbishop of Lyons from 814 to 840, against the Jews of that city in the late 830s. Many scholars have pored over them,[1] and if we were to attempt to review them all, this article would take on the dimensions of a book. We will therefore examine only the minimum necessary to support a suggestion which emerges from a rereading of Agobard's comments, namely, that they appear to reflect the cultural character of the Jews of Lyons in his time.

I

Apparently Agobard did not draw his remarks regarding the Jews from the writings of the Church Fathers. Hence, they constitute evidence of information that was supplied to him directly either by Jews[2] or, as seems more plausible, by converts.[3] They touch on three areas that are bound together by a single thread in an attempt to incite the Emperor's hatred of the Jews:[4] the Jews' religious customs that, according to him, are offensive to Christians;[5] their beliefs and opinions that are an insult to the pure conception of the Godhead as held by the bishop; and, lastly, the clearly slanderous remarks made by the Jews against the Christian God.

The difficulty in analyzing these passages—as well as other writings of a similar kind—lies principally in their general nature which discourages attempts to define their content with precision, and therefore reinforces the tendency to dismiss all of them as if they were nothing but a collection of ignorance, half-truths, and hostile propaganda. On the other hand, when an attempt is made at a textual analysis of Agobard's remarks, it becomes clear that they do not constitute a whole, and it seems impossible to point to one text which comprises them all. The natural tendency to identify one detail or another with a corresponding rabbinic text is likely to further complicate the analysis—the problem is strictly related to the more general one of transmission of the talmudic traditions.

For example, Agobard relates that according to the Jews there are seven firmaments, that the second is called "heaven" (*rakia*) and the seventh "skies" (*aravot*) which is where God dwells, as it is said in the Psalms (68:5): "Extol him that rideth upon the skies." But how can we argue that the source of Agobard's remark is the tradition in the Babylonian Talmud (Hagigah 12b), where it is said that according to Resh

Lakish there are seven firmaments? Indeed, this talmudic sage specifies that the second is called *rakia* and the seventh, where God dwells, *aravot* as in the Psalm quoted above; he also explains that the third firmament is called "clouds" *(shehakim)* and there "millstones stand and grind manna for the righteous." Agobard, however, has it that the millstones are supported by the second firmament and that they grind manna for the angels! How, then, can we be sure that it is indeed this particular tradition from the Babylonian Talmud that corresponds to Agobard's words?

Therefore, rather than seeking to acquit ourselves of our task by setting up an "apparatus" for the analysis of Agobard's writings,[6] we should try to draw from them an overall picture in which each detail would occupy its proper place, even if here and there we should be forced to admit that we are unable to find an irrefutable explanation of its origin. In other words, we should look at Agobard's writings in the broadest possible context, seeking to draw a picture incorporating the combined impression of the various elements, although each, taken alone, does not enable us to come to a conclusion regarding its source. Clearly, if we were to isolate each detail and examine it thoroughly before we felt entitled to use it, we would never get around to drawing the composite picture at all.

This approach is admittedly problematic in that it leads us to ask general, perhaps overly broad, questions before we have dealt with details. However, it should not be rejected a priori. First, even if a broad question posed prior to a discussion of details proves irrelevant, this should not prevent the question from being raised. Moreover, the broad questions referred to here are basic to the clarification of the historic portrait of any period. It may well be that the details in our possession cannot answer those questions satisfactorily; nonetheless, nothing should prevent us from raising them. Let us then turn again to the documents in the hope that we will find what we seek in some place which at the outset seemed the most unlikely.

In the light of these preliminary methodological premises, we will now examine Agobard's statements about the Jews and ask two broad questions:

1. If Agobard based his remarks on information acquired from Jews or converts in Lyons, what was the nature of the cultural environment of the Jews of that town in the third decade of the ninth century? Since we have no other information about this, apart from Agobard's writings, can the archbishop's statements be considered valid references to that environment, or are his remarks of so general a nature that, even taken together, they cannot help to form a coherent picture of that environment?

2. If all or at least part of Agobard's remarks together form an or-

ganic whole, do they point to the sphere of influence of one of the two centers that were struggling for supremacy within Jewry at that time—Palestine or Babylon? Indeed, one cannot assume a priori that, at the start of the ninth century, this struggle was over and that throughout the Jewish world the two schools of thought had merged. One must therefore ask to which of the two camps each locality belonged at that time.

Let us now turn to Agobard in our search for a possible answer to these two questions. His remarks concerning the beliefs and opinions of the Jews of Lyons are found in a short passage:

And they say further that their God has concrete form and is distinguished by limbs having concrete contours, and that like us He hears with one organ and with another He sees and with another He speaks or acts; and hence man's body was created in God's image. However His fingers do not bend but are stiff, like those of one who does not do anything with his hands. And, like a terrestrial king, He sits upon a throne, surrounded by four creatures, and a kind of great temple contains Him. He also thinks many superfluous and vain thoughts which become demons, because not all of them reach their aim. And, as has been said, they preach innumerable abominations about their God and they worship such an image, like the images which they have fixed and set up in their hearts, not the real God who is immutable and whom they do not know at all. They also believe that the letters of their alphabet have existed forever, and that before the creation of the world they fulfilled various functions; and therefore they (the Jews) are worthy to stand at the head of this world. And that the written Law of Moses existed for eons of time before the world came into being. And they also claim that there are many lands, many hells and many heavens; one of them they call *rakia* and according to them it supports God's millstones which grind the manna destined as food for the angels, and another is called *aravot* and there, they claim, dwells the Lord, and according to them this is found in the Psalms—"Extol him that rideth upon the skies *(aravot).*" Their God also has seven trumpets, one of which measures a thousand cubits at its center. (E. Dümmler, *Monumenta Germaniae Historica, Epistolarum Tomus* V, Berlin, 1899, pp. 189–90)

According to Agobard, these views held by the Jews deserve to be censured because of the anthropomorphic foundations underlying their conception of the Godhead, and because of the mythological character of the cosmogonic and cosmological conception.

Indeed, Agobard's arguments against the Jews constitute a systematic and coherent expression of his ideological struggle against anthropomorphism in the conception of the Godhead, and against magic which was still held in high esteem among his contemporaries. In fact, the anthropomorphic conception of the Godhead had an obvious bearing on the debate over the worship of images then taking place within the framework of the struggle against the remnants of paganism that were still extant, and the mythological conception of cosmogony and cosmology had a no less obvious relationship to the contemporary debate over magic.[7] Not only did the Jews ascribe a magical role to the Law of Moses and to the letters of the Hebrew alphabet in the creation of the world, but they also held that the magic power of the Hebrew letters (and, one should obviously add, the combinations of words of the Torah) never ended. Had Agobard built his arguments on some kind of scholastic syllogism, he would have presented them in this manner: The Christians are attracted to the heinous belief in magic; the Jews say that the letters of their alphabet (and words of their Torah) have magical power (which they know how to use); hence, close contact between Christians and Jews is likely to increase the Christians' longing for the heinous magic; or, conversely, the longing for magic is likely to encourage close contact between Christians and Jews and their Law and lead to a deterioration in the existing situation. In any event, the Jews' belief in the eternal existence of the Torah prior to the world's coming into being is equivalent to a denial of the Christian principle that the Law of Moses was given for its time and was nullified with the coming of Jesus.[8]

There is no doubt that each of the details which Agobard mentions as a composite group may be found in midrashic literature. In fact, when we apply a suitable "apparatus" to them, we immediately find that most of them are mentioned in the mystical Merkavah and Heikhalot literature[9] including, among other works, the *Shi'ur Komah*, the esoteric doctrine concerning the quasi-bodily appearance of God—as indeed the first scholars who examined Agobard's writings perceived.[10] It is well known that this literary corpus is not uniform. On the one hand, the mystical nature of most of the texts is obvious. On the other, Gershom Scholem, who left an indelible mark on research into early Jewish mysticism, also pointed to the fact that this entire literature is closely linked to midrashic-exegetic literature.

The Merkavah and Heikhalot texts are of two kinds: (1) those of theological and cosmogonic speculation and (2) those dealing with mystical experiences. The mystical experience and reflection on theology and cosmogony have been entwined since mankind's earliest existence and have ever accompanied human thought in the effort to reveal man's place and purpose in creation. Whatever terms are used to express this thinking, and from whatever source the cultural symbols and expressions derive, any effort to distinguish and define a link between the finite and the infinite, the relative and the absolute, the ephemeral and the eternal, will naturally find expression in speculation upon "what is below and what above, what is before and what after." It is in the nature of such speculation that it will attempt to break out of the physical framework and strike out toward the metaphysical. Rational speculation, pursued in categories which draw upon the system of cultural symbols and expressions in which the philosopher's world is anchored, is, in this context, bound to the aim of arousing mystical experience, and there is no immediately definable borderline between these areas.

The world of Jewish philosophers, anchored in the sacred letters and words of the biblical text, is in this respect essentially no different from the world of the Greek philosophers who wrestled with the very same problem since the first pre-Socratic philosophers. When the Jewish and Greek worlds met, terms, concepts, and symbols passed naturally from one culture to the other. Whoever sought to reveal the essence of the Godhead and the paths of the cosmogonic evolution did so "out of a desire to discover the essence and form of the soul, to know its status in the body and in the world, and to understand the relationship between Man and Creation and the Godhead."[11] Hence, Gershom Scholem's fundamental intuition regarding the link between exegetical-midrashic texts and mystical literature is anchored in the immanent ways of the human soul reflecting on itself in categories, terms, concepts, and symbols characteristic of the Jewish people.

The philological approach was most useful to Gershom Scholem and other scholars in discovering threads leading back from the texts, and attesting to the ways of Jewish mysticism, to the world of the midrash which expressed the speculation of Jewish sages in the centuries prior to and immediately following the redaction of the Talmud. However, that same application of comparative philology may lead equally to the identification of crucial distinctions between traditions, even to the point of taking issue with the basic assumption that one is in fact dealing with a single body of literature. Hence, a pressing demand arises to clarify the part played by each of the two great Jewish centers, Palestine and Babylon, in the formation of those traditions, as well as the chronology and concrete historical framework in which that process occurred.[12]

Even though most of the ideas mentioned by Agobard may be found in the Merkavah and Heikhalot literature, the general fashion in which they are expressed, and the problems involved in the analysis of the textual traditions connected with this literature, make it difficult to present an unequivocal characterization of the cultural environment of the Jews of Lyons. The fact that the anthropomorphic descriptions quoted by Agobard correspond to *Shi'ur Komah* ideas is not in itself sufficient to determine that these passages belong to a body of speculation anchored in mysticism, and not in some midrashic-exegetic tradition upon which mysticism also drew. On the contrary, Agobard's writings do *not* point to an esoteric speculative context, since he himself admits that the Jews did not conceal these things but rather displayed them to all as examples of the glory of their forefathers. Indeed, Agobard also admitted that he spoke with the Jews "almost every day" and heard from them "the secrets of their error." On the other hand, one cannot deny the existence of some mystic-magic element, in particular in the meditation on the letters of the Hebrew alphabet, whose practical repercussions Agobard forcefully stressed. However, this component is extremely obscure and cannot be identified with any certainty. It should be emphasized as well that the preoccupation with letters is also to be found in talmudic literature and is not exclusive to Heikhalot mysticism.

Thus, from these passages in themselves, we cannot find an unequivocal answer regarding the nature and roots of the Jewish culture in ninth-century Lyons. We can, however, learn the following from them:

1. We are dealing with a crystallized body of theological and cosmological ideas of the kind found in the Merkavah and Heikhalot literature.

2. These ideas entered the cultural tradition of the Jews of Lyons organically linked one to the other, for we cannot assume that Agobard heard isolated ideas and from them selected and put together for the purposes of his propaganda precisely those elements which are found together in a defined conceptual context as reflected in the Merkavah and Heikhalot literature.[13]

3. This conceptual context was neither esoteric nor occult in nature.[14]

4. It contains clear elements of meditation on letters which is characteristic of mystical meditation but not exclusive to it.

II

With this meager result, we turn to Agobard's other writings concerning the customs and way of life of the Jews. There a surprise awaits us that may perhaps make a significant contribution to our study. In addition to certain items whose general character precludes the possibility of drawing any conclusion from them, Agobard provides a body of information which initially appears to raise more questions than it answers. All this information concerns the ritual slaughter and examination of animals. Agobard writes:

Such is the custom of the Jews: When an animal is to be slaughtered for food, if when this animal is brought it has not been slaughtered with three cuts, or if in its exposed entrails a defect is found in the liver, or if a lung adheres to

the chest wall or is penetrable to inflation, or if the gall-bladder is not found
in it, and so forth—such animals are unclean and are rejected by the Jews and
sold to Christians. They are called by the offensive name "Christian animals."
(Drümmler, op. cit., p. 183)

This passage does not offer clear testimony regarding its source. One
cannot say that it originated in the writings of the Church Fathers,
since students of patristic literature have not found any church texts
dealing with such subjects. It is also difficult to suggest that the archbishop's evidence reflects eyewitness experience, since certain details
are extremely difficult to match with any actual practice. For example,
where do we find that an animal into whose lung air can penetrate is
"unclean" *(taref)*?! Nonetheless, it seems possible to propose a link to a
specific kind of Hebrew text, and consequently to suggest that the Jews
about whom Agobard gives testimony followed the Palestinian tradition. Let us look at the clues which may substantiate this hypothesis.

First, according to Agobard's description, the Jews of whom he was
speaking did not follow the custom of the Babylonian Jews who examined *only* the lungs of animals to establish whether they were *kasher*.
Rather, he lists other signs of impurity that the Jews of Lyons looked
for in the "exposed entrails" of the animal, that is, what the Hebrew
sources term "intestines." (Although it is recorded, regarding the differences between the customs of the Palestinian and the Babylonian
Jews, that "the Jews of Palestine examine eighteen forms of *terefot* [im-
purities]," there is sufficient basis to assume that by talmudic times this
meant only the "intestines," that is, the lung, the liver, and so on.)
The Mishnah in Hullin (3,1) mentions those same three signs to which
Agobard refers—liver, lung, and gallbladder. However, between the
passage about the lung and that regarding the gallbladder, the Mishnah mentions the piercing of the maw (stomach), whereas Agobard
makes no mention of the stomach. Furthermore, the order in which
the organs to be inspected are listed is slightly different. The fact that
Agobard does not mention the stomach makes no difference to our
study, because he did not intend to enumerate all the impurities, but
contented himself with a partial list, adding "and so forth."

As to the different order, it also can be explained quite reasonably.
For instance, one might say that Agobard's wording followed the order
in which each part was examined, and that the archbishop had in fact
occasionally been present in some actual examination of that kind. One
might also presume that the text that he was taught followed a different order. If our assumption that we might be dealing with Palestinian
customs is correct, it should be useful to note at this point that the
Palestinian *terefot* rules, which generally follow the order appearing in
the Mishnah, present a similar difference. Actually, it is not impossible

that such textual variants might reflect local variations regarding the order in which the examination was made. M. Margalioth, who has done important work in this field, already noted on this issue that "the ruling on the gall-bladder came first, in order to attach it to the liver which is connected with it, and is covered by a joint ruling."[15]

A more thorough study of the details of Agobard's writings may well lead to considerable progress in our examination of the nature of the religious rules followed by the Jews of Lyons. According to Agobard, an animal was unfit for eating if "a defect is found in the liver." On this issue, the Mishnah reads: "If the liver was gone and naught remained." From the Babylonian Talmud (Hullin 46a), it is clear that there was disagreement over this ruling. Some scholars said if there remained an "olive's bulk [i.e., a quantity of liver having the volume of an olive] in the region of the gall-bladder" and others "an olive's bulk in the most vital place." In any event, the discussion in the Babylonian Talmud does not refer to the state of the remaining "olive's bulk"—whether it is "sound" or "deficient"—but turns only upon whether or not that volume actually exists. Indeed, that was the ruling given by the early rabbis in the Babylonian Talmud: "If there remains an olive's bulk in the region of the gall-bladder and an olive's bulk in the most vital part, it is *kasher*."

Let us now look at the Palestinian ruling: "If all or almost all of the liver was gone it is unfit, but if a sound olive's bulk remains it is *kasher* on condition that the sound olive's bulk is close to the gall-bladder." This sentence points clearly to the discussion in the Babylonian Talmud and the authoritative decision which specifies one olive's bulk only and in the region of the gallbladder; here, however, the olive's bulk must be sound. The practical significance of the Palestinian ruling is that the examiner had not only to ascertain that the liver was present, but also that it was not defective. This is exactly what Agobard was saying about the liver, contrary to his statement about the gallbladder, namely, that they examine "if the gall-bladder is not found in it."

The manner in which the "gallbladder" is mentioned may add an important detail to the picture that is emerging. The Mishnah says "the gall bladder is pierced" and no more. As against this, the Palestinian ruling specifies:

If the gall-bladder was pierced, even if the perforation was no bigger than the head of a needle, it is unfit, and if it was pierced and the perforation was in the liver and did not spread outside it is *kasher*. And if the gall-bladder was not there, put your tongue in its place. If you have a bitter taste on your tongue it is *kasher*; if not, it is unfit. And if the gall-bladder was pierced and injured, or if the perforation is closed by a scab or by pus, it is unfit. (M. Margalioth, *Hilkhot Eretz Israel min ha-Genizah*, Jerusalem, 1974, pp. 113–14)

From all this it is clear that the Jews of Palestine were more meticulous about the rules pertaining to the gallbladder than would appear from the Mishnah. A reading of the Babylonian Talmud (Hullin 42a ff.) shows that they were also more strict than the Jews of Babylon. From the Babylonian Talmud we do not learn the ruling about the absence of the gallbladder. Moreover, there is even room to assume that the rule about the "pierced gall-bladder" mentioned in the Mishnah is an individual opinion and, in accordance with those who disagree, there is nothing relative to the gallbladder in the rules of examination regarding the eighteen forms of *terefot;* thus, even if the gallbladder is absent the animal is *kasher.* Indeed, many a medieval Jewish scholar followed the Babylonian approach to the absence of the gallbladder, ruled with leniency, and declared the animal *kasher.* However, in the final analysis, the tendency to reject the animal gained ground in accordance with the rule of *terefot* that if an organ is missing, whether through natural cause or by an inflicted wound, the animal is unfit.

Thus, paradoxically, the more stringent Palestinian ruling, as it was recorded by the medieval scholars in *Halakhot Gedolot,*[16] was interpreted with leniency! We may thus infer that examining whether the gallbladder was missing was certainly in accordance with the Palestinian rules; hence, if the Jews of Lyons did in fact proceed with their examination, they were observing the Palestinian rules.

Let us now refer to Agobard's comments about the lung: "(If) a lung adheres to the chest wall or is penetrable to inflation," it is unfit. As it stands, this passage makes no sense. The expression "penetrable to inflation" is certainly parallel to "swells when inflated," and the expression "adheres to the chest wall," in this context, undoubtedly points to the ruling concerning a case where "the lung was pierced but the perforation was covered up by the chest wall" (Hullin 48a). Louis Ginzburg has shown that the question which Rabbi Yehudai and the rabbis of his generation discussed and about which Rabbi Yehudai warned the Palestinian rabbis that they were acting "not according to the law but according to the custom of the apostates," was precisely regarding the lung that was pierced, but the perforation was covered up by the chest wall.

In the Palestinian *terefot* rules, there is an explicit criterion for this: "If part of the windpipe adheres to the ribs and the slaughterer finds it difficult to remove it [the windpipe] and the slime close to the ribs is detached with it, even though the windpipe has a perforation, if it is covered by the slime and can be inflated by blowing [into it], the animal is fit." (Margalioth, op. cit., p. 114)

On the face of it, the terms Agobard used, which are parallel to those of the Palestinian rulings (adheres to the chest wall / is attached to the ribs; penetrable to inflation / inflates by blowing), would seem a clear indication that this is what we are talking about. The problem is that Agobard's conclusion is opposite to the Palestinian rulings: Whereas according to the latter, such animals were *kasher*, according to Agobard, they were unclean! Are we to assume that the practice Agobard is referring to was a Babylonian one, in accordance with Rabbi Yehudai's opinion—in which case we should altogether dismiss our hypothesis as clearly untenable? I would maintain that this is not the case, for it does not stand to logic that a Christian cleric, who is presenting Jewish ways to Christians, would seize precisely upon the sole point of disagreement between Palestinian and Babylonian Jews, and would depict it as characteristic of the entire examination procedure. Of course, one could explain this by saying that this is a first sign of the radical changeover from the Palestinian to the Babylonian rulings, but even this argument appears to me to be ultimately unconvincing. I would rather propose one of the following two explanations:

1. Agobard gives an eyewitness account only of the examination itself. Hence, he is saying that the Jews examine the animal for adhesions in the lung; and, in fact, the first routine act in the examination of the lung is to find out whether this is evidence of a perforation of the lung; the essential element in this examination is whether the lung "inflates when blown into." If this is indeed an eyewitness account, then Agobard simply substituted the term *kasher* with *unfit*.

2. It may well be that Agobard is talking about the rules of examination as he heard of them from a convert to Christianity, who recited to him the rules of *terefot* observed in the environs in terms that were very similar to those of the Palestinian rules. Even if this is so, we must still assume that Agobard substituted *kasher* with *unfit*.

Though in both cases we must make an extremely farfetched assumption, I would prefer it to any other, since it may be coherently linked to the philologic findings already mentioned. Hence, I would conclude, though somewhat hesitantly, that Agobard's words echo a version very close indeed to the Palestinian rules of *terefot* (discovered in the Genizah). If this assumption is correct, we can add this evidence to what we have deduced previously; if not, the question will require further study. In any event, this conclusion would be preferable to the alternative possibility that what Agobard was talking about was a Babylonian custom.

Let us now take a look at what Agobard has to say about Jewish slaughter. As quoted above, he testifies that "when an animal is to be slaughtered for food, if when this animal is brought it has not been slaughtered *with three cuts* [emphasis added] . . . it is unfit."

This passage hardly corresponds with any reality. Who has ever heard of Jewish ritual slaughter "with three cuts"? One way to solve the problem is to emphasize certain of the archbishop's words which at first sight appear superfluous, namely, "this animal is brought." What do these words mean? It might be that the reference here is not actually to the ruling relative to slaughtering, but rather to that relative to meat that has disappeared from sight. Agobard might have heard about such meat, as he heard about all the other things he related, from someone who repeated to him a well-known and accepted custom. In the Babylonian Talmud (Hullin 95a–b) we find: "Rab said, Meat which had disappeared from sight is forbidden" (in case an animal not slaughtered ritually has been substituted for it). Toward the end of the discussion, the question is asked: "[According to this] how could Rab eat meat?" Three answers were given: "Soon [after the slaughtering] so that he did not lose sight of it; or only if it was wrapped up and sealed; or if it bore some distinguishing mark." The text then provides an example of such a distinguishing mark: "Thus Rabbah son of R. Huna used to mark [the meat] with a triangle." Now, the talmudic chain of tradition has it that Rabbah son of R. Huna, though a Babylonian *amora*, was linked directly with the Palestinian tradition.[17]

The distinguishing mark of a triangle (three cuts) mentioned in the Babylonian Talmud as a custom particular to Rabbah son of R. Huna indicates that this custom was worthy of mention, since the majority did not practice it. Given that it is referred to in the context of meat that has disappeared from sight, and in accordance with the opinion of Rab, who himself brought various Palestinian traditions to Babylon, one may infer that the three cuts were the manner in which the Jews of Palestine marked meat in order to ensure that it would not be forbidden if it disappeared from sight. In this case, whoever repeated to Agobard the rules pertaining to slaughter also must have told him about the three cuts as a mark distinguishing slaughtered meat that had disappeared from view.

Agobard reported this in an ambiguous manner ("when this animal is brought"!), as possibly referring to the slaughtering itself, yet also to the identification of ritually slaughtered meat as *kasher* after it has disappeared for a while. The ambiguity might well be rooted in the fact that the information given to him was itself not absolutely clear. Hence, we might have further evidence that the Jewish customs which Agobard reports correspond to the Palestinian traditions. Furthermore, in this particular instance, we would have a trace of a custom that is not mentioned either in the Jerusalem Talmud or in the midrashim, and that would have been preserved in the Babylonian Talmud only as a practice observed by a single individual.

Another way to make Agobard's comments coherent with actual practice would be to assume they meant that an animal slaughtered with three cuts is *kasher;* an animal slaughtered with more than three cuts is unfit. If this be the case, we might be dealing with a rule of the type Eldad the Danite reported.[18] Eldad prohibited slaughter if the knife was moved to and fro more than three times. This is contrary to the Talmud which permits slaughter even "if it took all day." It is not impossible that the rules of Eldad the Danite followed the Palestinian tradition. In any event, a link has already been established between various formulae in the rules of Eldad the Danite and those in *Halakhot Gedolot* where echoes of the Palestinian traditions have been preserved. Hence even in this case, Agobard's words are significant when related to a normative system similar to that applied by the Jews in Palestine.

Thus, without favoring either explanation regarding the question of slaughtering "with three cuts," each of which is plausible in itself, it would appear that the rules of slaughter and examination followed by the Jews of Lyons corresponded to the Palestinian tradition. There are even grounds to assert that Agobard's testimony contains an echo of a certain order of slaughter and examination similar to the Palestinian rules of *terefot* that have not come down to us in their entirety and whose loss we can only regret.[19]

Now that we have shown the plausibility that the traditions of the Jews of Lyons in Agobard's time were indeed Palestinian, we would also like to suggest that Agobard's comments correspond to the contents of the "Life of Jesus." The early version of this work was apparently written in the fifth or even as early as the fourth century. In any case, it was certainly written in an area that was under Palestinian influence during the Byzantine period.[20]

We may thus come to an additional conclusion: unless proof of the contrary is produced, we may suggest that the theological and cosmological views of the Jews of Lyons were rooted in Palestinian tradition. Consequently, it emerges that, to the extent that the mystic-magic strain of meditation on letters mentioned above is evidence of the character of Jewish theological and cosmological thought and that the whole constitutes an organic *Weltanschauung*, then that philosophy is of the type found in the Merkavah and Heikhalot literature, *but is not esoteric,*[21] and its source lies in the Palestinian teaching.

This conclusion has further, far-reaching, consequences. If there is substance to it, then the existence of such a *Weltanschauung* among the Jews in Europe need not have spread through the intermediary of Babylon. On the contrary, the fact that it appears in Lyons, which was certainly under Palestinian influence before the Babylon school had succeeded in gaining supremacy in the Jewish world, as well as the fact that this *Weltanschauung* was not esoteric, is consistent with the assumption (which is gaining acceptance) that the occult dimension was predominant in the area under Babylonian influence, whereas in Palestine, it was the exegetical aspect that predominated.

In other words, if all that has been said until now is correct, our conclusion calls for reconsideration of the generally accepted view that the ideological corpus known as early mysticism, which is reflected in the Merkavah and Heikhalot literature, reached Europe via Babylon.[22] If we assume the unity of the cultural phenomenon at all levels, and if we accept that Agobard's comments reflect a well-defined conceptual corpus, as indicated above, we must conclude that early Jewish mysticism stemmed from the same center that was the source of the normative system followed by the Jews of Lyons, as well as of the body of arguments that they employed in their discussions with the Christians—namely, Palestine.

If this conclusion is correct, it has far-reaching effects on our understanding of the intellectual life of the Jews of Europe in general during the Dark Ages, and of the process of change that took place therein as a result of the rise in influence of the Babylonian center. Clearly, in the struggle of supremacy between Palestine and Babylon, the mystic-magic character of Jewish theology and cosmology anchored in the Palestinian world was among the topics in dispute. Once it became clear to the Jews of Europe that Babylon had gained ascendance (about the end of the ninth century), the theology and cosmology referred to above took the form of occult mysticism and became shrouded in secrecy, disappearing almost completely from the mainstream of overt Jewish intellectual activity in Europe. Yet it continued to exist as an underground current, and surfaced again much later, with the development of the kabbalah.

Needless to say, the mystic-kabbalist tradition as it was formulated at the beginning of the thirteenth century shows considerable differences from that which was common in the ninth. Thus, the statement that Isaiah Tishby made forty years ago still holds true: "The manner in which the interpreters of the *aggadah* used the early mystic literature . . . deserves further discussion." Such a reappraisal will have significance for the study of the cultural history of the Jews of Europe.

NOTES

1. On Agobard and his attitude to the Jews see I. Levi, "Etude sur les juifs de France," in *Rapport au Séminaire Israélite pour 1903;* Th. Reinach, "Agobard et les juifs," *Revue des Etudes Juives* 50 (1905): L. I. Newman, *Jewish Influence on Christian Reform Movements* (New York: Columbia University Press, 1925), 50,

176–77, 399–400; A. L. Williams, *Adversos Judaeos; A Bird's Eye View of Christian Apologiae Until the Renaissance* (Cambridge: Cambridge University Press, 1935), 348–57; S. Katz, *The Jews in Visigoth and Frankish Kingdoms of Spain and Gaul* (Cambridge, Mass.: Harvard University Press, 1937), 66ff; A. Bressolles, "La question juive au temps de Louis le Pieux," *Revue de l'Histoire de l'Eglise de France* 28 (1942): 51–64; A. Bressolles, *Doctrine et Action Politique d'Agobard, Vol. I: Saint Agobard évêque de Lyon 760–840* (Paris: J. Vrin, 1949), 101–19; J. A. Cabaniss, *Agobard of Lyons: Churchman and Critic* (Syracuse, NY: Syracuse University Press, 1953), 63–71; B. Blumenkranz, "Deux compilations canoniques de Florus de Lyon et l'action antijuive d'Agobard," *Revue Historique du Droit Français et étranger* 33 (1955): 227–54, 560–82; B. Blumenkranz, *Juifs et Chrétiens dans le monde occidental, 430–1096* (Paris: Mouton, 1960), (see index s.v. *Agobard*); B. Blumenkranz, *Les Auteurs Chrétiens du Moyen Age sur les juifs et le judaisme* (Paris-la Haye: Mouton, 1963), 152–68; Ch. Verlinden, "A propos de la place des juifs dans l'economie de l'Europe occidentale au IXe et Xe siécle; "Agobard de Lyon et l'historiographie arabe," in *Storiografia e storia; studi in onore di Eugenio Dupre Theseider* (Rome: Bulzoni, 1974), 21–37.

2. See Bressolles, *Doctrine et Action*, 116; Cabaniss, *Agobard of Lyons*, 12; Blumenkrantz, *Juifs et Chrétiens*, 48; (note 1, above). It has been suggested that Agobard could read Hebrew, but this does not seem plausible. See Cabaniss, *Agobard of Lyons*, 11, 67, 117–18.

3. See Blumenkrantz, *Les Auteurs Chrétiens*, 161, n. 40.

4. On the main thrust and general ideological and political background of Agobard's missive, see Reinach, "Agobard et les juifs;" Blumenkrantz, *Juifs et Chrétiens*, 148 ff, 285–86; Blumenkrantz, *Les auteurs chrétiens*, 153–55; Cabaniss, *Agobard of Lyons*, 58–59, 63–71.

5. This is the age-old argument of Haman who, according to the Sages, secretly revealed to Ahasuerus that the Jews "eat and drink and despise the throne. For if a fly falls into the cup of one of them, he throws it out and drinks the wine, but if my lord the king were to touch his cup, he would dash it to the ground and not drink from it." (See Babylonian Talmud, Megillah 14a.)

6. This is a general problem concerning analysis of any text. However, it is not so acute for texts written in a period in which we can reasonably assume that known writings, such as the Babylonian Talmud, were in the hands of the authors, as it is for texts written at a time about which we cannot make such an assumption. Further, even after setting up some kind of "apparatus," there will still remain details for which we cannot find parallels in Jewish sources, neither prior to nor after Agobard's time, such as the evil thoughts of the Godhead. See note 10.

7. This formulation is not meant to imply that Agobard's battle against the worship of images and the practice of magic was exploited in his struggle against the Jews, or that the attack on the Jews was one aspect of a broader context. See the bibliography in note 1.

8. Clearly, this argument is significant if it is directed toward Christians who are drawn in some way to the magical activity of the Jews—one of whose foundations is, according to Agobard, the belief in the existence of the Torah before the world came into being. It is, however, impossible to determine from

Agobard's remarks whether Christians were in fact attracted to the Jews' magical activity or, indeed, if there was any such activity at all. Perhaps this is simply a very sophisticated use of the stereotypical image of the Jew as a sorcerer. In any event, this makes no difference to our study.

9. On that literature, see G. Scholem, *Major Trends in Jewish Mysticism* (New York: Schocken, 1954), 40–79; G. Scholem, *Jewish Gnosticism, Merkabah Mysticism and Talmudic Tradition* (New York: Jewish Theological Seminary, 1965); G. Scholem, *Kabbalah* (Jerusalem: Keter, 1974), 14–21; D. J. Halperin, *The Merkavah in Rabbinic Literature* (New Haven: American Oriental Society, 1980); I. Gruenwald, *Apocalyptic and Merkabah Mysticism* (Leiden: E. J. Brill, 1980); R. Elior, "The Concept of God in Hekhalot Literature," *BINAH 2: Studies in Jewish Thought* (New York: Praeger, 1989).

10. See Reinach, "Agobard et les juifs," cvi; Katz, *The Jews in Visigoth,* 115–16; Blumenkrantz, *Les auteurs* 175; Newman, *Jewish Influence,* 176–77. On the anthropomorphic conception in general, see the literature on *Shi'ur Komah*; J. Dan, "The Concept of Knowledge in the *Shi'ur Komah,*" in *Studies in Jewish Religious and Intellectual History Presented to Alexander Altmann,* ed. S. Stein and R. Loewe (Alabama: University of Alabama, 1979), 67–73.

11. Isaiah Tishby, *Mishnat HaZohar,* vol. 1 (Jerusalem: Hebrew University, 1971; Hebrew).

12. See Gershom Scholem, *Jewish Gnosticism,* 27–40.

13. See Bressolles, *Doctrine,* 114.

14. One should note here that we have yet to focus on the question of whether the Merkavah and Heikhalot literature was occult. It is clear that this literature contains obvious esoteric trends.

15. M. Margalioth has published valuable material from the Genizah about this issue.

16. *Halakhot Gedolot,* a halakhic code compiled probably in the eighth or ninth century, provides a comprehensive and systematic summary of all the talmudic laws. Based on the Babylonian Talmud, it also includes some material from the Jerusalem Talmud and incorporates responsa of the geonim.

17. Gershom Scholem notes this within his discussion of the transmission of mystic traditions from Palestine to Babylon; see *Jewish Gnosticism,* 28. Rabbah son of R. Huna is mentioned in connection with a quarrel with the followers of the *Resh Galuta* (the head of the Babylonian Diaspora) in the course of which he demonstrated his independence, on the basis of the authority vested in him by his father, and in his father by Rab, and in Rab by R. Hiyya, and in R. Hiyya by Rabbi; in other words, on the basis of the line of tradition from which he descended and which linked him directly with the Palestinian teaching.

18. Eldad the Danite was a late-ninth-century Jewish traveler whose legendary adventures were loosely based on the existence of various early medieval Jewish kings and kingdoms in Africa and central Asia. He also published *halakhot* concerning the laws of *kashrut* which resemble traditional talmudic law but seem to show other influences as well.

19. It is my personal conviction that were we to find the beginning part of the Palestinian rules of *terefot,* which is missing, we would also find there an unequivocal explanation of Agobard's comments.

20. On the "Life of Jesus" see E. N. Adler, "Un fragment araméen du Toldot Yéschou, *Revue des Etudes Juives* 62 (1912): 28–37.

21. Cf. note 14.

22. See Gershom Scholem, *Major Trends,* 41. Acceptance of this view would seem to be due to the traditions of Hasidei Ashkenaz who held that their ancestors received their mystic lore from Abu-Aharon who came from Babylon. The discovery of the so-called Scroll of Ahimaaz, containing the genealogy of the Italian family of Ahimaaz ben Paltiel from the ninth to the early eleventh century, brought Abu-Aharon out of the realm of the *aggadah* and added weight to the traditional view, despite the fact that its substance was never examined. Even Gershom Scholem, who, within the framework of a discussion of far-reaching assertions concerning the quality of Abu-Aharon's teaching, emphasized the obvious fact that mysticism existed in southern Italy prior to Abu-Aharon's arrival there, did not, as far as is known, retract his original view; nor did he go into the question of how Merkavah mysticism spread to Italy via Babylon if it was not Abu-Aharon who transmitted it. This is not the place for that discussion. Suffice it to say that our conclusion invites a reappraisal of the traditions concerning Abu-Aharon's arrival in Italy from Babylon.

2

JOSEPH DAN

Kabbalistic and Gnostic Dualism

Jewish mysticism has often been described by scholars of the nineteenth and twentieth centuries as being "gnostic." Sometimes this designation has been meant as a compliment, but more often it was not. The term referred, in most cases, to the kabbalists' concept of evil as an independent divine power, resembling the evil creator found in the works of several gnostic sects. This study is an attempt to analyze the analogy and the nature of the resemblance between these two major mystical schools.

A close link exists between the concept of evil in Jewish mysticism and the problem of the gnostic element in kabbalah and other mystic currents within Judaism. This perception occasionally leads to the indiscriminate equation of gnostic principles in kabbalah with the dualistic conception of reality as a struggle between the divine powers of good and evil—as if this dualism was the sole characteristic of Gnosticism. Thus, Gershom Scholem's designation of *heikhalot* and *merkabah* mysticism as "Jewish Gnosticism" was critically received,[1] primarily on the basis that early Jewish mysticism lacks a dualistic concept of good versus evil. It should be noted, however, that Gnosticism has many other distinguishing characteristics that are equal in importance to the dualistic principle. This article concentrates primarily on a comparison of gnostic dualism with the dualism found in various strata of Jewish mysticism.

Confusion results in part from the complexity and manifold interpre-

This article was first published in *Da'at, Journal of Jewish Philosophy and Kabbalah*, 19 (1987), 5–16. The translation/adaptation is by Dena Ordan.

tations of the term "Gnosticism" as used by scholars without specifying its meaning in a particular context. This article will distinguish between the historical and the phenomenological significance of the term.

Historically, "gnosis" or "gnostic" refers to a concept or trend associated with any of dozens of sects, flourishing in the Orient and subsequently in Europe, from the second to the twelfth centuries. In this context, the contention that early kabbalah is gnostic means, for example, that the early Provençal kabbalists were influenced by the Catharist and Albigensian heresies, or that some of their ideas (not necessarily in the realm of good versus evil, but the transmigration of souls, for example) were borrowed from their gnostic neighbors. *Heikhalot* literature is gnostic if we assume that the depiction of divine powers in *heikhalot* and *merkabah* treatises was influenced by the gnostic doctrine of the *pleroma* and the *aeons*.[2] This sense of the term gnostic ignores specific content to a certain extent, focusing instead on historical ties to phenomena commonly identified as gnostic in the history of heretical Christian sects.

In contrast, gnostic in the phenomenological sense focuses on content rather than history. It assumes the existence of an abstract gnostic type of mysticism, identifiable by such characteristic ideas as the bisexual aspect of God, a dynamic stratified pleroma of divine powers, a myth relating the detachment of part of the divine world and its displacement from its proper place, the saving power of esoteric knowledge (the gnosis), and, of course, the dualism of good versus evil. This is not a historical assessment, but rather a typological evaluation of religious thought. Kabbalah can be said to be gnostic if we find phenomenological similarity between kabbalistic mysticism and a particular gnostic doctrine as understood by the speaker; this does not imply a direct historical influence of Gnosticism on kabbalah. (In this context, no attempt is made to determine whether the kabbalists were subject to external influences, or whether their ideas were the result of internal developments in Judaism in general and Jewish mystical sects in particular.)

These two senses will be dealt with separately in the following discussion, and a distinction will be made between the assumption of historical ties between Gnosticism and Jewish mysticism, and of phenomenological-typological parallels between kabbalistic and gnostic thought-processes. In each case, the evidence must be relevant; historical claims must be based on pertinent historical parallels, while phenomenological arguments must show similarity in the central concerns of Gnosticism on the one hand and Jewish mysticism on the other.

The same distinction applies to the concept of dualism. Dualism in Jewish mysticism is open to historical analysis aimed at uncovering actual contact between Jewish mystics and Gnostics, or to phenomenological treatment, based on similarities between gnostic dualism and Jewish sources (without attempting to establish the existence of historical influence). This methodological distinction will be the guiding principle in the attempt to uncover the relationship between Gnosticism and Jewish mysticism.

GNOSTICISM AND MERKABAH MYSTICISM

Historians have not reached a definite consensus with regard to two basic questions concerning Gnosticism: a) the position of the dualism of good versus evil in gnostic thought in general, and b) the origins of this dualism. The earlier widely-held opinion that dualism, as derived from Persian Zoroastrianism, was the defining characteristic of historical Gnosticism is no longer accepted. Many extant gnostic texts lack clearcut dualistic views, and some important gnostic schools, like the Valentinian, did not assign a central role to the mythological struggle between divine forces of good versus evil. Moreover, the characteristics of Persian religion during the period under discussion are obscure, and it is debatable whether it embraced the extreme dualism found in later Persian sources.[3]

Nevertheless, recent discoveries and extensive study of the Nag-Hammadi texts demonstrate that, between the second and fourth centuries, certain streams of gnostic thought did develop a starkly dualistic myth. (However, this myth was not accepted by all gnostic sects.) At the core of this myth stands a creator—the demiurge—a rebel against the Divine, a satanic force opposed to the Good Deity of the upper realms and to His faithful terrestrial servants, the Gnostics. This myth also often has anti-Semitic overtones, identifying the biblical creator and God of Israel with the demiurge, and the people of Israel, His chosen people, as satanic. The lack of parallels of this extreme dualism among the Oriental religions and the absence of clear sources for this myth imply that it is the product of internal processes within the gnostic sects themselves, nurtured in part by the Christian nature of these sects and partly by the Jewish origin of some of the extreme views described above. The contention that the anti-Semitic nature of gnostic dualism negates the possibility of Jewish origins unfortunately does not hold water. Although not sufficiently verified, the hypotheses linking the emergence of gnostic dualism with the crisis of the destruction of the Second Temple and the appearance of apocalyptic concepts,[4] and/or with the spiritual phenomena found in the Dead Sea Scrolls,[5] remain under consideration.

Examination of the Nag-Hammadi and other gnostic texts has uncovered interesting parallels with *heikhalot* and *merkabah* literature. Although of secondary importance, the motifs are sufficient to prove the existence of a modest interchange of ideas between early Gnostics and Jewish mystics in the talmudic era.[6] In light of this mutual influence, it is significant that Jewish mystics did not adopt the dualistic aspect of Gnosticism even as the mystical school of thought incorporated other characteristic ideas such as a divine *pleroma*,[7] and perhaps the distinction between the Supreme Deity and the demiurge—the God of Genesis *(yotzer bereshit)*.[8]

Heikhalot and *merkabah* literature contain no descriptions of autonomous satanic forces opposing the Divine; rather such forces emerge on a contextual basis as in the "Legend of the Ten Martyrs," where Samael appears as the "Prince of Rome," one of the many princes of the nations who implement Divine will. By no means is he ascribed autonomous status.[9] Similarly, the mystical literature dealing with the story of the Flood, where the appearance of rebellious angelic powers would be natural, lacks independent forces of evil.[10] Moreover, although the conception of "two Divine powers" ascribed to Elisha ben Avuyah (Aher) is clearly dualistic, it relates to two complementary forces, not implacably opposed enemies. Aher's assumption, when he saw Metatron sitting on a throne in the seventh palace, resembling God in every way, that "Indeed, there are two Divine powers in Heaven!" is based on Metatron's similarity to God, not his disparity.[11] Furthermore, although early Jewish esoteric literature emerged in a historical environment containing strong dualistic elements, and dealt with ideational contexts in which such dualism would be apposite, our extant texts show not the slightest evidence of dualism. Thus, even if we postulate the existence of unpreserved texts and/or a suppressed stratum of radical Jewish mysticism—inferred from the polemical nature of certain aspects of extant *heikhalot* literature—our sources indicate that the dualism which opposed the God of Genesis to the Supreme Deity contained no ascription to the realm of good or evil.

No polemic against the dualism of good versus evil appears in *heikhalot* or *merkabah* literature; evidently, this train of speculation was foreign to its worldview. Thus, if Scholem's designation of this literature as gnostic is apt, it must have another basis. Scholem grounded his view mainly on phenomenological similarities (while suggesting interesting historical parallels as well), but gnostic dualism was not one of them. It is historically clear that even if Jewish mystics were familiar with gnostic dualism, their unequivocal rejection of this idea completely obviated the need to deal with it. (It may be suggested that, conversely, gnostic dualism can be seen as an offshoot of the Jewish concept of "two Divine powers;" this possibility does not, however, change the historical evidence regarding the attitude of Jewish mysticism to gnostic dualism.

SEFER HABAHIR

Medieval Jewish mysticism developed from earlier forms of Jewish mysticism, the *ma'aseh merkabah* and *ma'aseh bereshit*.[12] The combination of ideas from both *heikhalot* and *shi'ur komah* mysticism and *Sefer Yetzirah*[13] led to the creation of the kabbalistic doctrine of *sefirot*,[14] whose elucidation was the focus of the esoteric lore of the *hasidei Ashkenaz* of the twelfth and thirteenth centuries.[15] The appearance of dualistic doctrines in medieval Jewish mysticism was a contemporaneous development, because the doctrines bequeathed by early Jewish mysticism contained no hint of dualism.

There is, of course, a possibility that unknown traditional conduits conveyed dualistic ideas to the medieval sages. Even though early Jewish mysticism lacks such concepts, the influence of gnostic sources unknown to us, whether Jewish or gentile, on the early kabbalists is not entirely out of the question. Nonetheless, it should be stressed that even where our sources imply the existence of suppressed traditions, as in R. Eleazar ben Judah of Worms' mystical description of the "Crown called Akhatri'el," or the doctrine of *sefirot* in *Sefer haBahir*,[16] no traces of specifically gnostic dualism are evident. Moreover, the philosophical systems of sources associated with figures like R. Aaron of Baghdad or Joseph ben Uzziel contain no references to a mythological treatment of opposing forces of good and evil. In conclusion, at present we have no evidence that medieval Jewish mystics inherited a gnostic-dualistic myth from ancient sources, Jewish or gentile.

It is a moot point whether the concept of the Deity in *Sefer haBahir* incorporates dualistic elements. The pertinent section of the book (probably based on R. Abraham bar Ḥiyya), a commentary on the primal chaos (Gen. 1:2), appears to be a speculative cosmology. However, the equation of chaos, matter, and evil by the author of *Sefer haBahir* is probably based entirely on known sources, beginning with the midrashic statement linking chaos with evil (*Midrash Rabbah* Gen. 1,9) and extending to R. Abraham bar Ḥiyya's interpretation in *Hegyon haNefesh*.[17] Other passages in *Sefer haBahir* equate evil with the anthropomorphic figure of the Deity, especially his left hand and fingers. Even if *Sefer haBahir* contains overtones of the potency and independent existence of evil, no hint of the existence of a second anthropomorphic divine figure, antithetical to the Deity, is found; the work's anthropomorphism depicts evil as belonging to and purposefully emanating from the Deity, not as an autonomous rebellious force.

Another major passage in *Bahir* links evil with the tradition describing Samael, riding on the serpent, as the prime mover in the "fall from Paradise." (This tradition first appears in *Enoch*, but its most important

Hebrew version is found in chapter 13 of *Pirke de Rabbi Eliezer*.)[18] These bold mythological elements are apparently based on the internal development of known apocalyptic and midrashic motifs. The outstanding exception, *Sefer haBahir* (passage 199), testifies to the existence of the principles of good versus evil, identifying them with the male and female principles in the material world. I believe that both this passage and the passage concerning the "princess who came from afar" (*Bahir* 132) incorporate early gnostic doctrines of good and evil, thereby laying the foundation for the development of a dualistic theory of good and evil in later kabbalah. Nonetheless, the significance of these elements in the doctrines of *Sefer haBahir* should not be overrated, nor does evidence exist that later kabbalists adapted these specific passages in the development of a comprehensive doctrine of evil.

The doctrine of evil in early kabbalah is rooted primarily in the works of three kabbalists: R. Isaac the Blind's statements on evil, particularly his commentary on Amalek (Exod. 17:16), R. Ezra ben Solomon of Gerona's well-known treatise *Etz haDa'at* (The Tree of Knowledge), and Naḥmanides' commentary on the scapegoat (Lev. 16:8). R. Isaac the Blind's commentary exhibits primitive dualistic leanings, but no evidence of external influence. R. Ezra's text, of greater significance, contains a vehement rejection of dualism within the Deity, ascribing the roots of evil to Adam's "original sin." Based on the vehemence of his arguments, which have an almost polemical approach, we can postulate the existence of dualistic concepts not found in extant texts. In my view, it is precisely R. Ezra of Gerona's treatise that provides the earliest evidence of the eruption of forces inherent in kabbalah itself, leading to the formation of a pronounced dualistic mythology of the Divine realm—even if we have no direct knowledge of the exact nature of these trends.

In Naḥmanides' commentary, on the other hand, Samael appears for the first time as a cosmic force, identified with the "spirit of the sphere of Mars" and associated with destructive demonic forces.[19] Although Naḥmanides' comments are obscure, if taken in conjunction with R. Ezra's polemic, they point to the existence of a dualistic trend (albeit partly hidden) in the thought of the Gerona kabbalists. The anonymity of the material hinders the identification of its sources, leaving the scholar to establish through indirect proof that the appearance of dualistic tendencies in kabbalah did not result from historical contact with non-Jewish sources.

Unequivocal mythological dualism first appears openly in the works of R. Isaac ben Jacob haKohen of Soria (in the second half of the thirteenth century), especially in his *Treatise on the Emanations on the Left* and in *Ta'amei Ta'amim*. In other articles,[20] I have attempted to identify the sources utilized by R. Isaac, which ranged from Pseudo-Ben Sira (geonic period) to the works of R. Judah the Pious and R. Eleazar ben Judah of Worms, and to show how their concepts were adapted and transmuted. Examination of sources known to have been used by R. Isaac haKohen indicates that his creation of the myth of the "left emanation" and the hierarchy of the forces of evil is based on texts devoid of such concepts. The sources provided raw material for imagery, but the dualistic aspect was solely R. Isaac's innovation. Moreover, the singularity of R. Isaac's views is heightened by the fact that neither the writings of his brother, R. Jacob ben Jacob haKohen, nor his father, reflect these ideas. R. Isaac's disciple and interpreter, R. Moses ben Solomon of Burgos, minimized dualistic aspects, even in his presentation of the doctrine of the left emanation, *The Left Pillar*. The followers of the "HaKohen brothers" like Todros Abulafia, author of the *Or Zaru'a* similarly obscured the dualistic core of their mentors' thought. R. Isaac's mythical doctrines come into their own only in the *Zohar* (but surprisingly, not in the Hebrew treatises of Moses ben Shem Tov de Leon himself, nor of his colleague, R. Joseph ben Abraham Gikatilla), where R. Isaac's doctrine of the emanation on the left becomes the basis for the powerful myth of the *sitra aḥra* (the "Other Side"—meaning Evil).

THE EMANATIONS ON THE LEFT

Historically and phenomenologically, R. Isaac's doctrine of the left emanation is at the core of any attempt to understand kabbalistic dualism and its relationship to gnostic dualism. Due to the dominant role of the *Zohar*, this was the critical juncture at which the nature of the kabbalistic myth of evil was established, leaving its stamp on all later doctrines. Thus the questions posed earlier are crucial with respect to R. Isaac haKohen: (1) Was his dualism gnostic? (2) If so, did it result from historical contact with Gnosticism? and (3) In the absence of historical contact, can R. Isaac's doctrine be phenomenologically defined as gnostic dualism? Unfortunately, limitations of space do not permit a detailed discussion, but only presentation of essential points.

1. The similarity between the dualism of the left emanation and gnostic dualism is open to interpretation. On the one hand, the depiction of a world ruled by ten demonic forces identifiable by name and by individual characteristics, involved in a dynamic relationship centering on sexual rivalry (the competition between Samael and Ashmodai for Lilith's favors is one example), contains elements strongly resembling the concept of the Archons[21] in the most extreme gnostic doctrines, including the Manichean. Other central motifs paralleling gnostic themes are the never-ending battle of evil against good leading to the exile of the forces of good, and anticipation of the decisive mythic

battle between the Messiah and the forces of evil. It is also notable that in R. Isaac's doctrine, "original sin" does not mark the emergence or the intensification of evil; evil has a fully independent existence prior to creation. Emanations from heavenly forces are the origin of evil, unrelated to man or his deeds. The dissociation between evil and human actions (in sharp contrast to the view of R. Ezra ben Solomon of Gerona) is intrinsically gnostic in and of itself. It is also inimical to Jewish tradition in general, as well as to the Catholic tradition in Christianity.

On the other hand, it can be argued that significant differences separate R. Isaac's doctrine from typical gnostic dualism. For example, evil powers play no demiurgic role in R. Isaac's thought; on the contrary, they defy creation, leading to the destruction of the first worlds.[22] Although R. Isaac's ideas lack clarity, the forces of evil in his works can, nonetheless, be described as antithetical to material existence, with only the final redemption freeing the world from the bonds of evil and establishing the true creation. The conception of Messianism as the redemption of the material world diverges from the gnostic view of redemption as the freeing of chosen individuals from material existence and their unification with the Good Deity, who exists above and apart from the material world. Thus, the absence of the demiurgic aspect from R. Isaac's description of evil distinguishes it in principle from the usual gnostic systems.

Yet another innovative aspect of R. Isaac's thought differentiates it from gnostic doctrines. In his *Treatise on the Emanations on the Left*, R. Isaac links, apparently for the first time in Jewish mystical literature, the adversities of human existence with the forces of evil—for example, attributing rabies and leprosy to the influence of Samael's servants. His dualistic approach divides material reality itself into good and evil without ascribing reality entirely to either the realm of Good or Evil. The world as created by God is essentially good; however, it contains harmful phenomena caused by the activities of evil powers. Apparently R. Isaac here expands the view first expressed by Naḥmanides, a view far removed from the gnostic doctrine of evil as the dominant force in created reality.

Another less strongly stated yet significant difference should also be stressed. Jewish mysticism, as an integral part of Jewish tradition, affirms man's role (including that of the mystic) as the servant of God, King of the universe. Scholem emphasized this element of divine sovereignty in his treatment of *heikhalot* and *merkabah* mysticism; the "descenders to the chariot" *(yordei merkabah)* achieved mystical ecstasy by joining the ranks of the servants of God in the upper realms and by serving God on earth. Normative Judaism in general, and all branches of Jewish mysticism in particular, take divine sovereignty and human devotion for granted—a principle expressed by the centrality of prayer in Jewish mysticism, especially the *kedushah*.[23]

In contrast, in gnosticism the mystic aspires to spiritual-religious freedom from material reality which is enslaved by the forces of evil. Gnostic literature contains no positive descriptions of divine sovereignty, and the aspect of servitude always appears in its negative connotation of bondage to the forces of evil. Gnostic dualism embodies the longing for spiritual freedom; redemption is release. Whereas Judaism, including its mystical aspect and even its starkest dualistic treatises, celebrates the value of human worship of God the creator. The exception to this is the well-known aspect of Sabbateanism.

In summation, while R. Isaac haKohen's dualism is clearly gnostic in nature, his theological doctrines are not identical with gnostic dualism. It is now incumbent on us to establish whether historical contact with Gnosticism shaped the similarities between R. Isaac and gnostic dualism.

2. In his initial study of the doctrines of R. Jacob and R. Isaac haKohen of Castile, Gershom Scholem tended to accept the possibility that gnostic sources influenced the theory of the left emanation. However, it should be noted that this view antedated the crystallization of Scholem's thesis regarding the date of the composition of the *Zohar*. Therefore, he was inclined to interpret the gnostic symbols common to the *Zohar* and to R. Isaac haKohen as resulting from the mutual influence of earlier sources—Scholem then believing that the *Zohar* incorporated many earlier sources and was itself widely known prior to the medieval era—and not as the influence of the thirteenth-century kabbalist, R. Isaac, on that work. Subsequent to his positive identification of R. Moses ben Shem Tov de Leon as the author of the *Zohar*, Scholem did not return to a detailed analysis of the works of R. Isaac haKohen, nor did he examine the question of R. Isaac's sources once the historical-philological structure of the *Zohar* had been established.

With regard to the question of the historical influence of Gnosticism on R. Isaac, the historian cannot argue *ex silentio*. It is impossible to prove beyond the shadow of a doubt that R. Isaac haKohen did not possess additional sources similar to the ones cited in his detailed description of the chain of tradition reaching him, and to his references to the esoteric writings, especially *Heikhalot Zutrati*,[24] from which he ostensibly derived his ideas. Despite the absence of evidence, the contention that R. Isaac may have utilized sources unknown to us, retains its validity. Nonetheless, the weight of the argument turns up not a shred of evidence that R. Isaac haKohen derived his gnostic motifs from sources unknown to us and indicates that these motifs evidently represent his innovations. The strange names and innovative concepts used by R. Isaac are comprehensible within the context of his commentary on traditional sources; for example, the names of the destroyed worlds, *Kam*tiel, *Bel*iel, and *It*tiel are based on the phonemes of Job 22:16 *(kumtu belo eit)*.[25] Where R. Isaac utilized other sources known to us, the manner in which he injected dualism into texts totally lacking such principles is readily apparent.

Historically, R. Isaac haKohen is, in my opinion, the last figure among the formulators of the kabbalistic doctrine of evil for whom the question of the source of his doctrines is relevant. With regard to the subsequent development of the kabbalistic doctrine of evil, the obvious dependence of the *Zohar*, Lurianic kabbalah, and Sabbateanism on the doctrines of R. Isaac and his followers makes this question extraneous. The problem can be presented *a minori ad majus:* If in the case of R. Isaac no historical evidence exists for use of early gnostic sources, then *a fortiori* this is so with regard to the *Zohar*, R. Isaac Luria, and Nathan of Gaza. Rabbi Isaac's doctrine in *Treatise on the Emanations on the Left* amounts to only a few dozen pages, filled with obscurities. In contrast, the broad scope of the *Zohar* and Lurianic kabbalah, with their motifs reappearing in different contexts, facilitates analysis of their origin and development. Moreover, as the historical distance between the development of kabbalah and the flowering of Gnosticism increases, the likelihood of the influence of gnostic sources unknown to us and of contact between kabbalists and adherents of Gnosticism decreases.

Essentially, R. Isaac is the pivotal figure in the formulation of the kabbalistic doctrine of evil. The features added in the *Zohar*, Lurianic kabbalah, and Sabbateanism are secondary to the revolutionary character of the theory of the left emanations in Jewish thought, and there is even less justification for their ascription to external influence. Thus, if R. Isaac's doctrines are thought to be based on the sources known to us, it is farfetched to assume the eruption of gnostic influences in later periods. Consequently, the question of possible contact between R. Isaac haKohen and gnostic sources is crucial for the history of Jewish thought. As seen from the above, I clearly lean towards the view that R. Isaac haKohen's doctrines are an immanent development of pre-kabbalistic thought.

BETWEEN HISTORY AND TYPOLOGY

The third question, namely, the phenomenological definition of R. Isaac haKohen's doctrine of evil, remains to be determined. Scholem certainly defined R. Isaac's doctrine as typologically gnostic, regardless of whether he postulated the existence of historical influence as well. Whereas historical impact is accessible to historical and philological investigation, phenomenological assessment assigns greater weight to the preferences of the scholar. I intend to digress momentarily in order to present a concept pertinent to the understanding of this issue.

Nearly forty years ago, in his article "Paths of Materialistic and Abstract Thought in Kabbalah," Isaiah Tishby demonstrated that kabbalah is subject to cyclical changes between "mythological" and "systematic" tendencies, with the latter displacing the mythological bases to a large extent.[26] Tishby correctly classified the dualistic understanding of evil as a mythological concept, since it represents the most acute mythological aspect of many of the doctrines under discussion. To illustrate the cyclical interchange of trends, Tishby contrasted *Sefer haBahir,* a materialistic myth, with the outstanding abstraction found in the works of R. Azriel of Gerona; the mythological aspect of the *Zohar* with the systematic approach of its interpreters, especially the doctrines of R. Moses ben Jacob of Cordovero; and the extreme mythology of Lurianic kabbalah with the retreat from that approach by later commentators. Time has not detracted from the validity of Tishby's thesis; rather, it has been corroborated.

Building on Tishby's thesis, I wish to add that in the cyclical swing between mythology and abstraction, the dualistic myth in kabbalah does not return to the *status quo ante;* rather, at each stage of development of the kabbalah, the dualistic myth intensifies. The existence of scattered and undeveloped dualistic elements in *Sefer haBahir* is incontrovertible. But, despite R. Ezra of Gerona's subsequent rejection of this dualism, it reappears in more extreme form, first in the works of Naḥmanides, followed by R. Isaac haKohen, and then in the *Zohar,* which now incorporates a mythological struggle between opposing divine forces of Good and Evil, based on sexual rivalry—beginning with a description of Lilith and culminating with the imprisonment of the *shekhinah* by the *sitra aḥra.* This myth met with opposition on the part of fourteenth to sixteenth century kabbalists, first and foremost among them R. Moses ben Jacob of Cordovero. Yet the reemergent myth in Lurianic kabbalah was even bolder. Moreover, if Lurianic kabbalah itself was tempered at the beginning of the seventeenth century, the eruption of Sabbateanism carried the myth to new summits. Rather than a cyclical model, I propose to view the process as cylindrical, with each ring on a higher plane than its predecessor.

The inescapable conclusion is that the gnostic element in the history of the kabbalistic doctrine of evil was not fixed, but rather was dynamic in nature, increasing in potency in proportion to its distance from historical Gnosticism. The dualistic myth of R. Isaac haKohen was intensified by several degrees in the *Zohar,* and in Lurianic kabbalah acquired definite Manichean elements. In Lurianic doctrine, on the one hand, the seeds of divine evil are contained in the pre-creation Deity, thus intensifying the theological basis for dualism. On the other hand, the myth of the fallen sparks awaiting redemption, which played a minor role in early kabbalah, becomes the focal point of that doctrine's mandates for daily life, morality, and observance of the *mitzvot*. Nathan of Gaza's dichotomy between the "light which contained thought" and the "light which did not contain thought" is also clearly gnostic, albeit inversely, since evil plays no demiurgic role. Older gnostic concepts are extended to their logical extreme in the Frankist doctrine of the total domination of the world by evil and in various manifestations of Sabbateanism.

It is precisely the inverse relationship between the phenomenological intensification of the kabbalistic doctrine of evil and increased distance from historical Gnosticism that illustrates the spiritual independence and immanent development of kabbalah on the one hand, and the surprising phenomenological similarity, which increases with time, between later Jewish mystics and the Jewish and gentile mystics of antiquity. If R. Isaac haKohen's doctrine is original, it represents the closest phenomenological parallel in kabbalah to the doctrine of evil espoused by some historical gnostic sects. By analogy, if the Lurianic doctrine of sparks could have evolved without direct gnostic influence, it is within the realm of possibility for R. Isaac haKohen's doctrine of the left emanation to be entirely the result of internal development.

In conclusion, I would like to suggest an entirely hypothetical construct to explain the close phenomenological parallels between kabbalah and gnostic doctrines, and to establish whether they represent separate but parallel developments or the expansion of philosophical elements inherent within the very nature of Judaism itself. Recent studies have indicated that the origins of Gnosticism—or at least of several of its central aspects—are to be found in the period of the destruction of the Second Temple. I suggested above that the source for the evil demiurge found in Gnosticism may be derived from the God of Genesis *(yotzer bereshit)* who complements the Deity in Second Temple Judaism and the succeeding generations—the Jewish doctrine of "two Divine powers" being transformed by the Gnostics into a dualistic mythology of good versus evil.

Perhaps we can contend that the evolution of the doctrine of evil in kabbalah represents the activation of proto-gnostic kernels within Judaism. While these elements developed rapidly within the gnostic sects outside Judaism, within Judaism itself they flowered slowly, in stages, coming to fruition one thousand years later in the doctrines of R. Isaac haKohen, and subsequently in the *Zohar*, Lurianic kabbalah, and in the thought of Nathan of Gaza and Jacob Frank.

Although this hypothesis cannot be summarily dismissed, it lies outside the purview of the historian, who must concern himself with the historical ties between texts and doctrines. The question of whether phenomenological parallels are evidence of hidden meta-historical ties, or emerge from the basic needs of the human soul, must concern the psychologist of religion, not the historian.

NOTES

Additional explanatory notes have been provided by the translator/adapter.

1. Scholem's use of the title "Merkabah Mysticism and Jewish Gnosticism" for a chapter in his book *Major Trends in Jewish Mysticism* aroused little comment upon the book's publication (New York: Schocken, 1941), or upon its 2d edition (1954). However, considerable discussion followed publication of *Jewish Gnosticism, Merkabah Mysticism, and Talmudic Tradition* (New York: Jewish Theological Seminary, 1960). See D. Flusser, "Scholem's Recent Book on Merkabah Literature," *Journal of Jewish Studies* 11 (1960): 59–68; I. Gruenwald, "Knowledge and Vision," *Israel Oriental Studies* 2 (1973): 64, 88–107. *Heikhalot* literature describes the ascent of the mystic through the celestial palaces, while *merkabah* mysticism centers on the mysteries of the divine throne-chariot. Those who achieve the ascent are referred to as *yordei merkabah*, "descenders to the chariot." See *Encyclopaedia Judaica* (hereafter, *EJ*), vol. 10, 479ff.; G. Scholem, *Major Trends in Jewish Mysticism*, 46–47.

2. The gnostic doctrine of the *aeons*, especially as taught by the Valentinians, refers to the group of divine eternal beings that emanated from the Deity and serve as intermediaries between him and the world. On the *aeon* in kabbalah, see *EJ*, vol. 10, 506. The *pleroma* is the fullness of being of the divine life, held in Gnosticism to comprise the *aeons* as well as the uncreated monad or dyad from which they have emerged.

3. See R. C. Zaehner, *The Dawn and Twilight of Zoroastrianism* (London: Weidenfeld & Nicolson, 1961).

4. For the hypothesis linking Gnosticism and the destruction of the Second Temple, see R. M. Grant, *Gnosticism and Early Christianity* (New York: Columbia University Press, 1959), 313ff.

5. For a detailed bibliography and discussion of the relationship between Gnosticism and the Dead Sea Scrolls, see E. Yamauchi, *Pre-Christian Gnosticism* (London: Tyndale Press, 1973), 151–56.

6. See, for example, I. Gruenwald, "Jewish Sources for the Gnostic Texts from Nag-Hammadi," *The Proceedings of the Sixth World Congress of Jewish Studies* 3 (1977): 45–56.

7. In my opinion, the specific terminology applied to the divine powers in *heikhalot* literature—"God of Israel," "Yah, the Lord of Hosts"—and that accompanies the use of "angelic names"—Akhatriel, Zaharriel, etc.—demonstrates the significance of these powers as partners in the divine realm. The later concept that distinguishes between a divine power and a created angel has no relevance in *heikhalot* literature.

8. *Yotzer bereshit*—Creator of the world. For a brief discussion of the *yotzer bereshit* in *merkabah* mysticism, see Scholem, *Major Trends*, 65.

9. For a discussion of the "Legend of the Ten Martyrs," see J. Dan, "The

Concept of History in Heikhalot and Merkabah Literature," *BINAH*, vol. 1 (New York: Praeger, 1989), 47–58.

10. For example, Uzza and Azzael, the angels mentioned in this context in *3rd Enoch* and in other *heikhalot* tracts in connection with the fallen angels, lack independence and bow to the will of God. See H. Odeberg, *3rd Enoch, or The Hebrew Book of Enoch* (New York: Ktav, 1973), 10–13.

11. Odeberg, *3rd Enoch*, 44.

12. *Ma'aseh bereshit* refers to the esoteric traditions focusing on chapter 1 in Genesis.

13. *Shi'ur komah* mysticism, literally the "measure of the body" of God, is the esoteric doctrine concerning the appearance of God in a quasi-bodily form (*EJ*, vol. 14, 1417). *Sefer Yetzirah, The Book of Creation*, is the earliest extant Hebrew text of systematic speculative thought, a mystical discourse on cosmology and cosmogony (*EJ*, vol. 16, 782).

14. *Sefirot* is a fundamental term in kabbalah. It was coined by the author of *Sefer Yetzirah*, to designate the ten primordial or ideal "numbers" (*sefirot*). The term's meaning expanded to denote the ten stages of emanation that form the realm of God's manifestations in His various attributes (*EJ*, vol. 14, 1104).

15. *Ḥasidei Ashkenaz:* a pietist movement in Germany which produced original ethical and mystical thought (*EJ*, vol. 7, 1377–83).

16. On "the Crown called Akhatri'el," see J. Dan, "The Emergence of Mystical Prayer," *Studies in Jewish Mysticism*, ed. J. Dan and F. Talmage (Cambridge, Mass.: Association for Jewish Studies, 1982), 85–120. *Sefer haBahir* is the earliest work of kabbalistic literature and the earliest source that deals with the realm of the *sefirot;* see *EJ*, vol. 4, 96ff.

17. *Midrash Rabba*, trans. H. Freedman (London: Soncino Press, 1951). For an English translation of *Hegyon haNefesh*, see *The Meditation of the Sad Soul by Abraham bar Hayya*, translated with an introduction by Geoffrey Wigoder (New York: Schocken, 1969).

18. For an English version, see *Pirke de Rabbi Eliezer*, translated and annotated by Gerald Friedlander (New York: Sepher-Hermon Press, 1981).

19. For an English version, see Rabbi C. B. Chavel, trans., *Ramban Commentary on the Torah* (New York: Shilo, 1974), Leviticus, 220.

20. J. Dan, "Samael, Lilith, and the Concept of Evil in Early Kabbalah," *AJS Review* 5 (1980): 17–40.

21. See I. Gruenwald, "Jewish Mysticism and Gnosticism," *Studies in Jewish Mysticism*, 42.

22. Based on midrashim relating the destruction of earlier worlds (see, for example, *Midrash Rabbah* 9, 2). G. Scholem writes, "Isaac haKohen taught that the first worlds that were destroyed were three dark emanations, which perished because of the overly concentrated power of strict judgment that they contained" (*Kabbalah* [Jerusalem: Keter, 1974], 123–24).

23. The blessing, based on the verse in Isa. 6:3, which is central in the Jewish daily prayer.

24. *Heikhalot Zutrati*, "The Small Book of the Celestial Palaces," is a *heikhalot* tract whose main speaker is R. Akiva. It contains a detailed description of the world of the "chariot," the ecstatic ascent to that world, and the techniques used to accomplish the ascent.

25. According to R. Isaac haKohen, the previous worlds were evil, and he uses midrashic terms to denote a process of "inverse emanation." See J. Dan, "Samael, Lilith, and the Concept of Evil," 33.

26. See I. Tishby, "Mythological vs. Systematic Trends in Kabbalah," *BINAH* 2: *Studies in Jewish Thought* (New York: Praeger, 1989), 121–30.

3

JOSÉ MARÍA MILLÁS VALLICROSA

The Beginning of Science Among the Jews of Spain

The long period of Jewish cultural development in Spain is regarded as one in which Jews reached an unprecedented position in the forefront of scientific inquiry in the Middle Ages. They contributed meaningfully to the development of medieval science, especially in mathematics, astronomy, and medicine, and also turned their expertise to the understanding of Jewish traditional culture. This study describes the beginning of Jewish contributions to the development of medieval science in Spain, continuing previous achievements in Mesopotamia, and its integration within the cultural and scientific "golden age" in Muslim-ruled Spain.

This article will deal with the first steps taken by the Jews of Spain in the investigation of natural science. The history of Hebrew poetry in Spain, and the origin and birth of the science of Hebrew grammar in that country have been explored. However, we know almost nothing of the beginnings of natural science among the Spanish Jews, even though it is generally agreed that they participated in an active fashion in the dispersion of general knowledge, and of natural science in particular, during the Middle Ages.

In recent years it has become clear that the sciences of medicine and astronomy were widespread among the Jews of the Middle East—in Palestine (especially the Galilee) and in Babylonia—at an early period. Dr. Süssman Muntner proved clearly that the renowned Jewish physician Assaf lived either in Galilee or in Haran (Mesopotamia) in the

This article was first published in *Tarbiz*, 24 (1954): 48–59. The translation/adaptation is by Professor Norman Roth, Department of Hebrew and Semitic Studies, University of Wisconsin (Madison).

sixth century C.E.—and not in the tenth century as Steinschneider thought.[1] But Muntner also suggested that *Sefer Assaf* contains many earlier portions that were possibly written in the second and third centuries; these include the translation of one of the aphorisms of Hippocrates, sections of the *Prognosticon*[2] dealing with the oath of the physician, and references to Greek (e.g., Dioscorides), Syrian and Persian scholars.

It is probable that the book by Assaf was composed in connection with the work of the schools and medical institutes of the city of Jundîshâpûr, the scientific center founded by King Ardashir IV in the middle of the third century,[3] and of the institute of medicine in the city of Mahuza under the direction of the physician Benjamin, mentioned in the Talmud.[4] With the aid of this tradition, the Hellenic-Alexandrian wisdom was preserved, and additions and commentaries were appended, especially by the Nestorian scholars who fled from Byzantium to Haran and Persia, and who engaged not only in the science of medicine, but also in philosophy. Recently, Khalil Georr[5] has proven that the work of the philosophical commentators and translators from Greek to Arabic was preceded by the preparatory activity of the Syrian translators and commentators. They worked in the scientific centers of Edessa, Nisibis,[6] and Jundîshâpûr, and invented many scientific and philosophical terms that were utilized by later Arabic translators.

The continuity of the scientific tradition among the Jews clearly points to their diligent activity during the great scientific period of Baghdad. We find a Jewish translator who assisted the eighth-century astronomer Ya'qûb ibn Târiq in translating into Arabic the ancient books of wisdom of Persia and India, as well as Jewish experts in astronomy and astrology (e.g., Mâshâ'allâh and Ibn Bishr.[7] The Qaraites were also active—for instance, al-Qirqisânî.[8] In the wake of Aristotelian logic, the science of Hebrew grammar was formed, and Sa'adya Gaon, like the Muslim *Mutakallimûn* ("theologians"), was determined to arbitrate between faith and reason.[9] This scientific movement reached the Maghrib (i.e., Northern Africa), and within the Fatimid empire there were many outstanding Jews engaged in the study of medicine and grammar. The most important of these was Isaac Israeli (Isaac Judaeus).[10]

What was the cultural situation in Spain during the eighth and ninth centuries? First, we must distinguish, in all that relates to this period, between Muslim Spain (i.e., al-Andalus) and Christian Spain. Muslim Spain extended over the entire face of the Iberian Peninsula. Only the narrow valleys in the Pyrenees were saved from Muslim inundation, and in these valleys, where they fled to escape the harsh blow of the hand of the Muslims, the Christian dominions carved out a most modest existence. From the beginning, Muslim Spain was not a united or organized state, but rather a disorganized fusion of diverse and opposing elements. The eighth and ninth century in al-Andalus were marked by continual warfare: between Arabs and Berbers, and among the Arabs themselves. The Christians who lived in the midst of the Muslims (the Mozarabes) rebelled, first in Toledo and afterward in Córdoba. The Christians who converted to Islam also frequently rebelled against the central government in Córdoba. How, therefore, is it possible to speak of culture and natural science in that terrible period? Yet, it must be emphasized that, in general, the Muslims displayed tolerance toward the Christians and Jews who dwelled among them throughout this period.

At the end of the ninth century, when the central government in Córdoba grew in strength, and it became possible to engage in cultural matters, Córdoba began to follow in the footsteps of Baghdad and even to rival it. When the excellent Muslim musician Ziryâb—who was forced to flee Baghdad—was invited to come to al-Andalus by the ruler 'Abd al-Raḥmân II, he was greeted by a delegation of welcomers headed by a Jew named Mansûr al-Yahûdî.[11] This incident indicates that good relations existed between the Jews and the Córdoban government, and that there already were Spanish Jews who excelled in cultural activities. This tendency grew stronger during the tenth century, especially in the illustrious days of the Córdoba caliphate.

The cultural situation in the tiny Christian dominions in northern Spain, as in all the countries of Christian Europe, was modest and unpretentious. Only in the Benedictine monasteries was an attempt made to preserve a smoldering coal of the heritage of classical culture. Even in these tiny dominions of Christian Spain, tolerance toward the Jews prevailed. The politics of their princes was generally dependent upon the Frankish government that had granted the Jews living in southern France (Septimania) special privileges and even recognized the transference of these privileges from fathers to sons. This benign and desirable situation for the Jews also existed in Catalonia, which was dependent on Septimania. For instance, when the Frankish king Charles the Bald sent a letter to his subjects in the city of Barcelona, he sent it by the hand of one of his trusted messengers, Juda *hebreus*. The Jewish community of Barcelona, like other communities in Spain, maintained connections with the geonim[12] of Sura; in 875, Rav Amram Gaon sent to the Jews of Barcelona the manuscript of his prayer book. By means of these connections, Eastern culture was able to reach the Jewish communities of Spain.

But only when Muslim Spain became strengthened under the leadership of Caliph 'Abd al-Raḥmân III, who vanquished his enemies and brought peace and tranquility to all his subjects, was it possible for Spain to enter into the special world of culture and knowledge. Córdoba, capital of the western Spanish caliphate, began to rival Baghdad, capital of the eastern caliphate, and even to rise above and obscure it. Hasdai Ibn Shaprut, a Jew, served as *wazîr* (minister) in the service of the Córdoban caliph. Ibn Shaprut was an outstanding scholar, an excellent physician, and the protector and "father" of that entire generation of Spanish Jews—a generation of awakening culture, poetry, and scientific investigation. Hasdai Ibn Shaprut, who bore the honorary title *Nasi* (Prince), encouraged humanistic science—such as Hebrew grammar developed by Menahem b. Saruq and the Hebrew poetry of Dunash Ibn Labrat—and restored talmudic learning at the hands of Rabbi Moses b. Hanokh. He himself undertook investigations into the natural sciences and engaged in research in pharmacology. In Córdoba, Hasdai received King Sancho of Navarre who was ill due to excessive obesity and succeeded in healing him. When the Byzantine emperor Constantine VIII sought a treaty with Caliph 'Abd al-Rahmân, and sent him a special delegation, Ibn Shaprut requested that he be sent the famous book of Dioscorides on pharmacology. A Greek monk, Nicholas, translated this book from Greek to Latin, and Hasdai ordered it translated from Latin to Arabic. All this information was detailed for us by the Jewish historian in Toledo, Abraham Ibn Daud.[13]

There is, however, some doubt as to the reliability of this tradition. It is known that the work of Dioscorides was at least in part translated from Greek to Arabic earlier, in Baghdad; in the eighth century, the well-known Christian translator Hunayn b. Ishâq translated it into Arabic.[14] What, therefore, was the purpose of the translation undertaken by Hasdai? On the other hand, it is impossible to dispute the testimony of the Jewish historian Ibn Daud. It is possible to explain the puzzle in this manner: In the first Arabic translation, which was done in Baghdad, a large number of plants bore strange and unfamiliar names that were impossible to identify in Spain; therefore, another translation was needed. For this purpose, the Greek text, including drawings of the plants, was sent to Córdoba to enable the plants to be identified. Indeed, in the translation of the book of Dioscorides, the translators occasionally use Western (Latin and Berber) names alongside the Arabic names.

In addition to medicine and botany, Hasdai Ibn Shaprut engaged in other natural sciences, such as astronomy. Córdoba was then a great center for the investigation of natural sciences in general, and astronomy in particular. We know that Ibn Shaprut received a special work on astronomy from an Eastern land—written in Arabic—that was divided into three parts: (1) the form of the sphere of the heavens; (2) the calculations of the measurement of this sphere; and (3) the calculation of the path of the stars. Unfortunately, one important detail, the name of the author, is unknown. What was this book and who wrote it? It seems to me that this book conforms by and large to the contents of the majority of Arabic books dealing with astronomy. Usually these books deal first with the form of the earth and the heavens, and end with the calculation of the path of the stars. This general arrangement is found, for example, in books by Muḥammad b. Mûsâ al-Khwâr-izmî[15] and by Abraham bar Ḥiyya.[16] It is also probable that the above-mentioned book included a chapter dealing with the making and use of the astrolabe. It is known that Mâshâ'allâh, a Jewish scholar of Bagh-dad, composed books like these; and the Arabic books of Mâshâ'allâh were known in Córdoba not only among the Muslims and Jews, but also among the Christians. We also know that at the end of the tenth century, a Jewish astronomer in Córdoba, Ḥasan b. Ḥasan, investi-gated the movement of the stars.

I believe that this interest in the sciences, coupled with the good relations that then prevailed among the adherents of the three religions in Spain, which resulted in the participation of Spanish Jews in the cultural awakening that began in Córdoba, illuminate two facets of the cultural life of Spain that until now have not been sufficiently clarified.

First, from the days of Ernst Renan, scholars have held that the translations from Arabic to Latin began in the twelfth century in To-ledo. These translations served to demarcate the division of the cultural history of the Middle Ages into two periods: the early and late Middle Ages. Now we know that such translations antedated this time by at least two hundred years. Charles Haskins, a historian of medieval sci-ence,[17] writes about the first translators of the eleventh and early twelfth centuries who sought to bring into Christian culture, then only beginning to develop, the excellent fruits of Arab wisdom. Haskins mentions scholars such as Hugo Sactalliensis, Petrus Alfonsus, Ade-lard of Bath, who undertook this work in northern Spain, in the Ebro valley, in southern France, or in England. In truth, we are forced to assume—even though we have no direct proof—that in tenth-century Spain, translations from Arabic to Latin had already been done. Fur-ther, it is likely that both Jews and learned monks participated in these first translations.

A small, but very important and old manuscript is preserved in the library of the Archivo de la Corona de Aragón in Barcelona (listed there as No. 225). It dates from the middle or the end of the tenth century[18] and contains a rich collection of treatises on natural science: astron-omy, surveying, and intercalation. Several of these treatises come from a Latin source, the writings of the Benedictine Monk Bede,[19] but sev-eral other treatises are clearly marked by Eastern influence and may indicate an Eastern source. The treatises generally deal with astronomy and surveying, but these sciences are explained and formulated in a practical and utilitarian, rather than formal, manner. The chapters touching on the science of surveying offer practical instructions on how to calculate angles and corners, and how to measure ground; in these calculations, the author has been aided by an astrolabe and/or a quadrant. The longest chapters, devoted to astronomy, deal with the interesting questions of how to construct and use the astrolabe and quadrant. These chapters are arranged in the manner of known Arabic treatises on astronomy: the construction *('amal)* and the craft *(şan'a)*. The first translations from Arabic to Latin referred to these Arabic expressions by the established terms *De mensura* (construction) and *De utilitatibus* (use).

Who is the author, or authors, of all the treatises included in this manuscript? Nowhere is there a hint. The language is Latin, but full of Arabic words; occasionally the translator did not find in Latin a word matching the source, and therefore used an Arabic expression. It is strange that the manuscript contains different versions of the translation of these words. Some are extremely faithful and exact, and are couched in a language and style full of Arabic expressions; others are free translations in a style that is classical Latin with few Arabic expressions. But all these versions have come from one source. Who, therefore, is the author of this source? It is my conjecture that the author is the Eastern Jewish astronomer Mâshâ'allâh, who worked in Baghdad in the ninth century and who exerted considerable and continual influence in Europe throughout the Middle Ages. While the Arabic source of his work on the construction and use of the astrolabe has not been preserved, several translations of it were made during the Middle Ages, not only in Latin but also in English, the latter by the most famous English writer of the time, Chaucer. On the basis of these late translations of the work of Mâshâ'allâh, I examined the anonymous treatises in the manuscript in the Barcelona Archive and came to the conclusion that they give us the first translations into Latin of the book of that Eastern Jewish astronomer. This fact reveals the deep influence of Mâshâ'allâh on the beginnings of natural science in Europe in the middle or end of the tenth century. I venture to say the middle of that century, for this manuscript is not the original but a copy, as is evident from the errors found in it.

The influence of this manuscript on the construction and use of the astrolabe spread throughout Latin Europe during the eleventh century. It is possible to say that, in general, the oldest Latin texts in the libraries of Europe are only copies, free or exact, of the source preserved in the manuscripts of the library of the Ripoll monastery in Catalonia. I have compared a large number of Latin manuscripts of the eleventh and twelfth centuries and discovered complete agreement among them. It is necessary to add that at the end of the tenth century, when the book of Mâshâ'allâh was translated from Arabic into Latin, other treatises on the use of the astrolabe had already been written in Córdoba—for example, the book of Maslama al-Majrîtî and the similar book of his student Ibn al-Ṣaffâr.[20] However, the book of Mâshâ'allâh preceded the other books by a considerable time and, clearly, his influence preceded the influence of these other treatises by at least a hundred years.

Let us now consider who wrote the first Latin translation of the book of Mâshâ'allâh. Understandably, the Christians of Northern Spain, for example Catalonia, were not able to translate Arabic books; only the Christians who lived among the Muslims (the Mozarabes), or the Jews, were capable of translating or of participating in the translation of these scientific works. One may assume that this translation was done for the sake of Christians of northern Spain (Catalonia) and for the wealthy monastery of Ripoll, which needed the science of astronomy and the use of the astrolabe for its practical uses (measuring land, determining the calendar—the beginnings of the year and the months). It is probable that scholars of southern Spain, or men who came from there, took part in this first translation.

The introduction to the Latin translation was written in classical language and lofty style. Who was this translator? I suggest he was the monk Lupitus Barchinonensis,[21] who, according to the testimony of Pope Sylvester II, translated a book on astronomy from Arabic to Latin. I also maintain that in this translation he was aided by a Jew or Mozarab, for the style of the translation as a whole is completely different from that of the introduction, and in one place in the introduction he praises the wisdom of Abraham the Hebrew patriarch who influenced, as it were, the Greeks.[22]

This matter is tied to another question that aroused the attention of several scholars more than forty or fifty years ago, namely, the problem of what was called in German *"Joseph's Frage"* and was connected in turn with *"Gerbert's Frage."*[23] The Benedictine monk Gerbert, who later became Pope Sylvester II, was the first of the Latin scholars of Europe who at the end of the tenth century recognized Arabic wisdom and was able to benefit from it. While he was still young, a pupil in the monastery of Aurillac in France, he traveled to Catalonia to learn natural science, which then was unknown in Latin Europe. It was possible for Gerbert to learn science in Catalonia because, as we have seen, the scholars of the Ripoll monastery already possessed Latin translations from Arabic of the sciences of astronomy and surveying. Gerbert remained in Catalonia for some two years, and then returned to France, to the city of Reims. The new sciences of astronomy and numbers that he had acquired won him recognition and fame throughout Europe. We must note that Gerbert, and his Reims teacher Scholasticus, did not forget his companions in Catalonia. In 984 he wrote Bishop Bonfill in Gerona[24] and requested that he be sent the book of the scholar Joseph on multiplication and division, *De multiplicatione et divisione numerorum, libellum a Joseph Ispano editum.*[25]

Who was "Joseph the Spaniard"—*Joseph sapiens hispanus*—who in the tenth century wrote an excellent book on mathematics, multiplication, and division? Several researchers of the history of arithmetic investigated this question: H. Suter and M. Curtze saw in "Joseph Hispanus" an indication of a Muslim scholar; H. Weissenborn was inclined to assume that he was a Jew, possibly renowned in Barcelona, who was in the service of the Count. But the great historian of mathematics, M. Cantor, negated all efforts to solve this question solely on the basis of the mention of a name by Gerbert in his letters. It is, however, possible to assert that *Joseph sapiens hispanus*, was a Jewish scholar of Spain, in that "Joseph" is a biblical Hebrew name, and not Arabic—in the Arabic language it has the form Yûsuf; and in general, the Arabic writers are mentioned by their family name, or agnomen *(kunya)*. Nor did the Christians use the name Joseph during this period.

It should be emphasized that the book requested by Gerbert is not written in Arabic or Hebrew, but in Latin. It is possible that this was a translation of a practical work of mathematics written by the excellent Arabic author Muḥammad b. Mûsâ al-Khwârizmî, for during the tenth century this book began to exert an important influence in Christian Spain. According to this suggestion, at the request of Gerbert, Joseph was the Latin translator of this book. Thus, we are presented with the possibility that this translator—almost the first in the chain of translators from Arabic—was a Jew from Spain and that his name was Joseph. The fact that the translation was in Latin raises no difficulty, for we know that in Spain there were renowned scholars like Ḥasdai Ibn Shaprut, who knew how to write Latin. In Christian Europe, scholars like Gerbert and his students in Reims—and in the eleventh century in the schools of Lotharingia—felt a compelling need to learn mathematics with the aid of Arabic numerals. In Roman letters, it is impossible to multiply and divide numbers; only with Arabic (Indian) numerals is it possible to carry out these mathematical functions, and even more complicated calculations. In astronomy and in the use of the astrolabe and quadrant, it is similarly necessary to make use of Arabic numerals. Practical issues, it seems to me, were what aided in the development of the new mathematics of Arabic and Indian origin, while the old arithmetic of Boethius was slowly forgotten in Latin Europe.

There are other avenues in the development of natural science in Europe in which it is possible to distinguish traces of Hebrew influence—for instance, in the best-known science at that time, astrology. Generally, the influence of ancient astrology was not felt in Christian Europe of that period. The Church prohibited it and was opposed to all its forms. Until the twelfth century, not a single Latin manuscript of astrology is to be found. The only exceptions are the *Astronomicon* of Manilius and the *Mathesis* of Firmicus Maternus, which were permitted because of the poetic form of both of these books.[26] The introduction to the above-mentioned book on the use of the astrolabe translated by Lupitus expresses explicit and definite opposition to astrology. However, all of the Eastern wisdom of the Greeks and the Muslims was influenced in content by astrology, so that when the Eastern sciences first arrived in Christian Europe, there was no possibility of preventing the study of astrology. In the East, the Hebrew scholars—and some Arabic scholars as well—wanted to determine the relationship between astrology and their religion, and in order to preserve the concept of free will, they postulated that there is a limit to the influence of the stars. These authors determined that the influence of the stars is by permission of God, a mediation of divine power. This was the scientific basis for the work of many Jewish astronomers and astrologers including Mâshâ'allâh. In this form, astrology was accepted in Latin Europe, and it stands to reason that Jewish scholars were involved in its infusion from the East.

In a manuscript of the Bibliotheque National of Paris (No. 17868), undoubtedly written in the tenth century, there is a treatise (ff. 12–22) under the general title *Mathematica Alhandrei*, composed of separate parts, some of which show a very pronounced Hebrew influence.[27] It seems to me that the name Alhandrei is nothing but a transposition of the name of the famous Arabic author Alkindus (al-Kindî), who composed many works on science and astrological influence. However, the *Mathematica Alhandrei* is not an exact translation, but only an epitome, or free synopsis, of astrological problems.

It is interesting that in this Latin collection, the Hebrew names of the twelve zodiac signs and seven planets are recorded. They are transcribed in both Latin and Hebrew letters, except that the scribe of the Paris manuscript wrote the Hebrew letters not from right to left, but from left to right. These are the names of the zodiac signs according to the Latin transcription: *tale, sor, tumin, certan, arie, betula, mozenai, acrau, queset, gidi, deli, dagin.* The order of the planets is similarly transcribed, namely, Hebrew names in Latin letters. It should be noted that the transcription of the Hebrew names in this manuscript is not fixed; the name of the sun is sometimes transcribed *hama* and sometimes *hame;* the name of the planet Venus is sometimes *noga* and sometimes *nuge.* Even if we assume that this treatise shows some influence from Bede, whose book on intercalation also mentions several Hebrew names of stars, the source of the book is nevertheless Eastern.[28] It also includes the astrological theory of twenty-eight "houses" of the moon, and the Hebrew names of all these houses are transcribed, including illustrations of their forms. Clearly, this astrological schema came to

Europe from remote sources, Arabic and Indian, but it is probable that this was through the mediation of some unknown Hebrew translator.[29]

However, not all of the astrological theory in the book *Mathematica Alhandrei* is derived from Arabic and Indian sources. There is a definite foundation in which the signs of a Hebrew source are recognizable. For example, when the author lists the relationship between the first hours of the day or the night for all seven days of the week, and the seven planets, and he distinguishes the "order of the day" *(Ordo diurnalis)* and the "order of the night" *(Ordo nocturnalis)*, he occasionally uses Hebrew words constructed and composed (as in *gematria*)[30] from the first letters of the names of the planets. Since the author states the numerical value of the Hebrew letters, he also lists these according to their alphabetical order. Sometimes the author of the manuscript mentions that his astrological theory comes from an Arabic-Indian source which does not coincide with the Hebrew theory. For example, concerning the "dragons of the moon" *(Nodus Lunaris)*, he says that according to the opinion of Hebrew scholars, there is only one dragon.

This Parisian manuscript contains several matters dealing with astronomy and astrology, partly from an Arabic-Oriental source and partly from a classical source. The translations and material from the Eastern source came to Latin Europe during the tenth century by way of Muslim Spain, probably through the agency of a Jewish scholar who translated the Arabic teaching and added to it some information from a Hebrew source. I hold that the theory of astrology came by way of Spain, since the Hebrew words in the Latin transcription include recognizable expressions peculiar to that land. This work on astrology, *Mathematica Alhandrei*, exerted considerable and continuing influence in Latin Europe. It was preserved in several manuscripts throughout the Middle Ages, sometimes mixed with other similar astrological material. It was also translated into French and English.

We are able to see that with the assistance of these early translators, a particular kind of scientific and cultural atmosphere was created in Christian Europe at the end of the tenth and beginning of the eleventh centuries that enabled scholars to benefit from the fruits of Eastern wisdom. At that time, Christian Europe was only beginning to learn the natural sciences that came to it from the East by way of Spain. Scholars in France, England, and Germany discovered in Spain—both Muslim and Christian—a new center of culture and natural science, a center of richer and more complex knowledge than that found in the collections of Rhabanus Maurus, Bede, Isidore of Seville, etc. The culture of Europe began to turn more and more to Arabic knowledge, and the Jews generally were its translators and disseminators. Precisely at the end of the eleventh century, in the wake of the upheavals and tumults that took place in Muslim Spain, many Jews left and migrated to Christian (northern) Spain, bringing with them the seeds of Arabic culture. In Barcelona, for example, Abraham bar Ḥiyya ("Sabasorda," i.e., *sâḥib al-surṭa*)[31] wrote and also translated from Arabic many works, some of which dealt with philosophy, astronomy, mathematics, and surveying. All these books were intended for Jews and Christians who did not understand the Arabic language. Also living in northern Spain at that time was Moses ha-Sefardi, better known as Petrus Alfonsus. He too traveled to France and England, where he engaged in astronomy and medicine, and translated, or assisted in the translation of, Arabic works on science. At the beginning of the twelfth century, the famous Jewish scholar Abraham Ibn Ezra, from Tudela in northern Spain, traveled through Italy, France, and England. He shone "like the sun at noon," and taught Jewish and Christian scholars the principles of the wisdom of the East. This scientific awakening reached a climax in the translations done in Toledo in the middle of the twelfth and throughout the thirteenth centuries, and aided in the spread of science and culture in Latin Europe.

NOTES

Prof. Millás' original notes have been supplemented by additional bibliographical and explanatory notes by the translator.

1. Süssman Muntner, "The Antiquity of Asaph the Physician and his Editorship of the Earliest Hebrew Book of Medicine," *Bulletin of the History of Medicine* 24 (1951): 101–31.

2. By this title, Muntner apparently refers to the *Prognostica* of Hippocrates. There is a medieval Hebrew translation of this work.

3. See George Sarton, *Introduction to the History of Science* 1 (Baltimore: Carnegie Institute, 1927), 435, on the school there. But Millás made an error here, for the city of Jundîshâpûr was founded by Shâpûr I (241–272), son of Ardashîr, as we know from Tabarî's chronicle. Cf. Edward G. Browne, *A Literary History of Persia* 1, 10, but it is uncertain when the school was founded.

4. Cf. Sanhedrin 99b and Sabbath 133b.

5. *Les catégories d'Aristote dans leur version syro-arabes* (Beirut, 1948). The Hebrew article erroneously has "Geon" as the name of the author. See the definitive study of F. E. Peters, *Aristotle and the Arabs* (New York/London: University Press, 1968).

6. So the translator understands the Hebrew *Nisibiyn* in the text. On this important school, see De Lacy O'Leary, *How Greek Science Passed to the Arabs* (London: Routledge & Kegan Paul, 1949), 66 ff.

7. See *The Fihrist of al-Nadîm*, vol. 2, trans. Bayard Dodge (New York/London: Columbia University Press, 1970), 650–52 on Mâshâ'allâh and Sahl Ibn Bishr. Mâshâ'allâh's *Astrological History* has been translated by E. S. Kennedy and David Pingree (Cambridge, Mass.: Harvard University Press, 1971).

8. See Sarton, *History of Science,* 620, 623, 626 on al Qirqisânî.

9. See Julius Guttmann, *The Philosophies of Judaism* (New York: Holt, Rinehart, 1964), 61 ff.

10. Isḥâq b. Sulayman al-Isrâ'îlî (d. 932) should be distinguished from the later Spanish Jewish astronomer Isaac Israeli. Cf. Sarton, *History of Science,* 639. His *Tratado de las fiebres* was translated by Jose Llamas (Madrid, Barcelona: C.S.I.C., 1945), and his philosophical works by A. Altmann and S. Stern, *Isaac Israeli* (Oxford: Oxford University Press, 1958).

11. He was Abû al Nasr al-Mansûr, a Jewish musician at the court. See Eliyahu Ashtor, *The Jews of Moslem Spain,* vol. 1 (Philadelphia: Jewish Publication Society, 1973), 66–67.

12. These were the heads of the rabbinical academies of Babylon (Iraq), whose legal decisions were binding upon world Jewry.

13. See *Sefer ha-Qabbalah: The Book of Tradition,* ed. and trans. Gerson D. Cohen (Philadelphia: Jewish Publication Society, 1967), Index s.v. Ibn Shaprut.

14. Sarton, *History of Science,* 611.

15. Ibid, 563–64. See also two Hebrew versions of *Ibn al-Muthanna's Commentary on the Astronomical Tables of al-Khwarizmi,* ed. and trans. Bernard Goldstein (New Haven: Yale University Press, 1967).

16. See *Sefer ha-'Ibbur,* ed. Herschell Filipowski (London, 1851), in Hebrew.

17. Charles Haskins, *Studies in the History of Mediaeval Science* (Cambridge, Mass.: Harvard University Press, 1924), 8 ff.

18. J. M. Millás Vallicrosa, *Assaig d'historia des les idees fisiques i matematiques a la Catalunya medieval,* vol. 1 (Barcelona, 1931), 150 ff.

19. Sarton, *History of Science,* 510–11.

20. Ibid, 668, 716; cf. Vallicrosa, *Assaig,* 28.

21. On the possible identity of this writer, see the Note of Harriet P. Lattin in *Speculum* 7 (1932): 58–64.

22. On this legend and its appearance in Jewish sources in Spain, see Norman Roth, "The 'Theft of Philosophy' by the Greeks from the Jews," *Classical Folio* 32 (1978): 53–67.

23. See Millás, *Assaig,* 96 ff.

24. Letter No. 25 in the Havet edition, *Lettres de Gerbert (983–997)* (Paris, 1889).

25. No. 17 in Havet's ed.

26. See Sarton, *History of Science,* 237, 354 on these authors and the works mentioned.

27. Lynn Thorndike, *History of Magic and Experimental Science,* vol. 6 (New York: Columbia University Press, 1953), 710 ff., and Millás, *Assaig,* 246 ff.

28. See Sarton, *History of Science,* 671.

29. The Hebrew text here reads "Arabic translator," but this obviously is a misprint. "Arabic" and "Hebrew" are spelled almost identically in Hebrew.

30. Gematria is a Hebrew term for symbolic letter combinations where the numerical value of the letters reveals hidden meanings.

31. Literally, "minister of police," but generally a title for any court official. Abraham bar Ḥiyya (correctly: Ḥayya) apparently held a post in the Christian government at Barcelona.

4

WARREN ZEV HARVEY

Political Philosophy and Halakhah in Maimonides

After several generations of intensive study, if one tries to categorize Maimoni-dean philosophy in modern philosophical and disciplinary terms, it is still very elusive. It often seems that Maimonides includes everything scholars attribute to him, and much more than that. One of these celebrated problems is the relationship between the concept of halakhah, Jewish traditional religious law, in Maimonides' philosophy, and the political and social laws that seek to an-swer human needs. This study is a fresh attempt to formulate this relationship, based on recent studies of medieval philosophy, both Jewish and non-Jewish.

I

The most striking feature of Maimonides' definition of "divine law" (*al-sharī'a al-ilāhiyya*) in *The Guide of the Perplexed*, Part II, Chapter 40, is its strictly *political* nature. It contains no Jewish, nor even theological or metaphysical, bias (except for the one general presupposition under which knowledge of God is attained through knowledge of nature).

Maimonides' definition of divine law is given in the course of a gen-eral discussion of the subject of political law, *al-sharī'a*. According to this discussion, man's physical existence necessitates social organiza-tion,[1] which in turn requires political laws that impose peace and order upon individuals of different temperaments. The Aristotelian premise that "man is political by nature,"[2] leads Maimonides to the assertion that political law too "enters into that which is natural." Following his assertion that political law is a natural necessity, Maimonides distin-

This article was first published in *Iyyun*, 29 (1980): 198–212. The translation/adaptation is by Sam Friedman.

guished between two types of political law. The first is "nomic law" (*al-sharī'a al-nāmūsiyya*);[3] the second, divine law. While nomic law is defined as a law for the purpose of instituting peace and order in the polity (that is, to fulfill the basic social need that occasioned political law), divine law is defined as a law that is not satisfied with merely instituting peace and order, but also seeks to advance the life of reason as far as possible, "to make man wise, to give him understanding and to awaken his attention, so that he should know the whole of that which exists in its true form," and in that way direct him to knowledge of God. In short, divine law is a political law that is not content to concern itself with the practical realm alone, but concerns itself with the theoretical realm as well. Thus writes Maimonides (*Guide*, II, 40, pp. 383–84):

Accordingly if you find a Law the whole end of which and the whole purpose of the chief thereof, are directed exclusively toward the ordering of the city and of its circumstances and the abolition in it of injustice and oppression; and if in that Law attention is not at all directed toward speculative matters, no heed is given to the perfecting of the rational faculty, and no regard is accorded to opinions being correct or faulty—the whole purpose of that Law being, on the contrary, the arrangement, in whatever way this may be brought about, of the circumstances of people in their relations with one another and provision for their obtaining, you must know that that Law is a nomos. . . . If, on the other hand, you find a Law all of whose ordinances are due to attention being paid, as was stated before, to the soundness of the circumstances pertaining to the body and also to the soundness of belief—a Law that takes pains to inculcate correct opinions with regard to God, may He be exalted in the first place, and with regard to the angels, and that desires to make man wise, to give him understanding, and to awaken his attention, so that he should know the whole of that which exists in its true form—you must know that this guidance comes from Him, may He be exalted, and that this Law is divine.

Availing ourselves of Maimonides' terminology in III, 27 we can express the matter as follows: Nomic law is any political law that concerns itself solely with the welfare and perfection of the body, while divine law is any political law which concerns itself both with the welfare and perfection of the body and with the welfare and perfection of the soul. Perfection of the soul is the true human perfection (the "ultimate perfection") for which perfection of the body is a necessary condition: "[F]or a man cannot represent to himself an 'intelligible' . . . if he is in pain or is very hungry or is thirsty or is hot or is very cold."[4] Thus, of the two types of political law, only divine law leads one to true perfection. Moreover, it is possible to infer from Maimonides' words that nomic law, insofar as it directs man toward a material end, actually *diverts* him from his true perfection. It follows that the promotion of true happiness indeed requires divine law; for man, by nature, needs political law, and the divine law is the only political law that promotes his true happiness. This means that even though true human happiness is a personal matter, its attainment constitutes a political problem.[5] Since man, as a political animal, needs coercive political law, it is important that such law not hinder the attainment of his true perfection but rather lead him to it.

It must be emphasized that for Maimonides, the definitions of divine law and nomic law are based on the *purpose* of the law. Maimonides does not say that every law that comes from God is a divine law; he says something entirely different—that every law which is divine comes from God. Since the definitions are based on the purpose of the laws, they can be used to establish criteria for the evaluation of all laws. Obviously, a nomic law would be considered good if those who obey it live together in moral rectitude and peace, even if all are simple-minded ignoramuses devoid of any knowledge of the theoretical sciences. A divine law would be considered good only to the extent that those who obey it attain a knowledge of "the whole of that which exists in its true form."

Similarly, since the definition of divine law is based on its aim, the determination of whether a particular law is "divine" is not dependent upon any historical or religious faith, but rather upon empirical evaluation: Is this law limited to the physical wellbeing of the polity, or does it also encourage science? It is clear that the distinction Maimonides makes between nomic law and divine law can be used in the examination of every law. One may ask, for instance, if the constitution of the United States or of France is nomic or divine, or if the legal system of the modern State of Israel is nomic or divine.

It should not be at all surprising that Maimonides saw fit to give the concept divine law a patently political definition. He believed that divine law is vital for the promotion of true human happiness. In addition, he believed, following Alfarabi, that such questions as what real human happiness is and how this happiness is attained, fall within the scope of political philosophy. "Politics is the science which bestows upon those who possess it knowledge of true happiness, and shows them the means for achieving it" (*Treatise on Logic*, ch. 14.)

II

The distinction Maimonides makes at the political level between divine law and nomic law parallels his distinction at the level of personal conduct between one who directs all his actions to the intellectual knowledge of God and any other person who directs his actions to other goals.[6] Just as there is an individual who sets intellectual happiness as his ultimate goal and considers material happiness solely as a necessary means for achieving intellectual happiness, so there is political law which sets as its ultimate end the intellectual happiness of those who abide by it, and relates to their material success solely as a necessary means to that end. And just as this man is called divine,[7] so is this law called divine.

However, in Maimonides' thought, the connection between divine law and the divine man or *prophet*[8] who directs all his actions to the intellectual knowledge of God is not merely analogical. It is a general principle in Maimonides that "belief in prophecy precedes belief in the law."[9] This seems to mean that the possible existence of a law whose ultimate goal is the intellectual knowledge of God is dependent on the possible existence of a lawgiver with the same purpose. Similarly, one who directs all his activities to one of the perfections of the body (wealth, health, morality, etc.)—all imaginary ends, that is to say, one who acts not according to reason but according to the *imagination*[10]— will be incapable of making any law other than one which aims at the *imaginary* human end of the welfare of the body.[11] Accordingly, Maimonides remarked in the course of his discussion in II, 40, the makers of the nomic laws are "perfect only in their imaginative faculty."[12]

III

If it was as a political philosopher that Maimonides defined the concept divine law, it was as a Jewish thinker that he claimed that the Law of Moses illustrates the definition perfectly. In the words of the prophet Zechariah (8:19)—"Love truth and peace"—Maimonides saw an expression of the Torah's striving for the improvement of human abilities both in the practical realm (peace) and in the theoretical realm (truth).[13] And if you are inclined to see the *Guide* as the interpretation of Judaism according to political philosophy, you could even say that the sole intention of the entire book is to define divine law, to explain its vital nature for the attainment of true human perfection, to show that the Law of Moses is indeed a divine law and, what is more, that it is the original and authentic divine law—the "true Law . . . which . . . is unique."[14]

The general claim that Mosaic law coincides with the definition of divine law, that is, that it aims for the welfare of both the body and of the soul, is found in III, 27. The chapter begins with a presentation of the characteristics of divine law. The central idea concerns the connection between the aim of the law and the perfection of man: Divine law has a "first aim" and a "second aim," namely, the welfare of the soul and the welfare of the body. These parallel, in reverse order, the "first" perfection and the "ultimate" perfection of man which are, respectively, the perfection of the body and the perfection of the soul. Following these remarks about divine law in general, Maimonides addresses himself to the Law of Moses in particular (*Guide,* III, 27, pp. 511–12):

The true Law then, the Law of *Moses our Master*—has come to bring us both perfections, I mean the welfare of the states of people in their relations with one another through the abolition of reciprocal wrongdoing and through the acquisition of a noble and excellent character. In this way the preservation of the population of the country and their permanent existence in the same order become possible, so that every one of them achieves his first perfection [perfection of the body]; I mean also the soundness of the beliefs and the giving of correct opinions through which ultimate perfection [perfection of the soul] is achieved.[15] The letter of the *Torah* speaks of both perfections and informs us that the end of this Law in its entirety is the achievement of these two perfections. For He, may He be exalted, says: *And the Lord commanded us to do all these statutes [huqqim], to fear the Lord our God, for our good always, that He might preserve us alive, as it is at this day* [Deut. 6:24]. Here he puts the ultimate perfection first because of its nobility; for, as we have explained, it is the ultimate end. It is referred to in the dictum: *For our good always.* I mean the attainment of *a world in which everything is well and [the whole of which is] long.* And this is perpetual preservation. On the other hand, His dictum, *that He might preserve us alive, as it is at this day,* refers to the first and corporeal preservation, which lasts for a certain duration and which can only be well ordered through political association, as we have explained.

The syllogism which results from II, 40 and III, 27 is clear: A law that promotes the welfare of the body and of the soul is a divine law; the Law of Moses promotes the welfare of the body and of the soul; therefore, the Law of Moses is a divine law. This logic is irresistible! Nevertheless, the syllogism is not very convincing. The reader who demands more than patriotic propaganda (the reader, for instance, who learned in I, 71–76, to be wary of the tendentious arguments of the sages of Kalam) would certainly want to know the basis on which Maimonides claims that Mosaic Law promotes the welfare of both the body and of the soul. Is this a scientific conclusion based upon a fair-minded analysis of all the texts? If so, is the analysis limited to the Pentateuch, or does it include the entire Bible and the entire corpus of rabbinic literature? Is it an empirical conclusion based on Maimonides' personal experience with various Jewish communities? Or is it a conclusion based on Maimonides' own rationalistic philosophical interpretations of biblical and rabbinic parables? Perhaps it is based on something else, and perhaps it is based on nothing.

The decisive reason that Maimonides gives for the divine nature of Mosaic Law is, in truth, not to be found in chapter 27. It begins to emerge at the very beginning of chapter 28, as if Maimonides wanted to satisfy the questioning reader immediately, and it is elaborated throughout the remaining chapters of the book. This reason is neither textual nor scientific, not empirical nor even philosophical. It is *halakhic*.

IV

Before dealing with the words of Maimonides at the beginning of III, 28, and the halakhic reason he gives for the divine nature of the Law of Moses, we must make several general remarks about his analysis of the reasons for the commandments (III, 26–49). In these chapters, Maimonides studies the Law of Moses, and his study here treats the *Written* Law, the Pentateuch. At the end of this section he claims to have succeeded in giving the reasons for all the commandments of the Torah except for "a few slight details for which I have not given reasons, even though in truth we have virtually given reasons also for these."

It is obvious that in the chapters on the reasons for the commandments, Maimonides is concerned with showing that the commandments of the Torah direct one to the welfare of the body and the welfare of the soul,[16] and that therefore the Torah is divine. However, to the astonishment and consternation of many readers, Maimonides appears in these chapters more as an anthropologist, sociologist, or student of comparative religion, than as a theologian concerned with the advancement of religious interests. He deals with Mosaic Law as an ancient legal system which is to be understood in the context of its time.[17]

For instance, his hypothesis, in chapter 48, that the commandment "You shall not boil a kid in the milk of its mother" (Ex. 23:19, 34:26; Deut. 14:21) is intended to undermine an idolatrous ritual prevalent in the land at that time, is undoubtedly an interesting social–scientific hypothesis.[18] However, it would not easily convince a Jew of the twelfth, or twentieth, century that strict observance of the laws of milk and meat *(kashrut)*, all based on that commandment, will bring him closer to the "perfection of the body" or the "perfection of the soul." In general, when Maimonides tells his readers that "every commandment or prohibition of the Law whose reason is hidden from you constitutes a cure for one of those diseases [the beliefs and rituals of idol worshippers at that time] which today—thank God—we do not know any more" (III, 49), the words provide no reason for us to believe that Mosaic Law brings *us* closer to the perfection of the body and soul today.

Why did Maimonides take the liberty of analyzing Mosaic Law in social–scientific terms, without favoring theology and without attempting to enhance the facts in order to bring men closer to the service of God? To this question one must answer, first of all, that it is impossible to worship the God of Maimonides by means of lies: "For only truth pleases Him, may He be exalted, and only that which is false angers Him" (II, 47). However, one must say in addition that Maimonides had no reason to be wary of a scientific analysis of Mosaic Law, since, in his eyes, its divinity is, in the last analysis, dependent on the halakhah, not on the outcome of scientific inquiry. His social–scientific study of the reasons for the commandments of the Written Law can certainly give us an idea of how the Torah worked to improve the material and spiritual condition of the Children of Israel in biblical times. However, it is obviously not capable of determining whether or not the Torah is divine *today*.

V

In his remarks at the beginning of chapter 28, to which we now turn, Maimonides clearly alludes to the way in which the divinity of Mosaic Law is based on the discipline of the halakhah. In doing so he presents the justification for what he had said in chapter 27 and prepares the reader for the proper study of the reasons for the commandments.

III, 28 begins with an appeal for the attention of the reader:

Among the things to which your attention ought to be directed is that you should know that in regard to the correct opinions through which the ultimate perfection may be obtained, the Law has communicated only their end and made a call to believe in them in a summary way—that is, to believe in the existence of the Deity, may He be exalted, His unity, His knowledge, His power, His will, and His eternity. All these points are ultimate ends [= rational knowledge of God is the unique ultimate end], which can be made clear in detail and through definitions only after one knows many opinions. With regard to all the other correct opinions concerning the whole of being—opinions that constitute the numerous kinds of all the theoretical sciences through which the opinions forming the ultimate end are validated—the Law, albeit it does not make a call to direct attention toward them in detail as it does with regard to [the opinions forming ultimate ends] [= did not stipulate by name each theoretical science as it stipulated by name the knowledge of God, His unity, etc.] it does this in summary fashion by saying: *To love the Lord* [Deut. 11:13; 19:9; 30:6, 16:20]. You know how this is confirmed in the dictum regarding love: *With all thy heart, and with all thy soul, and with all thy might* [Deut. 6:5]. We have already explained in *Mishneh Torah* ["Basic Principles of the Torah" 2,2] that this love becomes valid only through the apprehension of the whole of being as it is, and through the consideration of His wisdom as it is manifested in it. We have also mentioned there the fact that the Sages, may their memory be blessed, call attention to this notion.

In this meta-halakhic passage, we see how the Law of Moses leads one to the perfection of the soul; this explains why the Law of Moses is not a nomic, but rather a divine law. The Torah is divine because *it calls for the intellectual knowledge of God.* However, we also see in this passage that the Torah calls for the intellectual knowledge of God in a general way only; the commandment by virtue of which the Torah is called divine is not explicitly defined in the Torah! The Torah indeed called for the knowledge of God, but it did not stipulate that this knowledge depends on knowledge of the various theoretical sciences, "the knowledge of the whole of that which exists." While the Torah called for the study of the theoretical sciences, it did not name them or specify their content; it confined itself to the most general commandment to "love God."

But *how do we know* that this poetic command obliges us to study the theoretical sciences? This question too has an answer in the passage before us: *Because Maimonides rules that it is so in the Mishneh Torah!* The obligation is not explicit in the Bible nor in the remark of the sages on this issue, in which Maimonides found support for his ruling. That remark is indeed quoted in the *Mishneh Torah* ("Basic Principles of the Torah" 2, 2), where he writes that he will explain "great principles of the works of the Sovereign of the Universe [= an outline of the theoretical sciences]," that they may serve the intelligent individual as an entryway to the love of God; even as our sages have remarked in connection with the theme of the love of God, "through it you will come to know Him who spoke and the world came into existence." However, the straightforward meaning of this remark in its original context (*Sifre on Deuteronomy*, Va'ethanan, 33) is not that the study of the theoretical sciences leads to the knowledge of God, but rather that turning our attention to the commandments leads to the knowledge of God![19] It thus emerges that, given Maimonides' definition of divine law, the divinity of the Law of Moses found no explicit expression in halakhah until the time of Maimonides.

What is more, it seems that if we examine the history of halakhah, we find that even the *general* call for the knowledge of God, mentioned at the outset of chapter 28, is not unequivocal in the Bible, and that it received no clear halakhic definition until Maimonides defined "I am the Lord your God," "You shall have no other gods beside Me" (Ex. 20:2–3; Deut. 5:6–7) and "The Lord is our God, the Lord is one" (Deut. 6:4) in the *Book of Commandments (Sefer haMitzvot)*[20] and in the first chapter of "Basic Principles of the Torah." In this connection, it is very significant that in the *Guide* III, 36, the chapter that deals with the basic principles of the Torah in the Written Law, there is no mention of the knowledge of God in general nor of any of the three aforementioned verses in particular. Thus, the theoretical laws which direct one to the "perfection of the soul" are made explicit for the first time in the halakhic writings of Maimonides, especially in the "Basic Principles of the Torah" in the *Mishneh Torah*. By virtue of these laws, the Law of Moses expressly and exemplarily fulfills the ultimate goal of divine law as defined in the political philosophy of Maimonides. The bold meta-halakhic conception according to which commandments directed to the intellect are possible, is already cited in the *Eight Chapters* as Maimonides' own private view.[21] In the *Book of Commandments* and, to a greater extent, in the *Mishneh Torah*, this private view becomes established law for all of Israel.

Maimonides, as a halakhic authority, insisted that the theoretical commandments are not only part of the Torah, but are the *basic principles* of the Torah. According to his halakhic approach, Judaism is characterized primarily by its theoretical content, that is to say, by the commandments directed to the intellect.[22] This attitude is prominent, for example, in his halakhic discussions about one who abandons the faith (the heretic) and one who embraces it (the proselyte). In the "Laws Concerning Repentance" 3, 7, he rules, without any explicit halakhic precedent, that "he who says there is but one Creator, yet He is corporeal or has a physical shape" is a heretic. Similarly, in the "Laws concerning Forbidden Intercourse" 14, 2, he rules concerning the education of the proselyte, again without any explicit halakhic precedent: "He should then be made acquainted with principles of the faith, which are the oneness of God and the prohibition of idolatry. These matters should be discussed in great detail."[23]

Maimonides found it necessary to make bold halakhic rulings in order to adapt Mosaic Law not only to the requirements of the perfection of the soul, but also to the perfection of the body. For instance, realizing that there is no systematic ethics either in the Torah or in the writings of the Sages, he made use of the writings of Aristotle and Alfarabi and ruled that Mosaic Law contains an entire moral system inherent in the commandment "And you shall walk in His ways" (Deut. 28:9).[24] On the importance of "Laws concerning Character Traits" in general to the welfare of the body, Maimonides remarks in the *Guide* (III, 35): "It is well known that through fine moral qualities human association and society are perfected, which is necessary for the good order of human circumstances." Further in chapter 38: "The utility of all [the commandments enumerated in 'Laws Concerning Character Traits'] is clear and evident, for all concern moral qualities by virtue of which the association among people is in good condition." It must be noted that of the fourteen chapters (36–49) that deal with the fourteen different groups of commandments in the Torah, chapter 38 dealing with laws concerning character traits is the only one that has no biblical quotation. This undoubtedly hints at the absence of a systematic ethic in the Written Law.

As a political philosopher, Maimonides analyzed Mosaic Law from an external point of view and examined it in the light of his political definition of divine law.[25] Obviously, as a political philosopher, he was powerless to do anything in case his analysis disclosed that, in one respect or another, Mosaic Law did not explicitly coincide with that definition. Yet as a halakhic authority, he was not at all powerless. He could act audaciously and make halakhic decisions so that Mosaic Law could effectively direct man to the perfection of the body and soul.

Maimonides' intention, which is manifest throughout his entire halakhic enterprise and particularly in his great work the *Mishneh Torah*, is to establish the divinity of the Torah. His intense need to do so is expressed in a letter written to Rabbi Joseph ben Judah, the student to whom he dedicated *The Guide of the Perplexed*. In the letter he explains why he wrote the *Mishneh Torah*: "I was zealous for the Lord God of Israel when I saw a nation without a true code of law and without true and precise opinions." A thorough, systematic analysis of the *Mishneh Torah* and his other rulings would certainly show that Maimonides issued his halakhic rulings with the two aims of the divine Law—the welfare of the body and the welfare of the soul—always before him.[26] Such an analysis would also allow us to determine the extent to which he was forced to make halakhic rulings boldly and without explicit precedents.

Needless to say, when I point out that Maimonides made halakhic rulings "without explicit precedents," I am not suggesting that these rulings are based on misrepresentation or arbitrariness. No one contests the fact that Maimonides was a great halakhic authority, perhaps the greatest since the time of the Talmud, and that his halakhic rulings are based upon amazingly intimate knowledge of the entire corpus of rabbinic literature and on excellent halakhic methodology. I am convinced that, even in situations where he made rulings audaciously and without explicit precedent, he always had some references in the halakhic literature in mind, as is evident from the traditional commentaries on the *Mishneh Torah*.

To conclude: The Law of Moses, according to Maimonides, is a divine law *by virtue of the halakhah*. As a halakhic authority, Maimonides was zealous for the Lord God of Israel, and acted so that Mosaic Law would be a divine law in the full sense of the term, as defined in his political philosophy. From this we may conclude that the statement "The Law of Moses is divine" is, according to Maimonides, no less prescriptive than descriptive.

VI

From all that has been said thus far, it is clear that Maimonides, the halakhic judge, was the executive arm of Maimonides, the political philosopher. The latter defined divine law, the former worked to adapt the Law of Moses to this definition. In general one can say that, in Maimonides' view, the task of political philosophy is to define the essence of divine law, and the task of the science of halakhah is to ensure that the Law of Moses indeed is divine law.

Contrary to the accepted view of certain circles both in the Middle Ages and today, there is no doubt that, for Maimonides, the discipline of halakhah requires a higher form of human perfection than that required by political philosophy. For according to him, the halakhic authority worthy of his position must also be a political philosopher. He must know what is the true happiness of man, knowledge which follows from the knowledge (to the extent that it is possible) of "the whole of that which exists in its true form."[27] But a halakhic judge is not content with knowledge alone. He is also active in this world in order to do kindness to other human beings:

It is as if you said, by way of example, that there is an individual who has wealth sufficing only for his own necessities, no residue being left over for which someone else might receive benefit; and that there is another individual who has enough wealth for a residue to be left over from it, sufficient for the enrichment of many people. (*Guide* II, 11 cf. II, 37; see also Appendix)

It is to the halakhic judge, not the ordinary philosopher, that Maimonides alludes at the end of the *Guide* in his discussion about the person whose way of life, once he has attained knowledge of God to the best of his abilities, "will always have in view lovingkindness, righteousness, and judgment in order to imitate *His actions.*"[28]

Did Maimonides see himself as a reformer seeking to add to Mosaic Law, contrary to the principle "You shall not add to it nor subtract from it" (Deut. 13:1); contrary to the "ninth principle" of Judaism that he himself formulated in the introduction to *Helek*; and contrary to what he writes in "Basic Principles of the Torah" 9, 1: "It is clear and explicit in the Torah, that it is an eternal commandment, changeless, with no subtraction nor addition"?[29] No!

Not only is the answer indubitably negative, but there is also reason to doubt that Maimonides, while making halakhic rulings, saw himself as someone *distinct* from Moses our Teacher. For according to a Maimonides meta-halakhic principle, the prophecy of Moses our Teacher was purely intellectual,[30] and as for the intellect, all men are "one in number."[31] I dare to present the matter as follows: if Moses our Teacher received the Torah through a unification (to the extent that it is possible) with the Active Intellect,[32] then Maimonides set down the laws of the Torah while also in unification (to the extent that it is possible) with the Active Intellect, which is to say, in unification with Moses our Teacher.[33]

In any case, it should be clear to anyone who looks at his halakhic writings that Maimonides in no way saw himself as the reformer of Moses our Teacher, but rather as his partner, his disciple, his vicar (cf. "the one who excels in wisdom . . . occupies the place of Moses our Teacher"),[34] or his interpreter (cf. "the precepts which Moses received on Sinai were given together with their interpretation").[35] So convinced was Maimonides that the Torah of Moses our Teacher issued from his own mouth, that he entitled his great work *Mishneh Torah*. And so convinced of this were the people, that they called this work *HaYad HaHazakah* (the Mighty Hand; cf. Deut. 34:12).

Throughout the generations, the Jewish people have been blessed with a great number of philosophers and an even greater number of halakhic authorities. However, Maimonides was exceptional in that he was both philosopher and halakhic authority. As such, he was able to do what an ordinary philosopher could not do, and he was able to know what an ordinary halakhic authority could not know. Maimonides was indeed exceptional in being both philosopher and halakhic authority, but he himself held that "It is the aim of the Torah that everyone should be such an individual" (*Guide* II, 39).

APPENDIX: THE PERFECTION OF MAN AND THE POLITICAL IMITATION OF GOD

In Maimonides' statement on the political imitation of God (*Guide* III, 54) Prof. Shlomo Pines finds support for the view that he held political activity to be the ultimate perfection of man.[36] However, it appears to me that Maimonides did not believe that the political imitation of God is the ultimate human perfection, but that the political imitation of God is a *byproduct* of man's ultimate perfection which is, in fact, the perfection of the intellect.

To my mind, the determining factor here is the ontological principle explained in the *Guide* II, 11:

Know that in the case of every being that causes a certain good thing to overflow from it according to this order of rank, the existence, the purpose, and the end of the being conferring the benefits, do not consist in conferring the benefits on the recipient. For pure absurdity necessarily would follow from this assumption. . . . It would . . . follow . . . that the existence of what is the

highest, the most perfect, and the most noble, is for the sake of what is inferior. . . . The matter is rather as I shall describe it. In effect a thing that is
perfect . . . [s]ometimes its perfection is within such limits that a residue of
perfection is left over from it for something else. . . . The case of being is
similar. For the overflow coming from Him, may He be exalted, for the bringing into being of separate intellects overflows likewise from these intellects, so
that one of them brings another into being and this continues up to the Active
Intellect. . . . Moreover a certain other act of bringing into being overflows
from every separate intellect until the spheres come to an end with the sphere
of the moon. After it, there is the body subject to generation and corruption.[37]

That is to say, the perfection of the fifth intellect, for example, is its
knowledge of the fourth intellect superior to it, and not its beneficial
influence on the sixth intellect inferior to it. Similarly, the perfection of
the tenth intellect, the Active Intellect (which is also the perfect, ideal
man who embraces it), is the knowledge of the ninth intellect above it,
and not its beneficial influence on the world of generation and corruption beneath it, that is to say, not in the political, legislative, and divine
activity of the prophet or the halakhic authority.

Maimonides applies the ontological principle explained in II, 11 explicitly to the problem of statecraft: "Sometimes the measure of what
comes to the individual [from the overflowing of the divine intellect]
overflows from rendering him perfect, toward rendering others perfect. This is what happens to all beings: some of them achieve perfection to an extent that enables them to govern others" (II, 37).

In that same chapter, Maimonides comments on the differences between "the class of men of science engaged in speculation," "the class
of prophets," and "the class of those who govern cities, being the legis-
lators, the soothsayers, the augurs, and the dreamers of veracious
dreams." This should also be compared with what he says in II, 39
on the distinction between the legislative prophecy of Moses and the
prophecy of Abraham.

In general, just as the perfection of God is His intellectual activity,
not His governance of the world,[38] so the perfection of one who imi-
tates God is his intellectual activity, not his governance of the state.

NOTES

1. Cf. *The Guide of the Perplexed* Part I, Chapter 46. There Maimonides says:
"The need of man for manufacturing work is due to its being required for the
preparation of his food, his clothing and his place of shelter. For this is bound
up with his nature, I mean his needing to prepare what is suitable for him"
(p. 102). In I, 72 he explains that this natural necessity requires social organization: "For the foods through which he exists require the application of some
art and a lengthy management that cannot be made perfect except through

thought and perspicacity, as well as with the help of many tools and many individuals, every one of whom devotes himself to one single occupation" (p. 191). However in III, 49 he speaks of another human need for society: "It is well known that friends are something that is necessary for man throughout his whole life. Aristotle has already set this forth [see *Nicomachean Ethics* VIII, 1, 1153a 3 ff.]. For in a state of health and happiness, a man takes pleasure in their familiar relationship with him; in adversity he has recourse to them; and in his old age, when his body is grown weak, he seeks their help" (p. 601).

Quotations herein are taken from *The Guide of the Perplexed*, trans. Shlomo Pines (Chicago: University of Chicago Press, 1963).

2. *Nicomachean Ethics* I, 7, 1097b 12. Cf. *The History of Animals* I, 1, 488a 7; *Politics* I, 2, 1253a 2.

3. From the Greek word *nomos*. By "nomic law," Maimonides means any political law which is not divine; cf. *Treatise on Logic*, ch. 14.

4. Cf. "Laws concerning Character Traits," III, 3.

5. Prof. Shlomo Pines has argued that, according to Maimonides, perfection of the soul is unattainable, for it is impossible to know "the whole of that which exists in its true form" or, in other words, to know the "Active Intellect," and thus it is political activity which is the ultimate human perfection. See S. Pines, "The Limitations of Human Knowledge According to Alfarabi, ibn Bajja, and Maimonides," in *Studies in Medieval Jewish History and Literature*, ed. I. Twersky (Cambridge, Mass.: Harvard University Press, 1979), 82–109.

In my opinion, however, one cannot conclude that Maimonides despaired of science or elevated the practical life above the life of knowledge (see Appendix). It seems to me that Maimonides saw perfection of the soul as an end which can be approached, yet never attained. It follows that when Maimonides speaks of the "perfect" man he means either the ideal, or a relative standing. On the relation between the individual and society, see David Hartman, *Maimonides: Torah and Philosophic Quest* (Philadelphia: Jewish Publication Society, 1976).

6. See, for instance *Eight Chapters*, chapter 5; *Guide* III, 8.

7. "[Man] should take as his end . . . solely the mental representation of the intelligibles. . . . These individuals are those who are permanently with God. They are those to whom it has been said: *Ye are gods, and all of you children of the Most High* [Psalms, 82:6]" (*Guide* III, 8).

8. See the description of the prophet in "Basic Principles of the Torah" 7, 1, and cf. *Eight Chapters*, ch. 5: "If an individual is found who is occupied with this, I do not say that he is less than the prophets! That is to say, one who employs all his spiritual powers, whose sole aim is the knowledge of God, may He be blessed, who does nothing that does not elevate." Also, *Guide* III, 51: "There are those who set their thought to work after having attained perfection in the divine science, turn wholly toward God, may He be cherished and held sublime . . . and direct all the acts of their intellect toward an examination of the beings. . . . This is the rank of the prophets!"

9. *Guide* III, 45. Also, prophecy is one of the fundamental elements of religion in general ("Basic Principles of the Torah," 7, 1) and precedes the belief in Mosaic Law in particular.

10. On the distinction between "true happiness" and "imaginary happiness," see *Treatise on Logic*, ch. 14; and compare Guide III, 23 and 54.

11. Even if a lawgiver who was not a prophet were able to make a divine law, he would certainly not *want* to make such a law. This would be so not only because truth is of no use to one who is not interested in it for its own sake—"the end of truth is but to know that it is truth" (Introduction to *Perek Helek*)—but also because truth is liable to endanger law and order. Compare the remark of R. Joseph ibn Kaspi (thirteenth century) on *Guide* I, Introduction: "The multitude could not tolerate the true theory but would go mad, run wild, and take complete leave of its senses." Just as there is political utility in the noble lie, so there is political danger in the encouragement of the life of reason, that is, the encouragement of free, critical thinking. Thus, only the lawgiver who is interested in the truth for its own sake would be prepared to take the risk of instituting a divine law. Moreover, only the lawmaker who is not satisfied solely with his own rational perfections, but wishes to spread rational knowledge among other humans as well, would be interested in making a divine law. The solipsistic philosopher is content with nomic law—for example, Plato's *Republic*—which will guarantee law and order in the streets and allow him to sit peacefully in his room and develop his reason.

12. Cf. II, 37, on the subject of the "three classes." On the distinction between imagination and understanding according to Maimonides, see my article, "Maimonides and Spinoza on the Knowledge of Good and Evil," *BINAH*, vol. 2 (New York: Praeger, 1989), 131–46.

13. *Eight Chapters*, ch. 4.

14. *Guide* III, 27. On the uniqueness of Mosaic Law, see II, 39. On divine law given by a plagiarist, see II, 40. Needless to say, after Mosaic Law there can be no other original divine law, unless it is made without any historical connection to Mosaic Law. Note that in II, 40, Maimonides speaks of the existence of "divine regimens" in the plural: "Accordingly I only want to give you knowledge concerning the regimens with regard to which the claim is made that they are prophetic; some of them are truly prophetic—I mean divine." (p. 383)

15. An interesting discussion (though I have reservations regarding its conclusions) of Chapter 27 can be found in an article by M. Galston, "The Purpose of the Law according to Maimonides," *Jewish Quarterly Review* 69 (1978): 27–51 (esp. 35–41).

16. "[E]very commandment from among these six hundred and thirteen commandments exists either with a view to communicating a correct opinion, or to putting an end to an unhealthy opinion, or to communicating a rule of justice, or to warding off an injustice, or to endowing men with a noble moral quality, or to warning them against an evil moral quality. Thus all [the commandments] are bound up with three things: opinions, moral qualities, and political civic actions" (III, 31).

17. "The knowledge of these opinions and practices [of the idol worshippers in biblical times] is a very important chapter in the exposition of the reasons for the commandments. For the foundation of the whole of our Law and the pivot around which it turns, consists in the effacement of these opinions from the minds and of these monuments from existence" (III, 29).

18. In Ugaritic writings, there is one fragment that, according to the interpretation of the first scholars to deal with it, provides an impressive confirmation of this Maimonidean hypothesis. However, the correctness of this interpretation has since been seriously questioned.

19. In the words of *Sifre:* "And you shall love the Lord your God with all your heart [Deut. 6:5], the question arises, how is one to manifest this love for the Lord? Scripture therefore says: 'And these words which I command you this day, shall be upon your heart' [ibid. 6:6]; for through this you will learn to know Him whose word called the universe into existence." Indeed, in the *Book of Commandments*, Positive Commandment 3, Maimonides interpreted the commandment to love God on the basis of this remark in *Sifre*. His explanation there, "to dwell upon and contemplate His commandments, His injunctions, and His works," is midway between the literal meaning of the remark in *Sifre* and the wider meaning he urges in the "Basic Principles of the Torah".

20. Positive commandments, 1–2; negative commandments, 1.

21. "[B]ut *I maintain* that [the ability to accept] a positive or negative commandment may also be present in this [rational] faculty, insofar as one believes a true or false doctrine." However, from his determination that *all* the positive and negative commandments of the Torah concern the sensitive and appetitive faculties, it follows that when he wrote the *Eight Chapters*, Maimonides did not recognize any theoretical commandments, but only practical commandments, as decided halakhah.

22. Maimonides does not mean (as many mistakenly believe) that philosophy is more important than the commandments. Rather, he means that the theoretical commandments are more important than the practical ones.

23. Maimonides' response to R. Obadiah the Righteous Proselyte allows the convert to pray to "Our God and the God of our fathers." Abraham, he explains, is the father not only of his descendants, but also of all his disciples who declare the unity of God: "And what is most important is that Abraham our father taught the people and enlightened them and informed them of the unity of God and rejected idolatry." This ruling did not follow the halakhah found in the Mishnah (Bikurim 1,4).

24. The sages had already interpreted "walking in His ways" as a general moral commandment (*Sifre* on Deuteronomy, Ekev, 49; Shabbat 133b; Sotah 14a; and more). In the introduction to his first systematic moral work, the *Eight Chapters*, Maimonides states explicitly that in writing the treatise, he made use not only of Jewish sources but also of "the words of the philosophers, ancient and recent."

25. Cf. Pines' words at the end of the introduction to his English translation of the *Guide*, p. cxxxiv.

26. Prof. Isadore Twersky, an authority on the *Mishneh Torah*, argues that "the basic, leading claim [in the *Mishneh Torah* is that] the commandments are means for the welfare of the body and soul," and that "throughout the great work we find an effort 'to correct our moral qualities and to keep straight all our doings' " (according to "Laws Concerning Substitute Offerings," 4,13).

27. Moses our Teacher possessed such knowledge (*Guide* I, 54) and "the call to the Torah followed necessarily from that apprehension alone" (II, 39) (p. 378). Compare the expression of Maimonides, "and I relied on the Rock" (in-

troduction to the *Mishneh Torah*) with his understanding of God's words to Moses our Teacher: "And you shall stand erect upon the rock" (Exodus 33:21): "Rely upon, and be firm in considering, God, may He be exalted, as the first principle. This is the entryway through which you shall come to Him." (*Guide* I, 16) In the writings of Alfarabi we find the idea that the true religious lawgiver must be an outstanding theoretical philosopher, and that the greatest human perfection is manifest not in philosophical knowledge itself but in the act of religious legislation which derives from it. Cf. article by Pines quoted in note 5 and the Appendix above.

28. L. V. Berman has written on the political definition of the notion of *imitatio Dei* in Alfarabi and Maimonides. However, he does not believe, as I do, that Maimonides saw halakhic legislative activity as an example of the political imitation of God. See L. V. Berman, "The Political Interpretation of the Maxim: The Purpose of Philosophy is the Imitation of God," *Studia Islamica* 15 (1961): 56–60; "Maimonides, the Disciple of Alfarabi," *Israel Oriental Studies* 4 (1974): 170–71. On Prof. Pines' argument that according to Maimonides the political imitation of God is the ultimate human perfection, see Appendix.

29. Cf. *Book of Commandments*, Positive Commandments 313–314. However cf. also *Guide* III, 41: "Inasmuch as God, may He be exalted, knew that the commandments of this Law will need . . . to be added to or subtracted from" (p. 562–63). See also G. F. Blidstein, "Maimonides on Oral Law," *The Jewish Law Annual 1* (1978): 118–20, cf. 114–15.

30. Maimonides did indeed distinguish between the ideal Moses, the receiver of the divine law (pure intellect), and the historical Moses (flesh and blood). However, this distinction does not concern us here.

31. *Guide* I, 74, The Seventh Method; cf. II, Introduction, premise 16; II, 12, first species. Similarly, Maimonides argues in the introduction to the *Commentary on the Mishnah* that there was hardly any disagreement between Hillel and Shammai in halakhah, "for insofar as any two individuals are equal in intellect and philosophy and knowledge of the principles that derive from opinions, there will be no disagreement in their views in any respect." However, "when the number of disciples of Hillel and Shammai—not well versed in all respects—increased, the number of disagreements in the House of Israel increased [Sanhedrin 88b]." Also: "In all things whose true reality is known through [rational] demonstration there is no dispute" (*Guide* I, 31).

32. On prophecy and the Active Intellect, see the introduction to *Helek: Sanhedrin, Chapter Ten*, Fundamental Principles 6 and 7; "Basic Principles of the Torah" 2, 7; 7,1 and 6; *Guide* II, 36.

33. It follows from our discussion that, according to Maimonides, the halakhic judge must be not only a philosopher, but also a prophet. (On the prophecy of Maimonides, see the writings of Abraham J. Heschel.) However, to avoid misunderstanding, it must be clarified that according to Maimonides, prophecy, like philosophy, though essential in the training of the halakhic judge, adds nothing to his formal credentials. The judge who is a prophet, like the judge who is a philosopher, must justify his rulings as must any other halakhic judge. And just as it is pointless for the philosopher-judge to claim: "The halakhah is as I say for I am a philosopher," so it is pointless for the prophet-judge to claim: "The halakhah is as I say for I am a prophet." On

prophecy and halakhic methodology, see Maimonides' introduction to the *Commentary on the Mishnah*, and cf. "Basic Principles of the Torah" 9,1.

34. "Laws concerning Sanhedrin" 1,3. On the connection between the wise men throughout the generations and Moses our Teacher, see the introductions to the *Commentary on the Mishnah* and the *Mishneh Torah*.

35. Introduction to the *Mishneh Torah*. For Maimonides, "their interpretation" = commandment = halakhah = Oral Law = *Mishneh Torah*. See section 3 in Isadore Twersky: "Some Halakhic Aspects of the *Mishneh Torah*," in *Jewish Medieval and Renaissance Studies*, ed. Alexander Altmann (Cambridge, Mass.: Harvard University Press, 1967), 106–11.

36. See his article cited in note 5 above, p. 100.

37. Cf. "Basic Principles of the Torah" 1–4; and *Guide* III, 53 on the interpretation of "The world is built up in lovingkindness" (Psalms 89:3).

38. See, for instance, "Basic Principles of the Torah," 1:3, 5; and 2:10.

5

SARA O. HELLER WILENSKY

The "First Created Being" in Early Kabbalah: Philosophical and Isma'ilian Sources

The Jewish medieval mystical movement known as the kabbalah first appeared in Provence and northern Spain in the last decades of the twelfth century and developed rapidly in the thirteenth century. It was rooted in various layers of Jewish tradition, but it was also deeply influenced by rationalistic philosophy, mainly the Neoplatonic schools that had great impact among Jews, Muslims, and Christians. Many terms that were originally philosophical and rationalistic were adopted by kabbalists as mystical symbols. The works of Rabbi Isaac Ibn Latif, a thirteenth-century Jewish thinker, present some of the most profound examples of this process, as the analysis in this study indicates.

The term the "First Created Being," which makes an appearance in kabbalistic literature in the thirteenth century, has its source in a Neoplatonic concept. In contrast to the view originating in Aristotle's *Metaphysics*,[1] which identifies God "the unmoved mover" with the Intellect in *actu* or, in the words of Maimonides, "He is the intellect as well as the intellectually cognizing subject and the intellectually cognized object,"[2] the Neoplatonic view originating in Plotinus maintains that God is the "absolute One" beyond the Universal Intellect.[3] According to the transcendental ontology of Plotinus, the absolute One is the source and cause of the Universal Intellect, which is in turn the first link in a chain of necessary, unwilled emanation from the plenitude of the absolute One. The Universal Intellect is coexistent with God and is identical with the World of Ideas. The Intellect emanates from its pleni-

This article was first published in *Mehkarim be-Hagut Yehudit* (Studies in Jewish Thought), ed. S. O. Heller Wilensky and M. Idel (Jerusalem: Magnes Press, 1989). The translation/adaptation is by Zipporah Brody.

tude the World Soul, the second link in Plotinus' chain of emanation. The World Soul is dual: a superior soul drawn to the World of Ideas, and a lesser soul turned to the material world, whose existence it forms according to the World of Ideas.

The Neoplatonic view of the Universal Intellect as the first emanation from God, from the superabundance of the absolute and infinite One, penetrated the literature of early thirteenth-century kabbalah via two terms. The "first emanation"—a term widely used in Neoplatonic literature for the Universal Intellect—appeared in the works of the early kabbalists, for example, R. Jacob Ben Sheshet of Gerona, who stated: "The first emanation *(ha-ne'zal ha-rishon)* which is emanated from the hidden Cause . . . is an extremely fine essence from which the median line begins to be drawn and extend."[4] The second term which also appears in early kabbalistic literature is the First Created Being *(ha-nivra ha-rishon)*, a paradoxical term which serves to designate the universal Intellect emanated from God.

In this study I shall devote myself to the meaning of the term First Created Being as it appears in the works of the earliest thirteenth-century kabbalists and, in particular, in the works of R. Isaac Ben Abraham Ibn Latif (c. 1210–c. 1280) in whose mystical system it plays a central role. The study will serve to illuminate the meaning of the term in the works of the first kabbalists and shed light on the sources upon which they drew.[5]

The First Created Being appears in Ibn Latif in three contexts: (1) his doctrine of the Divine Will, (2) the problems of the transcendence and immanence of God, and (3) the subject of prophecy. I shall outline his thinking regarding the First Created Being in each of these contexts.

THE DIVINE WILL

Ibn Latif was influenced by Solomon Ibn Gabirol's doctrine of the Divine Will, as I have pointed out in my study of Ibn Latif's philosophical sources.[6] This influence is expressed in his reiteration of all the characteristic aspects of Ibn Gabirol's doctrine of the Divine Will. Following Ibn Gabirol, Ibn Latif introduces the Will into the Neoplatonic doctrine of emanation, in order to make it a voluntary, spontaneous process and thereby remove the origin of the world from the category of necessary causality. Like Ibn Gabirol, Ibn Latif equates the Divine Will with the Divine Word, an identification which places his doctrine of the Will within the broad stream of the history of the Philonic Logos. To quote: "For the world was created by Will . . . and the Will is depicted by the Word," and "the literal interpretation of the creation is the Will depicted by the Word, and it is a great secret."[7] In his view, the doctrine of the Will and the kabbalah are linked: "In his search to find words of delight (Ecclesiastes 12:10) [*divre ḥefez*–taken here to mean words concerning the doctrine of the Will], he found the wisdom of the kabbalah."[8]

Ibn Latif is aware of the difficulty posed by the doctrine of the Divine Will for the Neoplatonic concept of the One as absolute unity beyond change and activity. Following Ibn Gabirol, on the one hand he identifies the Will with the Divine Essence, claiming it is preexistent and coexistent with God; on the other hand, he states that the Will is distinct from God, the first emanation, with regard to its activity in the world. The Will is identical with the Divine Essence, but is also a hypostasis, a subsistent essence. The unification of these two principles in Ibn Gabirol's philosophy is quite involved, and this is not the place to enter into its difficulties, which were recognized by all scholars who have studied his system. We are interested here in presenting Ibn Latif's interpretation of this complicated issue in Ibn Gabirol's doctrine of the Will.

Ibn Latif introduces a significant change in Ibn Gabirol's doctrine of the Divine Will. He splits it into two: a Will that is primordial and coexistent with the God who is described as the source of all reality, and a Will that is separate from God in His activities in the world—a hypostasis which is a subsistent essence, identified with the Divine Intellect, that he calls the First Created Being (*ha-nivra ha-rishon*). In describing the First Created Being which broke off from the Divine Will, Ibn Latif employs terms and symbols applied to the Will and the Logos, and depicts it as the source of all existence:

The First Created Being, may he be blessed, cognizes everything by virtue of his essence, for he is everywhere and everything is in him, as it is written: the whole earth is full of his glory (Isaiah 10:3); and all beings exist through him by way of emanation and evolvement, and nothing exists outside of him.[9]

Herein lies the paradox: "The First Created Being, may he be blessed"(!) is given all the appellations attributed to the Creator.

THE TRANSCENDENCE AND IMMANENCE OF GOD

A second aspect of the First Created Being relates to the problem of the transcendence and immanence of God. Ibn Latif adopted Ibn Gabirol's pantheistic system, developed in his philosophical work *Mekor Haim (Fons Vitae)*,[10] which Moses Cordovero (the sixteenth-century kabbalist of Safed) later formulated in his famous statement "God is all reality, but not all reality is God."[11] However, Ibn Latif applied all the pantheistic terms and expressions in his works not to the transcendent God, but to the Will and to the First Created Being. He maintained that the philosophers (i.e., Maimonides) had not succeeded in resolving the antinomy between the concept of a transcendent God, the absolute One as a metaphysical concept, the ineffable God beyond man's finite thought and beyond description in human language, of whom one can speak only through negation—and the personal God of religion, the God of Will and action, who creates and reveals Himself, who is immanent in the world, the Scriptural God of attributes. Ibn Latif attempted to resolve the dialectic of God's transcendence and immanence by differentiating between the transcendent, hidden God who is detached and impersonal—the *Ein Sof*[12] in the terminology of the early kabbalists, who is not the object of religious life where he has no place, and who does not appear in the biblical account of creation—and the immanent God, the God of Genesis who creates the world and dwells in it, the God of Scripture who reveals Himself and relates to man, to whom Ibn Latif refers with the paradoxical term the First Created Being. We have, therefore, two aspects of the Godhead: the transcendent God on the one hand, and the First Created Being or immanent God on the other.

Synonyms for this immanent God are the Will, the First Created Being, and the Supreme Intellect.[13] The major Hebrew terms and symbols employed in Ibn Latif's works for the First Created Being are fire (*esh*), first (*rosh*), house (*bayit*), convenant (*berit*), beginning (*bereshit*), the great Prince, glory (*kavod*), world, point, spiritual light, light of the garment, firstborn, voice, who (*mi*), face (*panim*), the First Angel, the High Priest, Michael, the Supreme Binding Force, the Fountain of Life, and Supreme Category (*sug 'elyon*).[14]

The significance of some of these appellations will be discussed here. Ibn Latif interprets the first verse of the Bible and the word *bereshit* in light of the symbolism of the term the First Created Being as follows. He explains the word *bereshit* as an anagram of *berit* (convenant) + *esh* (fire), and of *rosh* (first) + *bayit* (house). He writes: "The word *bereshit* alludes to Creation, and to the mystery of the covenant made, and to the secret of the First Created Being which passes between the parts (cf. Genesis 15), and to the fact of it being fire and being called first, and to the house in which He dwells."[15] He interprets Genesis 1:1 thus: *Bereshit* is the First Created Being, whose appellations are *esh*, *rosh*, *berit*, and *bayit*, all contained within that word; *bara*, that is, emanated, *elohim*, that is, the upper, immaterial world,[16] along with the *shamayim*, the intermediate world of the celestial spheres, and the *aretz*, the lower, sublunar world. It is clear that in his interpretation, the First Created Being is the Creator of Genesis, a sort of *demiurge*, and the source of the three worlds. The First Created Being is above the spiritual world in its ontologic position in the hierarchy of emanation; it is the source from which the world emanates.

Although Ibn Latif does not say so, one may infer that he held the First Created Being, called *bereshit*, to be identical with the first *sefirah* *(Keter)* from which the other *sefirot* emanated. This inference was stated explicitly by Judah Ḥayyat, who was familiar with Ibn Latif's thought and wrote a critical analysis of his work. Ḥayyat also cites Naḥmanides' opposing view, that *bereshit* is the second *sefirah (Ḥokhmah)*,[17] a view which prevailed in the mainstream of kabbalistic thought.

Ibn Latif maintains that there is a twofold link between the First Created Being and the world: the world is emanated from the First Created Being, this emanation constituting Creation; and the world is maintained by the superabundance that flows from it. This is the import of the word *berit* (covenant) that, according to Ibn Latif, has the dual significance of creation and immanence. The First Created Being is God revealed, God as Creator.

Ibn Latif describes the process of the emanation of the world from the First Created Being by means of two mathematical analogies common in Arabic and Jewish Neoplatonic literature. In the first analogy, the First Created Being is likened to the numeral "one," and the world that emanates from it is like the multiplication of numbers from the numeral one. In the second analogy, the First Created Being resembles the mathematical "point" from which develops a line, then surface, and then volume; "a deep mystery is posited in the point, the line, and volume."[18]

PROPHECY AND THE DIVINE REVELATION TO MOSES
(Exod. 33)

The First Created Being also functions as the source of prophecy. Ibn Latif claims that it is the "root" of the "prophetic soul." His reply to the question: how can a link exist between infinite God and finite and material man (a question posed by Judah Halevi through the Khazar),[19] is that there is no relationship between the transcendent, infinite God and finite man, and that the infinite God cannot be grasped by human thought. He quotes Plotinus, as formulated by Ibn Gabirol in *Fons Vitae*, and adds: "I say that the limit of cognition is when the intellectually cognizing subject is able to encompass the object of cognition; and He who is infinite cannot be encompassed by the finite intellect."[20] He maintains that the source of prophecy is not the transcendent, infinite, and hidden God, but the First Created Being. The paradox of prophecy can be solved by positing a link between the First Created Being and the prophetic soul (the intuitive soul). The latter term was adopted from the *Kitab al-Hada'ik* of the Andalusian philosopher al-Batalyawsi (1052–1127), who in turn borrowed it from the *Epistles of the Sincere*

Brethren (Ikhwan al-Safa), Neoplatonic texts closely connected to the Isma'ilia.

Ibn Latif maintains that the First Created Being is both the root of the prophetic soul as well as the upper limit of prophetic knowledge:

The faculties of the soul are five according to the philosophers, and they are vegetative, animate, rational, philosophical and prophetic. Their roots are five . . . and with the great Prince, the First Created Being, the prophetic faculty terminates. Study this, for it is very deep.[21]

Ibn Latif claims that the First Created Being has a dual countenance: the upper is turned to God, and is alluded to in the Bible by the word *panim* (face, or front), while the lower, turned to the world, is alluded to by the term *aḥor* (back). He interprets the Divine revelation to Moses (Exod. 33) accordingly. Moses requested knowledge of the face of the First Created Being, for it is inconceivable, Ibn Latif argues (in criticism of the *Guide* I, 54), that Moses, the greatest of all prophets and wise men, would naively request knowledge of the essence of the transcendent God, as Maimonides stated. What Moses requested was knowledge of the face, the upper aspect of the First Created Being. But God's response was that the upper aspect was beyond human cognition, and only the lower aspect, the back of the First Created Being, which is turned to the world, can be apprehended by man's intelligence.

Similar interpretations of the Divine revelation to Moses in Exodus 33 are found in two kabbalistic manuscripts from the late-thirteenth century: the *Likkutei HaRan*, ms. New York, JTS 1777, and *Eshkol Ha-Kofer*, ms. Vatican 219. To quote from *Likkutei HaRan*: "And that which is written 'And thou shalt see My back but My face shall not be seen' (Ex.33): 'My back' refers to everything from the First Intellect and below, and 'My face' [refers to] all that is above it, which is the First Cause."[22]

In *Likkutei HaRan*, the First Intellect is identical with the First Created Being. G. Scholem, who published several passages from *Likkutei HaRan* as classic examples of "neoplatonic speculation in the kabbalist camp," and of "philosophical kabbalah," does not explain the acronym *HaRan*. M. Idel suggests that the author is R. Nathan, a student of Abraham Abulafia and teacher of R. Isaac of Acre, and detects Sufic influences in his writing.[23] R. Nathan and Ibn Latif may have shared common sources, but it seems to me that traces of Ibn Latif's influence are discernible in R. Nathan's commentary on Exod. 33.

An interpretation identical to Ibn Latif's is found in the anonymous kabbalistic work *Eshkol HaKofer*. The commentary is an almost literal rendering of Ibn Latif's interpretation:

Moses did not wish to know and see the essence of the Creator, Blessed be He, for he knew that this could not be grasped . . . rather Moses requested to know the emanation of the First Created Being. . . . This was [the meaning of] his entreaty "make known to me Your Glory." God responded that this was impossible to achieve and said, "thou may not see My face"; for the aspect called "face" cannot be grasped by man, but the other aspect called "back" can be comprehended, as it is written, "and thou shalt see My back."[24]

In my opinion, a careful study of *Eshkol HaKofer* would reveal Ibn Latif's strong influence, which is also expressed in that work's appellations for the First Created Being: "The First Created Being is the secret of the covenant *(berit)* between the Creator, blessed be He, and created beings, and 'he passed between the parts', for he is the beginning of creation and therefore all beings exist by his causation."[25] Furthermore, like Ibn Latif, *Eshkol HaKofer* also equates the First Created Being with the universal Intellect and the *Kavod*.

This is not the place to discuss the sources and problematics of the doctrine of the *Kavod* which have been extensively studied. Let us note, however, the parallel between the above views of the kabbalists regarding the dual aspect of the First Created Being and their commentary on the Divine revelation to Moses, and the doctrine pronounced by Hasidei Ashkenaz (twelfth–thirteenth centuries), regarding the dual countenance of the Divine *Kavod:* the upper face turned towards God, and the lower face called the back, turned to the world, that was revealed to Moses. Of import for our discussion are the statements of the "second scholar" who participated in a debate by three scholars over the essence of the *Kavod*, found in ms. Oxford 1567, and cited by J. Dan.[26] It is possible that the kabbalists drew their above interpretation of Exod. 33 from Hasidei Ashkenaz, and it is noteworthy that parallels exist between Ibn Latif's mystical doctrine and the esoteric teaching of that group.[27] However, both groups probably drew upon common sources, such as Saadia Gaon's doctrine of the *Kavod* and his distinction between the upper *Kavod* revealed to the angels, and the lower *Kavod* revealed to the prophets, as well as Abraham Ibn Ezra's commentary on Exod. 33, which posits a hidden aspect called *panim* and a revealed aspect called *ahoraim*. They may also have been aware of other ancient traditions concerning the doctrine of the *Kavod*.

We may point to an additional parallel to the dual nature of the First Created Being, found in Neoplatonic literature, namely, the well-known doctrine expounded by Plotinus in the *Enneads*.[28] In that work, the World Soul is dual; a superior, upper soul, turned to the World of the Intellects above it, and an inferior, lower soul, turned to the material world below it, which it forms. Indeed, Plotinus' doctrine is found in *Bustan al-'Aqul (Garden of the Intellects)* by Nathanael ben al-Fayyumi (twelfth century) of Yemen: "For the [universal] soul has two poles; one pole is attracted to the Intellect from which it draws beneficence and blessing, and the second serves to draw towards that which is below it in degree."[29]

The term First Created Being appears as well in Nahmanides' writings, in connection with the famous statement in *Pirkei Rabbi Eliezer the Great*, 3: "Whence were the heavens created? From the light of the garment with which He was robed." In the *Guide* (II, 26), Maimonides rejected R. Eliezer's statement for in his opinion it reflected the Platonic view of creation, while the Gerona kabbalists interpreted R. Eliezer's statement in accordance with the theory of emanation. Naḥmanides, in a covert attack on Maimonides, explained that "the light of the garment" with which God was robed and from which He created the heavens is the First Created Being. To quote: "Do not find difficult R. Eliezer the Great's statement 'whence were the heavens created? From the light of God's garment' . . . for the light of the garment is the First Created Being."[30]

Nahmanides' statement is enigmatic, as was his practice when writing about kabbalistic matters, and the cryptic prevails over the explicit. In my opinion, his remark should be interpreted so that the First Created Being is the subject of the sentence rather than the predicate, that is, the First Created Being is analogous to the light of the garment in *Pirkei Rabbi Eliezer the Great*. If I have understood Nahmanides properly, a correlation of his hints and his explicit statements[31] would make the First Created Being, which is analogous to the light of the garment, analogous to the *sefirah* of *Ḥokhmah*, the beginning of creation. The *sefirah* of *Ḥokhmah*, *Bereshit*, is the First Created Being, which is the source of the world, the first link in the chain of emanation, since the first *sefirah*, *Keter*, the Will, is primordial and coexistent with God.

ISMA'ILIAN SOURCES OF THE FIRST CREATED BEING

It has become evident to me that all the characteristics of the concept First Created Being in early kabbalah, including the term itself, are found in the theology of the Isma'ilia.[32] The First Created Being has a central place in Isma'ilian literature, particularly in the works of Muhammad al-Nasafi (executed in 942) and Ahmad al-Kirmani (died after 1021). The Hebrew term *ha-nivra ha-rishon* is a literal translation of the Arabic term *al-mubda' al-awwal*, a widely used *terminus technicus* in the Isma'ilian doctrine of creation; both terms express an identical concept.[33] Almost all the definitive characteristics of the early kabbalistic doctrine of the First Created Being are found in the theologian Al-Nasafi who introduced Neoplatonic philosophy into the Gnostic theology of the Isma'ilia.[34] According to Al-Nasafi's doctrine of Creation, the hidden and infinite God, the absolute One beyond the grasp of human thought or description by human language, created *(abda')* by means of the Divine Will which is equated with the "Word" *(amr)*, the Supreme Intellect, which is the First Created Being *('al-mubda' al-awwal)*. From the Supreme Intellect—the First Created Being and the Cause of Causes—the Universal Soul was emanated *(inbi'ath)*. From the Universal Soul were emanated the seven spheres. It is noteworthy that Al-Nasafi identifies the Neoplatonic terms with scriptural terms as well.

Al-Nasafi's main work, *Kitab al-Maḥsul*, is lost; its contents are preserved in other authors, in particular al-Kirmani, whose major work *Raḥat al-'Aql*[35] is largely extant. Al-Kirmani states that the first Intellect is the First Created Being *(al-mubda' al-awwal)*, which was created *ex nihilo*. From the first Intellect, a second Intellect was emanated, which is the first emanated being *(al-mumba'ith al-awwal)*. He develops a system of ten Intellects, three upper and seven lower. The seven lower Intellects are the movers of the celestial spheres, the last one being the Active Intellect.

The concept of the First Created Being in Isma'ilian theology, and the term *al-mubda; al-awwal,* also appear in R. Nathanael ben al-Fayyumi's work, *Bustan al-'Aqul,* which was written in Arabic in 1164, under Isma'ilian influence.[36] He states in this work that the First Created Being is the "Universal Intellect." R. Nathanael uses various expressions for the First Created Being, for example, the Cause of Causes, the First Cause, Fountain of Life, the One, the Point, *Hokhmah,* and the First Light; he describes it in terms usually applied to the Creator. He claims that the First Created Being was created *ex nihilo* "by the Word and Will of God." It is the First Cause and the Cause of Causes, and God is "He who causes the Cause of Causes." R. Nathanael maintains that the "Universal Soul" is emanated from the First Created Being: "The First Created Being is of the first degree [of emanation], and the Universal Soul is of the second degree." The World of Nature, of the seven celestial spheres, is emanated in turn from the Universal Soul.[37]

The question of how the Isma'ilian concept of the First Created Being penetrated the kabbalah has a number of possible and complementary answers. One possibility is that the kabbalists became aware of Isma'ilian theology, either directly or through literature which drew from Isma'ilian thought such as the *Epistles of the Sincere Brethren,* and from Sufic literature, or through Jewish thought originating in the East that was influenced by the Isma'ilia. Ibn Latif knew Arabic and was well-versed in Muslim philosophy and theology. R. Nathan, author of *Likkutei HaRan,* knew Sufic literature, as M. Idel has pointed out,[38] and recently it has been suggested by R. Jospe that Naḥmanides and his circle knew Arabic as well.[39]

A second possibility is that they had in common Neoplatonic sources in Arabic, such as *The Book of the Five Substances* by Pseudo-Empedocles, where the term First Created Being appears. (Shem Tov Ibn Falaquera, who translated the book into Hebrew and believed it to be one of Ibn Gabirol's sources, translates it as the "first created.") Another possible Neoplatonic source common to the Isma'ilia and to kabbalah is *The Theology of Aristotle* in its longer version (recently discovered by A. Borisov and not yet studied), as S. Pines suggests.[40]

Still another possibility is that Isma'ilian ideas entered kabbalah through magical and astrological literature. The term *al-mubda' al-awwal* appears in an astrological-magical work by the Isma'ilian author 'Abd al-Khazaraji, found in Ms. Paris Arabe 1360, a passage of which Pines cites.[41] It is also possible that Isma'ilian thinkers were in turn influenced by Jewish sources and that this is an instance of reciprocal influence, a common phenomenon in the history of ideas. Al-Kirmani, for instance, apparently debated with Jewish scholars, as evidenced by the Hebrew citation found in his work.[42]

In any event, it seems clear that the Isma'ilian sources, which scholars discovered only in the past fifty years, can shed light on some kabbalistic concepts and terms. Their close study by future scholars of the early kabbalah is a major desideratum.

NOTES

1. *Metaphysics*, Book XI, chapters 7–8.

2. *Guide of the Perplexed*, I, 68. trans. S. Pines (Chicago: University of Chicago, 1963), 163.

3. *Plotinus*, Enneads, Fifth Ennead, 3, 11.

4. See *Meshiv Devarim Nekhohim* (Jerusalem: Israel Academy, 1969), 113. On the analogy of the "line" and the "point," see n.16, below.

5. The term First Created Being is prevalent in the Renaissance as well—in the works of Judah Moscato and Pico Della Mirandola, who were possibly influenced by Ibn Latif. See, M. Idel, "The Magical and Neoplatonic Interpretation of Kabbalah," in *Jewish Thought in the Sixteenth Century*, ed. B. D. Cooperman (Cambridge, Mass.: Harvard University Press, 1983), 186–242.

6. For the influence of Ibn Gabirol's doctrine of the Divine Will upon Ibn Latif, see my article "Isaac Ibn Latif—Philosopher or Kabbalist?" in *Jewish Medieval and Renaissance Studies*, ed. A. Altmann (Cambridge, Mass.: Harvard University Press, 1967), 200–210. It is also possible that he and Ibn Gabirol had common sources.

7. Ibn Latif, *Zurat ha-'Olam* (Vienna, 1860), 21, 24.

8. Ibn Latif, *Commentary on Ecclesiastes* (n.d., n.p.) 56a.

9. Ibn Latif, *Ginzei haMelekh, Kokhvei Yizhak*, vol. 28 (Vienna, 1862), ch. 3.

10. The Latin translation was widely circulated in Christian circles in the Middle Ages without its Jewish authorship being known.

11. Moses Cordovero, *'Elimah Rabbati* (Brody, 1881), 24b.

12. The term *Ein Sof,* widely used in the early kabbalah for the hidden God, does not appear in Ibn Latif's works. He generally uses the philosophical term "First Cause." It is noteworthy that he uses the verbs "created" and "emanated" interchangeably.

13. The term "Supreme Intellect" is Neoplatonic.

14. The term *sug 'elyon* is Neoplatonic, the *sug* (category) having an ontic significance. Plotinus equates it with the Universal Intellect.

15. Ibn Latif, *Sha'ar haShamayim,* ms. Vatican 335.1, part 2, chap. 3, 45a–b. A similar anagram of the word *bereshit* is found in Baḥya ben Asher: "The word *bereshit* contains *esh* and *berit; Commentary on the Torah,* vol. 1, ed. H. D. Chavel (Jerusalem: Mosad Harav Kook, 1966), 18 (Hebrew). Cf. Zohar on Genesis, 1, 15b, where the word *bereshit* is divided into *bayit* and *rosh.*

16. Compare Maimonides' statement (*Guide* I, 2) concerning the multiple, equivocal designations of the term *elohim* as referring to both the Deity and the angels, that is, to separate Intellects. It is noteworthy that Ibn Latif equates the ten separate Intellects with the ten *sefirot.*

17. See *Ma'arekhet Ha-Elohut* (Mantoba 1558) 42a.

18. This geometric parable, which entered early kabbalistic literature and is found in the works of Jacob b. Sheshet, Naḥmanides, Isaac HaCohen, and the Zohar (see G. Scholem, *Major Trends in Jewish Mysticism* [Jerusalem: Schocken, 1941], 241, 394–95 nn.42, 43), originated in the works of Albinus and Plotinus. See H. A. Wolfson, "Albinus and Plotinus on Divine Attributes," *Harvard Theological Review* 45 (1952): 118–19. This analogy is also found in Al-Batalyawsi (1052–1127), who may have served as the kabbalists' source.

19. Kuzari I 4.

20. *Sha'ar haShamayim,* 17b. Compare Ibn Gabirol, *Fons Vitae,* part I, 5.

21. *Rav-Pe'alim* (Lemberg, 1885) 5, *Sha'ar ha-Shamayim,* 33a. This view of the role of the First Created Being in prophecy is found in the Isma'ilian doctrine of prophecy. See, H. Corbin, "De la philosophie Prophetique en Islam Shi'ite," *Eranos Jahrbuch* 31 (1962): 49–116.

22. See G. Scholem, "An Inquiry in the Kabbalah of R. Isaac ben Jacob Hacohen," *Tarbiz* 3 (1931):33–66 (Hebrew).

23. See M. Idel, "Mundus Imaginalis and Likkutei HaRan," *Studies in Ecstatic Kabbalah* (New York: SUNY, 1988), 73–89.

24. *Eshkol HaKofer,* ms. Vatican 219, 9b–10a.

25. Ibid., 11a. He is also referred to as "the great Prince," p. 7a.

26. J. Dan, *The Esoteric Theology of Ashkenazi Hasidism* (Jerusalem: Bialik Press, 1968), 129–33 (Hebrew).

27. For example (in contrast to the mainstream of kabbalah, which identifies the *Kavod* with the last *sefirah, Malkhut*), Ibn Latif's identification of the First Created Being with the first *sefirah* parallels the German hasidic identification of the *Kavod* with the first *sefirah.* Furthermore, the doctrine of the ineffable Name, comprised of ten letters equal to the ten *sefirot* and containing the three tenses of the verb "to be" that have the same letters as the ineffable Name, is found in both Ibn Latif and Eleazer of Worms. A detailed comparison should elicit additional parallels. It is quite possible that the mystical circles that,

according to Ibn Latif, rejected him early in his career with the accusation that "you are a stranger" (*Zurat Ha-'Olam*, 5) were Hasidei Ashkenaz.

28. See Plotinus, *Ennead* 3, 5,2; 8,5; *Ennead* 4, 2,6,7,18; 8,2,7; *Enead* 5, 3,4,7,12,22.

29. *Bustan al-'Aqul*, ed. Y. D. Kapaḥ (Jerusalem: Agudat 'Am Israel, 1984), 55 (Arabic and Hebrew).

30. Naḥmanides, *Commentary on Genesis* 1,8.

31. Cf. ibid., 1,2; "Beur Ma'ase Breshit BeDerekh haKabbala misod ha-Ramban," published by G. Scholem in *Kiryat Sefer* 6 (1930):415; ibid., *Commentary on Sefer Yezira*, 401–10.

32. The theology of the Isma'ilia flowered in the East in the ninth century and reached the apogee of its influence in the tenth, eleventh, and twelfth centuries. It is phenomenologically close to kabbalistic literature both in its esoteric nature and in its unique synthesis of Gnostic and Neoplatonic sources. The Isma'ilia sect was persecuted for certain antinomian elements of its doctrines, and its writings were discovered by scholars only recently. G. Scholem hesitantly alluded to the possible influence of the Isma'ilia on the kabbalistic doctrine of the *shemittot* (in which each of the six days of Creation has a corresponding millennium in history) in his *Origins of the Kabbalah* (Princeton: Jewish Publication Society and Princeton University Press, 1987), 465, and S. Pines mentioned it in his article "Shi'ite Terms and Conceptions in J. Halevi's Kuzari," in *Jerusalem Studies in Arabic and Islam* 2 (1980): 243–47. I have shown, in my study of the doctrine of the *shemittot* in Ibn Latif ("Messianism and Utopia in Thirteenth-Century Spanish Kabbalah," in *Messianism and Eschatology* [Jerusalem: Mercaz Z. Shazar, 1983], 221–37 [Hebrew]), the deep influence of the Isma'ilian doctrine of cosmic cycles on his theory, which is expressed philologically in identical *terminus technicus* (ibid., 230 n.38a).

33. See P. E. Walker, "The Isma'ili Vocabulary of Creation," *Studia Islamica* 40 (1974):75–85; D. R. Blumenthal, "An Example of Isma'ili Influence in Post-Maimonidean Yemen," *Studies in Judaism and Islam presented to S. D. Goitein* (Jerusalem: Magnes Press, 1981), 161; W. Madelung, "Isma'iliyya," *Encyclopedia of Islam*[2] IV (Leiden, 1987), 203–204; Al-Hamadani, "A Compendium of Isma'ili Esoterics," *Islamic Culture* 11 (1937): 210–20; W. Ivanow, *Isma'ili Literature* (Teheran: Teheran University Press, 1963), 40–45.

34. See S. Stern, *Studies in Early Isma'ilism* (Jerusalem: Magnes Press, 1983), 5, 31.

35. Leiden, 1952; See S. Pines, "Nathanael ben al-Fayyumi et la thèologie ismaelienne," *Revue de l'histoire Juive en Egypte* I (1947), 5–21; 13 n.2; 13 n.2; 14 n.3. See as well, P. E. Walker, "The Isma'ili Vocabulary of Creation," note 33 above, pp. 75–85.

36. For R. Nathanael's Isma'ilian sources, see S. Pines, "Nathanael ben al-Fayyumi," 5–22; R. Kiener, "Jewish Isma'ilism in Twelfth-Century Yemen: R. Nethanel Ben Al-Fayyumi," *JQR* n.s. 74 (1984):249–66.

37. Cf. *Bustan al-'Aqul*, 20, 21–22, 26, 55.

38. Cf. note 23, above.

39. See R. Jospe, "Naḥmanides and Arabic," *Tarbiz* 57 (1988): 67–93.

40. Cf. Naḥmanides, *Commentary on Genesis*, 245.

41. S. Pines, "Shi'ite Terms" note 32, above, 246–47.

42. The Hebrew citation equates the ten *ma'amarot* by which the world was created (Tractate Avot 5) with the Ten Commandments. See P. Kraus, "Hebraische und Syrische Zitate in Isma'ilitischen Schriften," *Der Islam* 19 (1931): 243–63. A similar parallel between the ten *ma'amarot* and the Ten Commandments is found in Ibn Latif's *Zurat ha-'Olam*, ed. Z. Stern (Vienna, 1860), 30.

6

ISRAEL J. YUVAL

A German-Jewish Autobiography of the Fourteenth Century

The literary genre of autobiography is a rare one in Hebrew and is almost nonexistent in medieval Jewish literature. From a historical point of view, such writing is very important, revealing in a direct, immediate, and personal way the cultural and historical circumstances in which people lived during a certain period. The document analyzed in this study is also unique in its being a personal account by an otherwise unknown figure of adventurous spirit. The work reflects the life and thought of an ordinary person in the last decades of the fourteenth century.

THE MEDIEVAL AUTOBIOGRAPHY

Autobiography emerged as a literary genre, in both Jewish and European literature, only during the transition period between the medieval and modern world. While autobiographical works were written in Antiquity, for example, the biblical book of Nehemiah, Julius Caesar's *De bello gallico,* as well as Augustus' *Res gestae,* or Josephus' *Life,* these and others like them are not autobiographies as we know them in later periods. They do not contain a broad retrospective of a personal history, but present instead a narrowly defined description of the narrator's political activities.

The two major examples of medieval autobiography are those of Augustine and Abelard. Augustine's work, *Confessiones,* represents the last of ancient autobiography, rather than the forerunner of medieval autobiography. It was only in the twelfth century—in particular the

This article was first published in *Tarbiz* 55 (1985–86): 541–66. The translation/adaptation is by Zippora Brody.

autobiography of Guibert de Nogent, written in 1155—that Augustine's book became the archetype for Christian autobiography. This is also the period in which Abelard unfolded the tale of his sufferings, *Historia clamitatum mearum*, in epistolary form, to an anonymous friend, real or imaginary. This is not coincidental; the twelfth century was a period when individual self-awareness began to stir. The emergence of auto-biographical literature is a primary indication of this awakening.

Mystical autobiographical literature which took little heed of the ac-tivities of the outside world developed concurrently in the twelfth–fourteenth centuries. Hildegard von Bingen (d. 1179) and Mechthild von Magdeburg (1212–1280)—the latter wrote *Das fliegende Licht der Gottheit (The Flowing Light of God)*, the first autobiography in German—and later, Heinrich Seuse (1295–1366), described their path to God, ac-companied by visions, revelations, and ecstasy. These were autobiog-raphies of personal religious experiences, inner turmoil, suffering, and redemption, rather than the experiences of the authors in the world around them.

Also among the forerunners of autobiographical literature in the late medieval period, are travelogues of pilgrims and merchants, chronicles and family genealogies, and wills and business documents. In general, however, the Middle Ages were poor in autobiographical works; from 1400–1500 no more than ten such books were written in Christian Europe.

The secular-bourgeois autobiography begins to develop at the end of the fourteenth century. Its inception is thus described by George Misch, one of the major historians of the genre:

The son writes for the benefit of his family what he heard from his father. He compiles from old documents and family records his genealogy, paying special attention to the economic relationships between the family members. [He] adds his own life history and that of his children and grandchildren, and binds it all together with worldly advice and ethical exhortation.[1]

The narrator's personality is evident more in his interaction with ex-ternal events and other individuals than in a description of emotions or a subjective expression of personal experiences. The "I-world" inter-action reflects the medieval perception of reality, where the individual saw himself as part of a mystical chain of generations. This is primarily true for bourgeois autobiography, but religious autobiography is also characterized by didactic writing, whose aim is to disseminate religious and ethical lessons. The real protagonist in the biography is not the individual, but the beliefs that he represents and that are realized throughout the course of his life.

Examples of this type of work in medieval Jewish literature are *Obad-*

iah's Scroll (twelfth century), describing the Norman proselyte's conversion to Judaism, and *The Notebook of No Amon*, by the poet Moses son of Abraham Dar'i, which describes his path to Karaism, the Jewish sect which rejected the authority of the Oral Law. However, medieval Jewish literature bequeaths to us only a short list of autobiographies, insufficient to define a genre. Not one of them gives an entire life history; each focuses on specific biographical incidents that the author thought worthy of mention—the *Chronicle of Eviatar* by the Palestinian Gaon Eviatar the Priest, or the Memoirs of R. Eleazer ben Judah, famed as the author of the Ashkenazic halakhic codes, the *Rokeah*, who records the tragedy that befell his family in the Crusade of 1197.

Similar to these are biographical notes included by various authors in their works, most often in the introduction. Thus, for example, Shabbetai Donnolo (913–c. 982), an Italian physician, opens his *Sefer Ḥakhmoni*, an astrological commentary on the early mystical book, *Sefer Yetzira*, with a selective personal biography, whose sole purpose is to trace the course of his studies in medicine and astrology rather than to create a literary or historical document. Even in an obviously biographical work such as the *Scroll of Ahima'az*, an eleventh-century Italian-Jewish composition, the author is interested in proving the importance of his genealogy and extolling his ancestors, rather than in describing his own life.

R. Judah ben Asher, son of the *Asheri* (the renowned talmudic scholar who first meshed the halakhic traditions of Ashkenaz and Spain), mentions several details of his family biography in his will and explains their inclusion thus:

The second plan is for me to write something of the history of my saintly progenitors, for the edification of those that come after us. Seeing that the Lord, blessed be He, "hurled us with a man's throw" to Toledo, that great and renowned city, and that a little later the Jews were expelled from France, possibly some may think that we were among the exiles, or that we left our country in consequence of some whispered suspicion. Therefore it seems desirable to me to disabuse everyone of such an imputation. And further, when our posterity regards the upright lives of our ancestors, they will be ashamed if they walk not in the same paths. Rather will they strive in all things to imitate their fathers, thus finding grace and good favor in the sight of God and man. Otherwise, better were it for them never to be born.[2]

A will is the natural place for R. Judah's stated objective in writing: to uphold the distinguished reputation of his family in their new environment, following their emigration from Ashkenaz, and to exhort his descendants to follow in their ancestors' footsteps. However, he also relates certain personal incidents that have no bearing on his family history or its glorification. He describes his mother's dream before his birth, and the eye disease which he contracted in childhood and which never was healed. These and other incidents are apologies for not having attained the scholarly stature of his father and brothers and for not having composed halakhic works as they did.

A few autobiographical descriptions can be found in that popular medieval form of rhymed prose, the *maqama*, the most famous examples of which are the *Taḥkemoni* of Judah Alḥarizi (1170–1235) and the *Maḥbarot* of Immanuel of Rome (c.1261–after 1328). Some were written specifically for autobiographical purposes. A twelfth-century work found in the Cairo Geniza opens with these words: "These are the events of Moshe ben Levi [of Egypt], occurring during his lifetime." Another *maqama*, also of twelfth-century Egypt, whose publisher called it "[t]he autobiographical chronicle of a lad," seems to be more an imaginative parody than a realistic biography. Its author, a young man, tells of his father's second marriage, resulting in the birth of two daughters and a son. The author (their stepbrother), hated them, and expressed in his work his lack of emotion at their deaths. He even went so far as to compose a poem of thanksgiving to the Lord, and to pray for their mother's death as well. These strange excesses contribute to the impression of literary fiction, rather than a true story. In other works as well, autobiographical remarks serve literary purposes and may be fictional.

Our interest here is in factual rather than literary autobiography; this type, however, was not prevalent in the Middle Ages. Those isolated fragments of factual autobiography that we do find emanate from the East, rather than from northern Europe. Jewish autobiographical literature really begins in the sixteenth and seventeenth century, with Leon de Modena's (1571–1648) *Life of Judah* and Isaac ben Jacob Min Ha-Leviyyim's [of the Levites] (1621–1670) *Medabber Tahapukhot*. German Jews also contributed to the flowering of this genre; for example, the memoirs of Josel of Rosheim (1471–1547), Yom Tov Lippmann Heller's (1579–1654) composition *Megillat Eivah*, and Glueckel of Hamlin's (1645–1724) life story.

Because of the paucity of medieval Jewish autobiographies, special importance must be attached to a short anonymous autobiography written in the second half of the fourteenth century by a Jew born in the German city of Düren, who lived in Andernach during its composition. It is found in a manuscript of the Bodleian Library, Oxford, and appears in translation at the end of this chapter.[3]

Most of the Oxford manuscript was written before 1333 and contains various Ashkenazic works, among them the *Sha'arei Dura*, by Isaac ben Meir also of Düren (but not a contemporary of our author). In the colophon of the latter work, the scribe notes that he copied the manuscript for Shemariah of Zülpich, a neighboring city. The manuscript apparently circulated in the area, and eventually reached the author of our autobiography, who attached it to the end of his own life story.

This document is unique in three ways:

1. It is the first document in Jewish literature that comprehensively describes in chronological order the major biographical events of the author's life, from childhood to adulthood.

2. It is an exclusively personal autobiography, few of which exist from the medieval period. Despite its dry chronological order and its prosaic style, it illuminates in a warm and naive manner intimate, authentic, at times trivial, incidents of the author's life, which nevertheless occasionally echo more significant general events that had an impact on his biography.

3. The author is ordinary in terms of his social status and education. Until now the work of Abraham Yagel, *Gay Hizayyon*, written in Italy in 1577–1578, was considered the "first example in Jewish literature of the autobiography of a simple man [of the Renaissance period] with no literary, political, or historical pretensions, who is not interested in dealing with major philosophical problems, but with his own small, personal world."[4] The document presented here is a literary find which advances this genre by 200 years and places it in pre-Renaissance Germany.

A description of the content of the document, and a discussion of its literary and historical implications, follow.

AN ANONYMOUS JEWISH AUTOBIOGRAPHY

The author mentions only the names of his father, Samuel the Levite, and of his two sisters: Gutchen and Devla. As we shall see, the author was related to several wealthy families in the southern Rhineland.

He opens his autobiography in the spring of 1370, when he left his parental home in Düren in order to study in Mainz. This is the first documentation found of the existence of Jews in Düren after their expulsion from the city in 1350. In Mainz, he studied Pentateuch with a *haver* Isserlin (or Asherlin), otherwise unknown. As was customary, he started the summer semester, which the author called *zeman* (the traditional term for a period of Torah study in the yeshivah), on the first day of Iyyar (April–May). Another Jewish document lists the names of five scholars who lived in Mainz at the time. Two held the title *morenu* (our teacher): Moshe Moellin, father of Jacob Moellin (1375–1427), known as *Maharil*, the foremost talmudist of the generation, and Abraham Durinqa, father-in-law of *Maharil;* an additional three were designated *ḥaver.* Isserlin is not one of them, from which we conclude that he had a less distinguished status. From this fact, and the fact that our author was studying the Pentateuch, it seems that he was just starting his studies and was quite young; we estimate that he was approximately thirteen—a relatively late age to begin such studies. He seems to have been no great scholar. His parents apparently sent him away from home for his early education because there was no teacher closer, which gives us an idea of the havoc wreaked upon the Rhineland communities in the wake of the Black Plague.

His studies in Mainz were not of long duration: after three months he was notified that his father was terminally ill, and he returned home accompanied by a messenger, another indication of his youth at the time. The journey lasted three days, until he reached the Cologne area, where an informer delivered him into the hands of "bandits." A rich Jew by the name of Simon of Siegburg, a relative of the author, lived in the area at the time. Upon hearing of the boy's captivity, he presented himself to the Graf von Berg, with whom he had business dealings, in order to ransom his relative. This took a month, during which time the author's father passed away. The author returned home and lived there for a year.

In the summer of 1371, he decided to join the forces that had organized under Duke Wilhelm II of Jülich against Herzog Wenzel of Brabant, out of either a youthful taste for adventure or a well-developed business sense. In any event, this was unacceptable for a Jewish youth, and his mother was very angry. He therefore decided, upon returning, to once again leave home and study in Koblenz, an indication that the community had a scholar who was able to teach Torah, a fact unknown from any other source. It is doubtful that intellectual curiosity led the author to renew his studies; perhaps it was another example of youthful rebellion. In Koblenz, he became affianced to a girl from Trier, but changed his mind, apparently under pressure from relatives who lived in the city. He does not even mention his mother's opinion. He was fifteen at the time, an age when marriage arrangements were customarily made.

His studies at Koblenz also did not last long. He travelled to Rothenburg to study, and there joined forces with another youth and wandered further, to Austria, then the center of Jewish learning for all of Germany. In Austria, in the summer of 1375, at the age of eighteen, he married a woman whose family was important and adds "as everyone knows." The wedding took place far from home, with no parental guidance or family interference. Ten months after his marriage he ended his wanderings and returned to the Rhineland with his wife, a journey which lasted two months rather than the usual three weeks.

His return home with a wife, and his transformation into a family man, mark a new chapter in his life, although not an end to his travels. He settled first in Siegburg, but after only five months left for Düren. There he lived for a year-and-a-half, until the spring of 1378, when he returned to Siegburg for a number of months. In the summer of 1378, according to his testimony, two of the relatives mentioned previously, Simon of Siegburg and his brother-in-law David, were executed. The following day, he, his mother, and all his family living in Siegburg (aside from his wife) were arrested and all their property confiscated. He was under arrest for two months; after his release in the fall of 1378, he left with his mother for Andernach.

The author then decided once more to travel for the purposes of study. He was twenty-one at the time and a married man. This journey was also not of long duration. In 1381, both his sisters—the younger of whom lived with his mother in Andernach, and the older who lived in Cologne—died within a short period of time, and he decided to return home; but in the spring of 1382 he had already moved to Koblenz. There he became a community functionary: *hazan*, *shohet*, and keeper of the local hostel (apparently maintained by the community for the benefit of the poor), whose existence is first attested to in 1356. This appointment indicates that he was not a scholar, nor was he wealthy, perhaps because of his family's losses connected with the incident of Simon of Siegburg. In the summer of 1387, he returned to Andernach where he lived "until today." There he quarreled with his friends and was imprisoned in 1390, for the third time in ten years.

From this point on, the manuscript is damaged and only isolated sentences can be retrieved. He seems to have been freed from prison thanks to testimony given by some friends on his behalf, but he had to pay a fine. However, this was not the end of his troubles. A Christian attacked and wounded him, and apparently left only after thinking him dead. The author mentions other problems that befell him because of the *Kellner*, an administrative official of the Bishop who appeared before the Cardinal and his advisers. He ends his narrative with the pious hope that he will have the privilege of travelling to Jerusalem and of building the Temple, as befitting a Levite. Despite the defective state of the last lines of the manuscript, this celebratory and comforting ending indicates that the autobiography is whole. The signature also hints at the author's motive for writing the autobiography: he feels that his life until then (he was thirty-three at the time) was full of troubles that he wished to record. This view is understandable in someone who was orphaned at age thirteen, imprisoned three times, wandered many years far from home, and was badly wounded—although similar incidents befell many individuals in the Middle Ages, both Jews and non-Jews.

SOCIAL AND HISTORICAL IMPLICATIONS

What can this biography teach us about the social history of the Jews in Germany? The aspect most apparent to the reader is demographic instability. The author changes his dwelling-place twelve times in the space of twenty years. His frequent wanderings are not the result of an expulsion policy against the Jews, one of the hallmarks of the period, but of personal, familial, or economic considerations. It is notable that the author opens the description of his life with his departure from his parental home and his travels to Mainz to study. This departure, not the usual rites of passage (bar-mitzvah, marriage), signifies the start of an independent life, whose concrete expression was wandering. This independence is apparent later as well. After the mourning period for his father, the narrator does not return to his studies, but remains at home for a year-and-a-half, until he joins the army. The impression is that this adventure and his later travels for study purposes are attempts to assert his independence.

While he was a young bachelor, the geographical area of his travels was quite extensive: Mainz, Koblenz, Rothenberg, Austria. His marriage returned him to his family and restricted his travels to a much smaller geographical radius, while not reducing their frequency. In this respect, the author is not unusual among the Jews and non-Jews of his time.

Of special interest are his travels for purposes of study. This phenomenon, which became widespread among Christian students primarily during the humanistic period of the sixteenth century, had a uniquely Jewish background. Talmudic tradition advised against learning Torah from only one teacher (*Avodah Zarah* 19a). During the Middle Ages, this dictum had very practical applications. In contrast to the universities that were distinguished by their abundance of teachers and their stability, the more prominent drawing students from all of Europe, Jewish centers of Torah generally revolved around one teacher who was responsible for their rise and fall. This explains why the quest for knowledge involved taking a travelling staff in hand. Even married men undertook travel for purposes of study exactly as did our author; this is no doubt a consequence of the early marriage age then customary in Jewish society. For example, *Maharil*, already a married man, reached Italy in the south and Cologne in the north, and left his wife alone for long periods of time during the course of his studies. Similarly, two men, one of Enns and the second a student in Wiener Neustadt, are mentioned in a halakhic work as having left their wives for uninterrupted periods of eleven and twelve months. The latter work attempted to prove that a pregnancy can last longer than nine months! Travel by married men was so common that such arrangements were formalized and agreed upon by the families of the couple. The marriage settlement often included an agreement that the bridegroom could continue his studies after his marriage.

Little is known of the life of these wandering students. The author tells of joining another young man in Rothenburg and arranging to travel with him to Austria. In a Jewish writing manual (*Iggeret Shlomim*, n.43) printed in Augsburg in 1534, which contains examples of letters of the previous century, there is a letter written by a youth to his friend in which he notifies him of the establishment of a yeshivah in Erfurt (evidently before 1453–54, the date when the Jews left the city). The writer expresses his desire to travel there, and invites his friend to join him. "Let me know if you will accompany me, and I will go, and we will share a purse, and your horses will be as mine, and all your needs will be my responsibility. There will always be a compact between us, and no stranger shall interfere . . . for two are better than one."

This journey was not only for purposes of study; both young men had been invited to a wedding feast in Erfurt. In order to convince his friend to join him, the writer also suggested several attractive business propositions: a large fair was scheduled in Erfurt at this time, and he suggests a partnership in buying goods there and selling them elsewhere at a profit. It seems then, that a journey for study did not preclude two young men enjoying themselves and making a profit as well. Such travel, whether as youthful adventure or for serious study, is also mentioned in passing by *Maharil*. He notes that one of the advantages of a married youth continuing his studies after his wedding is financial support from his parents or in-laws in order to "go out with the boys."

These travels often spanned long distances. One of those who travelled for study was R. Shimshon, a prominent talmudist and author of the halakhic works *Kizur Mordechai* and *Yeriot Izim*, born in Düren circa 1330 and also the son of Samuel (perhaps he and the author of our autobiography were brothers?). In 1349, he studied in Heidelberg with Isaac Halevi *Assir HaTikvah* (Prisoner of Hope; see Zech. 9:12) of Beilstein. A year later, the teacher and pupils, including Shimshon, travelled to Jerusalem. In the spring of 1359 Shimshon left Eretz Israel, and on his way home spent some time in Famagusta, Cyprus, studying with another Ashkenazi teacher, Eliezer Pirna. That same year he was once again in Germany, apparently in Worms. At the age of thirty he ceased his travels, remaining in Worms at least until 1377 and continuing his studies with a local scholar, R. Meir Halevi. From 1380 on he served as the rabbi of Dortmund, and in 1383 he is mentioned as living in Sankt Goar in the Rhine Valley. He may have left there for a while to live in Bresse, Savoy.[5]

Long journeys are also mentioned in a book of Jewish magic attributed to Abraham ben Simon of Worms.[6] The author met a Bohemian

Jew by the name of Samuel and arranged to travel with him to Constantinople and to Eretz Israel, to learn magic. They travelled through Hungary, Greece, reached Egypt, and then returned to Constantinople. From there the author continued on to Venice, and on his way home managed to take a short side-trip to Paris where he made the acquaintance of an apostate who knew magic. According to the author, all this took place in 1387—although the entire book may be a fictional work of the sixteenth century. Nonetheless, imaginary characters also reflect reality:

I decided to return home, until I met a man of our nation from Bohemia called R. Samuel, whose good qualities bear witness to his desire to follow the path of God. I therefore made a compact with him and he told me of his desire to go to his uncle in Constantinople, and from there to the land of our holy forefathers. I wished to accompany him and we both swore not to be parted one from another. On the thirteenth of Adar [year left blank in original manuscript] we left and travelled through all of the land of Ashkenaz, Bohemia, and Austria, and from there through Hungary and Greece until we reached Constantina, and I stayed there two years. Were it not for R. Samuel's contracting a fatal illness I would not have left. (Ms. Oxford Bodleian Library, cat. A. Neubauer, no. 2051, vol. 2v–3n)

The late fifteenth-century works of the Alsatian scholar Yohanan Luria recommend travelling for study purposes. He maintained that a youth should begin to learn Talmud with one teacher from the age of fifteen, for five years. After gaining a basic knowledge during this time, the student was advised to travel from one teacher to another, and from one yeshivah to another, "for he who studies with one teacher cannot be compared to one who studies with many," since each scholar has his own area of expertise.

Other important information emerges from our autobiography concerning the history of the Jewish family and of education in the Middle Ages. As mentioned above, the author was not particularly well educated. On the other hand, he cannot be considered a simple man, for he writes Hebrew in a pleasant and coherent style. Whatever the degree of seriousness he attached to his studies, he nevertheless spent six years of his life (from age thirteen to nineteen) in study. Even after his marriage, at the age of twenty-two, he left his wife to study in yeshivot. His later appointment as a *hazan* and *shohet* indicates his status as one of the minor intelligentsia of the Jewish community.

Like many Jewish youths of his age, and unlike his Christian counterparts, the author was not apprenticed to learn a trade; this was due to the ban on accepting Jews into the Christian guilds and the restriction of Jews to the business of money lending. This had implications for Jewish education and for marriage arrangements which could therefore take place at a relatively early age. As will be recalled, our narrator's first engagement in Koblenz was at the age of fourteen, and his marriage took place at the age of eighteen. A systematic study of the marital age customary in Jewish society at that period has not yet been made, but the impression is that the average age for marriage, at least in well-established families, was between fifteen and twenty.

The author's life did not, however, conform to societal norms in all aspects. His engagement to a woman from Trier and his wedding in Austria (to someone else) were both a result of his own initiative, without the involvement of his mother or other relatives. This departure from the usual practice of the time can be explained by his having been orphaned at an early age, and perhaps by the cool relationship with his mother. However, his marriage to a woman from such a distant place was not unusual. Due to the small size of the Jewish communities in Germany (about thirty families in a large community and ten in an average one), it was difficult to find an appropriate partner in the locality. This may also explain the development of the institution of arranged marriages, which became a major source of income of several rabbis. In some cases, we hear of marriage agreements being signed by families separated by a distance of hundreds of miles. To cite a famous case, *Maharil* married a local girl during his studies in Austria, although his family lived in Mainz.

Here and there, the author unveils a bit of the ethical and marital norms of his time. He mentions, as cited above, that his wife comes from a family of "the descendants of important people, as everyone knows," from which it emerges that family pedigree was an important factor in marriage arrangements. The author does not bother to tell us which family his wife actually belonged to, perhaps because there was no real pedigree; the phrase "as everyone knows" sounds more like an apologetic evasion than a definite source of pride. For this very reason, his words clearly indicate the norm of the time. This is expressed in other sources of the period as well. In a matchmaker's letter found in the writing manual cited above, the writer extols the virtues of the match he proposed: the girl comes from a good family; her father and uncle are scholars; the girl is pretty, well-behaved, healthy, bright, and sociable. In addition, the family is prepared to guarantee a large dowry. In another case, the father of the bride complains that the bridegroom's father did not provide his son with new clothes for the wedding. The bride's father did not want to return with a bridegroom dressed in rags, for fear of being mocked by "the crowd." Marriages were a matter of public prestige, and the honor of the family, and particularly of the head of the household, was a major consideration.

The short life span during the Middle Ages is also testified to in this autobiography. The father of our author died when his son was thirteen. Two of his sisters passed away when he was twenty-three. He mentions his mother with the blessing for dead, meaning that she died before the year 1390, when he was thirty-three. It is surprising that he did not bother to mention the circumstances of her death and its date. Did he have so little affection for her?

THE INCIDENT OF SIMON OF SIEGBURG

The incident narrated by the author concerning the execution of his relatives Simon of Siegburg and David, is also related in other sources, both German (the city chronicles of Cologne) and Jewish (a Hebrew lament on their death). According to the German chronicle this incident occurred on the 5th of August 1377, while our narrator gives a Jewish date later in the year—the 29th Av, 138 (=1378). The two sources agree on the day of the month, but this only fits the year 1377, when August 5 was also the 29th of Av. Our author was apparently not careful with dates, which is not surprising since he wrote his personal history at least fourteen years later.

The details of the incident are as follows: Simon of Siegburg, one of the wealthy Jews of the Rhineland during that period, and his brother-in-law David were arrested in 1375 by the court of the Archbishop of Cologne and convicted of informing on other Jews and of delivering them into the hands of two brigand nobles, the brothers of Öfte, who attacked and robbed them on the road from Bonn to Cologne. Since Simon and David were subjects of the city of Cologne, it demanded their release. When this was to no avail, the city applied pressure by imprisoning the representative of the Archbishop. The quarrel rapidly escalated into the war known as the Schöffenkrieg, where the real issue was the secular jurisdiction of the Archbishop over the city of Cologne. After two years of war, a compromise was reached on February 16, 1377, in the framework of which the city rescinded its original demand for the release of the two imprisoned Jews. The two were executed, and Simon's considerable wealth (around 27,000 gulden) was confiscated and divided between the Archbishop and the city of Cologne. In accordance with the request of Graf von Kleve, Simon's wife was saved from death and converted to Christianity. We learn from the autobiography that the incident did not end with the execution of Simon and David. The family of the author, related to Simon of Siegburg, was imprisoned after the two were hung, and their wealth was also confiscated. Thus, the author was indirectly involved in this incident, which was one of a chain of events in the struggle by Cologne for political independence.

The Cologne chronicle couches the accusation against Simon of Siegburg as an informer in a vague statement. The charge seems dubious and cannot be accepted at face value, since it is difficult to imagine that the execution of informers was occasion for the composition of a Jewish lament for the Ninth of Av. Moreover, if the testimony of a relative can be relied upon, our author calls Simon "the holy *zaddik*" (e.g., martyr), an appellation unsuitable for someone executed as an informer. It does seem, however, that there is a kernel of truth in the narrative of the German chronicle. Its author knew vaguely that the accusation against Simon was in some way connected to an incident that occurred several years earlier, during which some Jews were arrested on the way from Bonn to Cologne because of informers. This is apparently the incident in which our author was involved in the summer of 1370 on his way back from Mainz to his home: "On the way an informer delivered me into the hands of bandits"—the robber nobles described by the German chronicle. According to the author, the event occurred close to the home of Simon of Siegburg, that is, between Cologne and Bonn, and the latter rescued him by virtue of his good connections with Graf von Berg. In other words, all the facts related by the German chronicle as the reason for Simon's execution are found here, except that the informer was not Simon, but someone else. It seems likely that with the passing of time, the German chronicler faintly remembered the incident, and meshed it with the executions of Simon and David. This might account for our author also being arrested after the execution of his relatives.

The execution of these two wealthy men during the month of Av, the time of tribulation and mourning for the destruction of the Temple, was of special significance, and explains why their being put to death was described in a lament for the Ninth of Av. The author of the lament, R. Menahem Zion, was a resident of Cologne at the time. He signs his name in an acrostic: Menahem Zion son of Rabbi Meir *miloh davar*. The phrase *miloh davar* is strange but R. Menahem also used it in his Hebrew signature on a receipt to the city of Cologne, preserved in the historical archive of the city. In documents of Frankfurt and Cologne, he is called several times: "Man von Spire" (the name of his birthplace, or that of his family). It has been suggested that the phrase *miloh davar* is the Hebrew translation of the ancient name of his birthplace, Speyer, namely, Nemetum [=nowhere].

It is also known that in the 1350s, R. Menahem travelled to Jerusalem and studied in a yeshivah of Ashkenazic scholars who had emigrated from Germany. His pilgrimage to Jerusalem earned him the appellation "Zion," which later became a family name. While he was in the East, R. Menahem was introduced to kabbalistic mysticism and was one of the first German scholars to synthesize in his works Ashkenazic and Spanish mystic approaches. He was also the first in Germany to make extensive use of the *Zohar*, the seminal work of Spanish kabbalah. His stay in the Land of Israel extended at the latest to the 1360s, for during 1364–1368 he was registered as a resident of Frankfurt. In 1372 R. Menahem settled in Cologne as one of the first Jews who returned there after the Black Plague. There, in 1384, he wrote his main *oeuvre*, the *Zioni*, a mystical commentary on the Pentateuch. This is the latest documentation for his dwelling in Cologne. By 1387, he had already settled in the vicinity of Venice where he participated together with three other people in floating a loan of 19,500 ducats. We last hear of him in Northern Italy in 1399.

R. Menahem's lament on the murder of Simon of Siegburg and David is written in the best tradition of religious poetry, joining sorrow for the destruction of Jerusalem with the troubles befalling the Jewish nation throughout the generations. Alongside a general lamentation over the fate of the nation, the author wove in concrete references to the tragedy befalling two members of his city and faith. The metaphors make a clear understanding of these references difficult at times. At the beginning of the lament, the author speaks words of eulogy for those murdered by "Christians," a phrase that obviously does not refer to the destruction of Jerusalem.

References to the "plucking of two berries from the top of the tree" refer to the murder of the two men, while "non-Jews besieged the beautiful daughter of the Hebrews" suggests the attempt to convert Simon's wife under threat of death. "The priests who officiated . . . inherited as well as murdered" suggests the confiscation of the victims' wealth. References to an "unclean animal and a rat" apparently are symbols for the Archbishop and for the city of Cologne. The former was the representative of the "unclean religion," as Christianity was called by Jews in the Middle Ages. "Rat" seems to be a play on words: *Rat* was the designation in German for town council. Thus the city of Cologne was accused of abetting the crime.

LITERARY ASPECTS

This document's poor literary quality is in inverse ratio to its value for the history of autobiography and the study of the mentality of the ordinary person in the Middle Ages.

The narrator attempted a full chronological description of his life history. He opens with a declaration of intention: "These are the chronicles and the happenings," meaning all the events that he deemed important, from the time he became a mature individual with an autonomous biography. His omission of his childhood and the date of his birth hints at the possibility that he did not consider them important enough to record. The dimension of time in his descriptions is not personal; he does not mention his age, but records only impersonal calendar dates. As P. Ariés has already noted, people in the Middle Ages rarely specified their age; this consciousness appeared only in the sixteenth century.[7] For medieval man, time had a universal, not an individual, rhythm.

No autobiography lacks a purpose. People chronicle their life because they believe it serves some useful purpose. Our author recorded his life history because he found some worthwhile aspects to it, his troubles being enough of a reason to do so. It is a mistake, however, to think of this autobiography solely, as a chronicle of suffering. The author reported various incidents that were unrelated to his suffering. He saw fit to write his personal biography, because he felt it to have intrinsic value.

If we compare this narrative to later Jewish autobiographies such as Leon de Modena's, or to contemporaneous German autobiographies, the unique characteristic of the narrator's style becomes apparent: he is enclosed in his own personal world and even omits events in his immediate environment or in his family that do not directly affect him. He apparently reports his father's death only to explain the chain of events that led to his arrest and does not record his mother's death at all. He does not bother to mention whether he has children and what their names are. We do not learn who his teachers were in Austria during the five years he spent there. He totally ignores the political events of his time, unless he is physically and financially involved. It is possible that his omission of his own name is a consequence of this introversion. He does not record his genealogy or family history, nor leave any message for posterity. He deals only with the present. His account lacks all ethical pretension, practical purpose, or desire to exhort his family. This is a completely personal account, whose author was aware only of his private life.

On the other hand, his narrative exhibits no self-awareness. A person's search for identity takes place against a hostile or nurturing background, within a certain political climate and social horizon. Our author, however, tells little of this, probably because it did not seem of value to him in relating his life story. The events happening to him are recorded in a broad, objective, rather than subjective, manner. They read as dry facts, and the modern reader looks in vain for some emotional or personal reaction. The verbs most used by the writer are: I left, I returned, I rode, I came, I settled, I was imprisoned. There is a great deal of external activity, but the narrative is static on the experiential level and includes very little descriptive adjectives. The author uses "and it transpired" three times while relating the same incident, indicating his passivity regarding what happens to him.

The real protagonist of this life history is not the narrator "I," but the events that overtook him. We know a good deal concerning the facts of his life, but very little of his personality; his image remains completely veiled. His interest lies in a dry recounting of facts, not in the impression they made on his memories. He is a person who tells of going to war, but not what motivated him to do so, nor what a fifteen-year-old boy saw on the battlefield. He reports his various imprisonments, without telling of the reasons for them or of his feelings as a prisoner. He is attacked and wounded, and we do not know why. Of his wife, he relates only that she was of a good family, not if he loved or hated her; he does not even mention her name. His being orphaned at an early age is recorded as an event without consequences. This is not the style of a person who seeks to define his identity through an autobiographical description. There is an overflowing cup of suffering in this chronicle, but no inner turmoil. It tells of wandering, but not of adventure. It lacks any attempt to impart psychological significance to the events of life, any development of the author's personality. His life proceeds smoothly from childhood to adulthood, with the same descriptions and atmosphere in both; it would be possible to reverse the order of events without any noticeable difference.

That which perhaps most characterizes modern biography is the retrospective view of one's life, making of the sequence of events a coherent whole. An autobiography is essentially an attempt to create a commentary on one's life, looking backward. These qualities are totally absent in the report before us.

The uniqueness of this work is apparent when compared with German autobiographies of the period. Scholars of German literature agree that the first secular Germany autobiography is that of Ulman Stromer, an aristocratic native of Nuremberg. The tale of his family and adventures covers the years 1349–1407, exactly the same period dealt with by the Jew of Düren. Perhaps it is not accidental that the beginning of German autobiography and of its Jewish Ashkenazic counterpart occurs at the same time. Is it possible to see in this phenomenon an expression of a new self-awareness by the generation after the Black Plague? However, the similarity between the two compositions, both in terms of style and author, is minimal.

First, the status of the narrator: Stromer was a wealthy man of considerable political consequence in his city, who served on the town council and was its head for a time. In contrast, the Jew from Düren was of secondary social status, with a mediocre education, who served in minor community offices, and did not belong to the higher economic echelons of the Jewish society of his day. This basic difference also determines the dissimilar content of the two autobiographies.

Stromer devotes a good deal of space to an exhaustive genealogical description of "his family and adventures"—the name he also gives to his work *(Puechel von mein geslechet und von abentewr)*—in order to prove his family's prominence, while the Jewish author describes only his adventures and not his family. In this our autobiography is closer to that of Burkard Zink of Augsburg (1396–1475), who described only his parents and did not relate his earlier family history. This characteristic distinguishes the autobiography of the Jew from the German family chronicles widespread among the bourgeoisie and nobility from the early fourteenth century onward (for example, the detailed genealogies of Erasmus Schürstab and the memoirs of Bertold Tucher); it is more similar to later autobiographies that put the narrator at the center of the action.

In Stromer's work, as in many other bourgeois chronicles, there is still a strong link between the autobiographical chapters and the financial and trade lists on which they were based. Stromer integrated into his work detailed information concerning prices, coins, weights, and the cities in which the merchants of Nuremberg were exempt from taxes. Other authors mentioned in their chronicles their income, expenses, and debts, and included various financial documents. In this way, the bourgeois values of the time were expressed, with wealth a central factor in evaluating an individual. The author of our narrative, on the other hand, showed no interest in detailing his financial dealings. He related laconically that he was rescued from his first imprisonment "with no financial loss." During his second arrest "all that he owned was taken from him;" the third time: "I sustained some losses." Aside from this, we learn nothing about his economic activities. This indifference is not necessarily common to his Jewish contemporaries. However, a person who served for five years as a *hazan, shohet,* and hostel-keeper was certainly not wealthy, nor did he make a living by money lending. Perhaps for this reason, his report lacks all the business and financial information that characterizes the German bourgeois autobiography.

Stromer's perspective is quite broad; incidents relating to the history of his city and of the Reich merit detailed description. It is noteworthy that he related in his work the fate of the Jewish community in Nuremberg during the Black Death. The Christian includes this major cataclysm, while the Jew (who was born shortly after the Plague) does not mention it or its consequences! Stromer also records another event, perhaps the most important in the history of German Jews in the latter half of the fourteenth century: King Wenzel's annulment of Jewish debts in 1390. This is not mentioned in the Jewish composition written at the same period.

The breadth of Stromer's knowledge and horizons is also evident from the length of his work, which is five times longer than our document. On the other hand, half of Stromer's composition is not autobiography for its own sake, while our work is devoted only to that.

Stromer's personal life serves as a background to the history of his city; his identification with his city and the Reich is deep and precludes his placing himself in the center of the narrative. This characteristic is true of most German autobiographical journals of the fourteenth and fifteenth centuries. Biographical details are almost always included in connection with external events, not as independent descriptions.

Stromer's work lacks literary unity as well; he passes from one topic to another without transitional statements. It is apparent that the chronicle was written in stages, in contrast to our document whose descriptions are coherent, and where the chain of events is clear, probably because it was all written at one time.

Nonetheless, there are several points of similarity between the two authors: the time framework for both is general chronology, not their own lives. Both dwell on incidents that they report in an impersonal style, without relating any experiential or emotional details. Most significantly, both believe that their life story is important enough to merit telling; it is not a literary means serving an ideological-religious end, as is common in the autobiographical literature of the Middle Ages.

In summary, we have been considering a document of an ordinary man, one of the minor intelligentsia of the Jewish society of his day. It is perhaps the first example of the literary genre of Jewish autobiography, describing in prosaic language an entire life story in chronological order, having no didactic purpose aside from the importance the author assigned to writing it down.

May we conjecture that the motive for composing it was a conscious search for identity? Did the author have the self-awareness which marked the transition to Renaissance man? The answer seems to be negative. This is a unique document, the like of which is not known either earlier or later. The author emerges, on the one hand, as a person with little sensitivity to his own individuality, and on the other hand, as egocentric and introverted, one who does not appreciate all that occurs around him as having value for his own story. Jacob Burkhardt, the first to point out the link between the appearance of biographical literature in Renaissance Italy and the development of the self-aware and self-critical individual wrote, "Much of what, till the close of the Middle Ages, passed for biography is, properly speaking, nothing but contemporary narrative, written without any sense of what is individual in the subject of the memoir, or any desire to tell of his greatness."[8] The document before us tells us nothing of the events of the time, only of the life of the author, yet he did not seek to glorify himself. It is not a pre-Renaissance mentality that emerges from this work, but rather the practical, sober, ambiance of the fourteenth century and of the generation after the great plagues.

APPENDIX: MS. OXFORD, BODLEIAN LIBRARY, MICHAEL 74 (Neubauer Catalogue, no. 1171), 154b

These are the chronicles and events from the day I left the house of my father, R. Samuel the Levite of the city of Düren. [I] left the house of my father of blessed memory on the 25th of Nissan, Sunday, 1370, and studied at that time in Mainz, before the ḥaver R. Isserlin [or Asherlin], a commentary on the Pentateuch. R. Moses son of R. Meshullam studied together with me before the ḥaver R. Isserlin. On Friday, 25th Tammuz 1370, a special messenger came to return me to my father's house, for he was fatally ill. I returned with the messenger, and on the way an informer delivered me into the hands of brigands on Monday, 28th Tammuz 1370, who held me for a month. The messenger went to my father of blessed memory to notify him, and my father died five days later on Friday, 3rd Av 1370. When my relative the saintly Simon of Siegburg realized that I had been captured one mile from him, he acted with the help of the noble Graf von Berg, who released me from my captivity with no financial loss, and returned me to the house of my mother of blessed memory.

Then I rode with the soldiers on Friday, 10th Elul 1371, in the war between the Duke of Jülich and the Duke of Brabant. When I returned from the war, my mother of blessed memory was angry with me. I went from her to study in Koblenz, and there became affianced to the daughter of Bruna of Trier. My relatives prevailed upon me not to marry her. I went from Koblenz to Rothenburg to study there. From Rothenburg I went with an important man named R. Jonah Geisel, and came with him to the province of Austria and studied there, until I became affianced to a descendant of important people, as everyone knows. The wedding took place on Shabbat Ekev 1375, and I remained there until after Passover 1376.

I came to Siegburg with my wife on Thursday, 28th Sivan 1376, and settled in Düren for a year-and-a-half, from the first day of Heshvan 1376 until Passover 1378. Then I settled in Siegburg from Passover 1378 until the first day of [name of month missing in ms] 1378.

Because of our many sins, on 29th Av, Wednesday, 1378, my relatives the honored R. Simon and the honored R. David were executed by the authorities in Cologne, and the next day I and my mother of blessed memory and my brother and sisters and brother-in-law, the honored Aaron of blessed memory, were imprisoned and all our possessions were taken from us.

Then I settled with my mother of blessed memory in Andernach on the first of the month of Heshvan 1378. I went to study in the yeshivahs of [unclear in ms] until my two sisters died: on the eve of Kippur

1380 my younger sister, Mistress Gutchen passed away in Andernach, and on the second day of the year 1380, my sister Mistress Devla passed away in Cologne.

And it came to pass that I settled in Koblenz on the first day of Nissan 1382, and I became the *ḥazan*, *shoḥet* and *bodek*, and hostel-keeper for the community there until the first day of Elul 1387. Then I returned to settle in Andernach to this day.

In Andernach I quarrelled with some of my friends until it transpired that I was imprisoned on Shabbat Teshuvah 1390, and praised be God, one of my friends testified on my behalf so that the informers could not carry out their hatred of [. . .] and the matter was annulled with only a slight financial loss. It transpired that a non-Jew came on Monday [. . .] and wounded me and ran away, thinking he had killed me. Praised be God and with His help I recovered from all my wounds and who [. . .] salvation, etc., and one says this and one says that. I still have not reached a conclusion why he wounded me, and for all the above incidents, those whom I trusted [?], who ate my bread [? see Ps.41:10] to [. . .] and overcame me by informing about me to the *Kellner*, and the *Kellner* evilly stood before the Archbishop [at Cologne or Trier] and his advisers.

May God in His mercy and goodness [. . .] like [. . .] peace, cause that I may stand and build the eternal house with the rest of my relatives, and to sing there in the eternal house. Amen, Selah, so may it be.

NOTES

1. *Geschichte der Autobiographie*, vol. 4 (Frankfurt: Verlag G. Schulte-Bulmke, 1949–1969), 585.

2. I. Abrahams, *Hebrew Ethical Wills* (Philadelphia: Jewish Publication Society, 1976), 163–200.

3. This autobiography first appeared in print in the Appendix to the Hebrew original of this article, *Tarbiz* 55 (1985–86).

4. D. Ruderman, *Kabbalah, Magic, and Science: The Cultural Universe of a Sixteenth-Century Jewish Physician* (Cambridge, Mass.: Harvard University Press, 1988). See also, *Encyclopaedia Judaica*, vol. 4 (Jerusalem: Keter, 1978), 1011.

5. E. Reiner, "Between Ashkenaz and Jerusalem," *Shalem* 4 (1984), 27–62 (Hebrew).

6. Oxford Bodl. ms. no. 2051 includes the Introduction to this work. The book was translated into several European languages. See *The Book of the Sacred Magic of Abra-Melin the Mage*, trans. S. L. MacGregor-Mathers (London: John M. Watkins, 1899). The English edition was translated from French, which notes that the original was written in Hebrew.

7. P. Ariés, *L'enfant et la vie familiale sous l'Ancien Regime* (Paris: Edition du Seuil, 1973), 29–34.

8. J. Burkhardt, *The Civilization of the Renaissance in Italy*, vol. 2 (New York: Harper-Torchbooks, 1958), 324.

SUGGESTIONS FOR FURTHER READING

A major study of the history of the autobiography is K. J. Weintraub, *The Value of the Individual—Self and Circumstance in Autobiography* (Chicago/London: University of Chicago Press, 1978).

A study of the history of Jewish autobiography, as well as a comprehensive bibliography of works in print and in manuscript, is still a desideratum. For an English anthology that includes several Jewish autobiographies, see L. W. Schwarz, *Memoirs of My People through a Thousand Years* (Philadelphia: Jewish Publication Society, 1960).

For a study of twelfth-century autobiography, see J. F. Benton, "Consciousness of Self and Perception of Individuality," in *Renaissance and Renewal in the Twelfth Century*, ed. by R. L. Benson and G. Constable (Oxford: Clarendon Press, 1982).

Little research has been undertaken in the lives of the lower classes of European Jewry. Mention should be made of C. Roth, "The Ordinary Jew in the Middle Ages: A Contribution to His History," in *Studies and Essays in Honor of Abraham A. Neumann*, ed. M. Ben-Horin (Leiden: Brill, 1962), 424–37; H. Pollack, *Jewish Folkways in Germanic Lands (1648–1806)—Studies in Aspects of Daily Life* (Cambridge Mass./London: M.I.T. Press, 1971).

The most comprehensive book on the subject is R. Glanz, *Geschichte des niederen judischen Volkes in Deutschland—Eine Studie uber historisches Gaunertum, Bettelwesen und Vagantentum* (New York: Leo Baeck Institute, 1968).

16TH AND 17TH CENTURY JEWISH AUTOBIOGRAPHIES

Mark R. Cohen, *The Autobiography of a Seventeenth-Century Venetian Rabbi, Leon Modena's* Life of Judah (Princeton: Princeton University Press, 1988). See the comprehensive introduction by Natalie Z. Davis, "Fame and Secrecy: Leon Modena's Life as an Early Modern Autobiography."

I. Kracauer, "Rabbi Joselmann de Rosheim," *REJ* 16 (1888): 84–105.

A. Marx, "A Seventeenth-Century Autobiography, A Picture of Jewish Life in Bohemia and Moravia," *JQR* n.s. 8 (1918): 269–304.

C. Roth, "The Memoirs of a Siennese Jew, 1625–1633," *HUCA* 5 (1928): 352–402.

Beth-Zion Abrahams, trans. and ed., *The Life of Glückel of Hameln 1646–1724, Written by Herself* (New York: Thomas Yoseloff, 1963).

7

YITZHAK F. BAER

Rashi and the World Around Him

The figure of Rabbi Shlomo Yitzhaki (Rashi) is a dominant one in the period in which the cultural centers of Judaism in western and central Europe were emerging and taking form. His commentaries on the Bible and the Talmud, and the school of halakhists and commentators which he founded, became identified with Ashkenazi Jewish culture. Rashi's works reflect the economic, social, and cultural circumstances in which Jews lived, and many details therein enlighten us as to the relationships between Jews and non-Jews in early medieval Europe. This study outlines some of the main features of these relationships based on material found in the works of Rashi and others.

About two generations before Rashi (the acronym for Rabbi Shlomo ben Isaac, 1040–1105),[1] in the days of the rabbis and religious poets of the calibre of R. Kalonymus of Lucca and his son R. Meshullam, R. Gershom Me'or Ha-Golah ("who sheds light upon the Jewish Diaspora"), R. Simeon bar Isaac, R. Joseph Bonfils, and others, the patterns unique to Jewish life in Christian Europe—methods of Torah study, patterns of prayer, social life, and communal organization—were developed and infused with vigor. Jewish religious law *(halakhah)* and traditional rabbinic interpretation of the Bible *(aggadah)* that had developed in the Land of Israel were transported by the Jewish community that had left its nest, to the new "homeland" it had found in the forests and the emerging commercial centers of Europe at the very time that early Christianity was being reconstituted within the feudal frame-

This article appeared in *Sefer Rashi*, published on the 850th anniversary of Rashi's death, ed. Y. L. HaKohen Maimon (Jerusalem: Mossad HaRav Kook, 1956). The translation/adaptation is by Nathan Reisner.

work. One of the numerous historical questions arising in this context is that of the mutual relationship between the organization of the Jewish community and the beginnings of the Christian city.

It was precisely in the period of transition to the Middle Ages, when the last traces of freedom had long disappeared from the Greco-Roman city that in the end was totally destroyed, and when the Christian religious community, democratic in its early days, had become an artificial hierarchical institution, that the Jewish community overcame the destruction that threatened it as well as the entire world. In a quiet development that had begun in the ninth century C.E., it proceeded to organize itself anew until, in the tenth century, it succeeded in acquiring some of the basic functions that were not to appear in the emerging Christian city until the twelfth century, as well as other prerogatives of civil law not found among the gentiles. The Jewish community was a fellowship of people of similar religious, national, and social (mainly commercial) status. It was a religious community empowered to judge its members, to legislate in matters of internal and "foreign" affairs, to impose its authority by means of bans and fines and, *inter alia*, to exact punishment for physical injury or for personal defamation. In particular, the community assumed responsibility for the constant monetary demands made upon the Jews by the feudal lords, by paying those rulers one jointly negotiated tax that was then proportionally imposed upon each individual by "trustees" elected from among all the members of the community.

The latent inner strengths that operate in the history of mankind surfaced among the Jews much earlier than in Christian society, and as a more enduring commitment. In the Jewish communities of France and Germany, the buds of the European "bourgeois" culture which illuminated urban social life with a light of calm inner religiosity appeared early, in a period when Christian society was still driven by the deep conflict between the peaceful tendencies of the devotees of the Church and the licentious lives of the nobles—and a legitimate urban class to mediate between them had not yet arisen.

This dichotomy did not exist in the academy of Rashi and his teachers. The intimacy of the relationships between teachers and pupils encompassed all the family members—husband and wife, children, and grandchildren. With the wife ranking high in the family economy and in the community's relationship with the Christian officials, the woman's voice was at times even heard in matters of halakhic tradition. Certainly the wife was influential in household matters and in the education of the children.

The academy served as the center and basis for the life of the entire community in every aspect. This framework explains a number of fine points raised by modern students of Rashi in their deeply penetrating works. Every page of Rashi's commentaries attests to the spirit prevailing in the study hall and the community: simplicity, modesty, preciseness, vivacity, and observation of all aspects of life—from nature and the tools used in daily existence, to the social and communal patterns of both Jews and gentiles.

This modest Jewish community was, from the very first, at serious odds with the Christians. At the turn of the tenth century, religious disputations between Jews and Christians increased. Kings and prelates were seeking to convert Jews, and there were outbursts of mob violence against them in various districts. There were also signs of anti-Semitism stemming from the undesirable side-effects of the economic patterns of the Jewish society, and the first examples of the medieval-type blood libel were evident. For a while, this interreligious struggle was stilled because of the polemic that had arisen within Christianity over the movement for inner reform and the struggle over investiture. However, the aggressive forces of the Christian Church were again aroused at the time of the First Crusade (1095), that is, during the last period of Rashi's life.

From what remains of Rashi's halakhic decisions and responsa, it is clear that he participated in communal life with his unique enthusiasm and alertness. Although he was the acknowledged leader of his generation, he saw no need to innovate anything crucial or to deviate from the course of the two preceding generations of rabbis. We do not intend to reopen this question here, nor to exhaust the historical material found in Rashi's responsa, but to focus on two issues that illustrate the gravity of the Jewish situation in his day and are subject, in our humble opinion, to further explanation even after much has been written about them.[2]

One matter touches upon the relationships between the Jews and the feudal lords. One of Rashi's responsa (Miller, #30–31; Elfenbein, #240) deals with the following situation: Leah and Jacob (party of the first part) gave their son Reuben and his wife Rachel (party of the second part) a wedding gift of a vineyard that they owned in the city and "the tithe of seven liters that comes from one village, that had been given them as a pledge, to enjoy its fruits each year, and to receive the principal [money lent to the lord] whenever the lord should wish to redeem it [the pledge]." This tithe, according to Rashi's responsum, "does not have any legal status from year to year as does land, since it is not a boundary-defined field . . . but is rather a contribution to idolatry given by the gentiles as tithes from their crops." It was apparently an ecclesiastical tithe (*decima* to the Church) which the violent lords of northern France took for themselves as part of their feudal rights, against the wishes of the Christian faithful.

Reuben then went to a foreign country and Simon (a third party) took possession of the principal, enjoying the fruits of the tithe for a number of years. As one learns from the rest of the question put to Rashi, the old lady, Leah, was "established in the city and known to the nobles," and Reuben and Simon had business connections with the "lord" and "the city rulers." Apparently, in return for providing credit, such Jews received pledges from the lord of the city and in turn pawned them to a particular gentile. "When the lord claimed his pledges and they could not pay, he imprisoned Simon." The principal and the tithe returned to the lord, whereupon Leah requested the lord "to return the tithe to her as a *feudum* (a feudal benefice) which she would hold" as a dependent of his "like the others who receive a *feudum* from the lords;" and this was done. After Leah died, the lord took the tithe back, but a year later returned it to Simon on the same conditions as his mother's.

Some time thereafter, the gentile with whom the lord's pledges had been pawned, sought to return them to the lord in exchange for the vineyard and the tithe held by the Jews. "I am greatly distressed that the property of my fathers be possessed by the gentile," argued Simon and, with the community's consent, he purchased the tithe and the vineyard and returned them to his absolute possession.

The legal question raised here concerns Jewish land stolen by one of the violent lords, which another Jew subsequently received from him. This question was dealt with in a number of actual cases in feudal France. Rabbenu Gershom Me'or Ha-Golah (c. 960–1028) had already ruled in the case of a Jew's house taken by force by a non-Jew and subsequently purchased from the latter by another Jew, that the purchaser was not to return it to the original owner without indemnity, but was to be paid the amount by which he had benefitted. As we know, Rashi had ruled to the contrary in his commentary on the Talmud (Gittin 58b): if a gentile obtained possession of a Jew's property through seizure, as payment for a debt or as a forfeiture, and subsequently sold it to a Jew, the *sikarikon* law (the law concerning the purchase of confiscated property), namely, that if the land had been in the hands of the (gentile) holder for twelve months, the Jewish purchaser must give the original owner one-fourth (of the land or of the purchasing price) does not apply; rather, he must return the land to the original owner without any indemnity.

One can theorize that the difference in the halakhic positions of these great rabbis came about because the use of force by the lords was more common in Rashi's time than in the time of Rabbenu Gershom. In this responsum, Rashi also ruled in keeping with his general approach. For instance, he explains the text found in the talmudic discussion—"the law concerning partial payments [i.e., an agreement of term-payments with the condition of forfeiture on missing one term, especially such an agreement forced upon a Jew by a gentile individual or authority] does not exist in Babylonia [under the Persian government]"—to mean that "there were regular courts in Babylonia that did no evil and judged truthfully [to which an aggrieved party could turn for redress], *but these* [courts in France] *take things by robbery and violence; he who cries out is not answered and especially if a lord is involved and against whom no one is more powerful.*"

In the same vein, Rashi ruled in a responsum (#660) found in a collection of responsa of *Maharal* (Rabbi Judah Loew of Prague):

Reuben abandoned his place of residence because of a violent man and left behind him his wife and children; his home was stolen from him and the robber sold it to Simon. The community decreed that Simon not inform on Reuben concerning the house or anything else that might cause him loss, and that he not acquire the land.

Again,

Reuben complains about a book and utensils that were in his home in Orleans. He had a gentile creditor pressing him for payment of interest, whom he entrusted with his house to take care of its contents and upon whom he depended to collect his monies while he set out to wander *because the lord had seized his funds*, until he should be pardoned from above and be able to return.

Of him it was said: "You were totally dispossessed by the lord's appropriation." Another responsum of Rashi deals with acts of capricious malice that harmed the entire community. The "ruler" ordered the imprisonment of a number of community members (or all of them) in order to extract heavier than usual taxes from them. The specific question adjudicated was whether Reuben was permitted to redeem himself with money that belonged to others but that was in his possession as a result of a business arrangement. He claimed that "they had exempted him from any coercion that he might meet at the hands of the city and its servants." Rashi responds:

His argument is not acceptable, since the lords of the cities did not normally act this way and it would not occur to anyone to specify such a coercive act as a precondition, and he would not worry that the regime would make a demand of each one individually, since the usual procedure is to make a demand of the entire community collectively, and each one would exempt his money according to the decree (= ban) wherever he be.

The system of robbery that the lord adopted this time was of such proportions that one could say: "Now the members of the community are an empty vessel;" their situation was undermined to the very foundations.

And especially was the hand of the gentiles strengthened, seeing that the ruler was hostile to the community. The Jews no longer had significance in their eyes and were forced to forgo [part of their claims on the gentile borrowers] in order to collect [the rest]; . . . and he must remain in the city and collect the money remaining with gentiles as long as the rest of the community is detained.

From this responsum, there emerges a picture of the situation of the Jewish community that we have generally tended to attribute to a later time. Moreover, Rashi's responsa indicate that the Jews of his day were increasingly compelled to restrict their economic pursuits to money-lending at interest. They were tied to the lords and rulers through their provision of loans and other services; they even needed the lord's assistance in collecting what was owed them. In any event, the Jews were completely subject to the caprices of the rulers and to their increasing acts of pillage.

The difficult plight of the Jews was, to a certain extent, part of a general social phenomenon. Pope Gregory VII complains in his letter of September 1074 to the bishops of France about the internal wars that have wrought total confusion in France: the wickedness of the people has reached a peak; relatives imprison one another and confiscate each other's property. In particular, they seize the "wanderers" *(peregrini)* on their way to visit the tombs of the Apostles in Rome, imprisoning them and torturing them most cruelly. First and foremost among these evil-doers is, "at Satan's instigation," King Philip I, "who should not be called 'king' but 'tyrant.' " In predatory fashion "as does an armed robber" *(more praedonis),* he took a huge sum of money from the merchants who came to one of the fairs in France; the one who should have been the defender of law and justice has, of all things, become a plunderer. Historians have found in this document an early allusion to the famous fairs in the Champagne district, just as Jewish scholars thought—in this case without justification, as we shall see below—that they had found reference to these fairs in Rashi's commentaries. The main point is that capricious acts of malice, such as those mentioned, were already common practice with regard to Christian traders. How much more was this true concerning Jews. It was so prevalent that such acts of robbery on the part of the King of France and of the other lords were judged by the great Pope to be of the Devil *(diabolus),* in keeping with the standard typological and theological-historical outlook among the Christians. Let us see if we can discover analogous views in Rashi's works. But first we must examine another problem that caused a deterioration in the situation of the Jews in Rashi's period, namely, the persecutions they experienced as a result of the decree of 1096, at the time of the First Crusade.

Scholars have discovered signs of these events in Rashi's responsa. He mentioned Jews who were killed "in a day of great killing," or who changed their religion "at the point of the sword." Matters having to do with forced converts *(anusim)* are dealt with in a spirit of forgiveness in Rashi's responsa, as they are in the tales of the 1096 decree from Ashkenaz. Except for the few references of Rabbenu Gershom Me'or Ha-Golah, Rashi is the first to deal with halakhic issues involving the forced converts, and he usually does so leniently: "Though [a Jew] has sinned, he remains a Jew; and especially so the *anusim*, whose heart is directed to Heaven." One can learn from Rashi's responsa that the problem of the forced converts was a severe, ongoing religious-social problem which weighed upon that generation for many years, because the Christians did not permit them to return quickly to the Jewish fold. A similar situation later pertained in a number of European countries after other persecutions. But one may assume that the questions discussed by Rashi came from the nearby French communities, not from distant Ashkenaz.

Another of Rashi's responsa dealt with "the families who were vying with one another in calumnies and vituperation. Their complaints were heard by the community and they were ordered not to continue." Then one of them jumped up and reminded the other that "he had been baptized," whereupon someone else stood up and said: "Be still! That is forbidden to be mentioned!" It turns out that he was referring to the "Ban of Rabbenu Gershom" (Me'or Ha-Golah). In a passage apparently appended to this responsum, Rashi warns the disputants: "Set your hearts to pursuing peace; and note that because of our sins those around you were roundly smitten and are already gorging themselves among the gentiles. But peace will get you help from the enemy and Satan will be unable to prevail over you, etc." This incident took place in Châlon-sur-Saône, about midway between Clermont and Troyes. It does not require farfetched theories to connect the aforementioned act of apostasy and the famous Church Council at which the First Crusade was proclaimed; these events took place not far from where Rashi lived.

From a Christian source, we learn of persecutions that occurred in the city of Rouen, in the district of Normandy. Just as was to happen later in Germany, the Crusaders there came to their own conclusion: "Here we are going a long distance to the East to do battle against the enemies of God, and here before our eyes there are Jews, than whom there is no nation more hostile to God." The Crusaders then gathered the Jews of the city into one of the churches and killed all of them except those who agreed to convert to the Christian faith. This is described in the interesting memoirs of Guibert who, in 1104, toward the end of Rashi's life, was chosen to be the abbot of the Santa Maria monastery at Nogent, not far from Rashi's home. Among the forced converts of Rouen there was a Jewish lad who was raised as a Christian. Father Guibert wrote a special work to strengthen him in his new belief and to refute the claims of the Prince of Soissons who tended to view Judaism and the Catharist heresy favorably, praising the Jews and their religious teachings. Guibert, the author of an important book on the history of the First Crusade, also wrote *Tractatus de incarnatione contra judaeos*, a general work against the Jews who, he held, attacked the teachings of Christianity and had a bad influence upon its faithful. This book is one of the first in the long line of polemical works written by Christians against the Jews, starting in the last decade of the eleventh century.

The literary polemic between Judaism and Christianity was renewed during the last period of Rashi's life, within the context of the general development of Christian theology and scholasticism. It is against this background that one must understand and interpret some of the things that Rashi wrote during his last years. Scholars believe that most of his commentaries on the Bible belong to this period, although they still hesitate to admit that the events of the period really determined the purpose which should be attributed to Rashi's commentaries in general, and not only to those places where "to respond to the heretics" is specifically stated.

Entire chapters of Rashi's commentary on Isaiah, Zechariah, and other prophets, on the Book of Daniel, and particularly on the Book of Psalms, must be understood as an anti-Christian polemic. Often, for apologetic reasons (for defense and also for attack), Rashi abandons his midrashic (basically allegorical) method of interpretation; and there are other signs, overt and covert, of his polemic intention (see his interpretations of Psalms 2:21, 22, 45, 68, and further examples that we shall cite below). On occasion, as with Psalm 110 which has served as a basis for Christian doctrine ever since the Gospel according to Matthew, he starts with the midrashic method, first offering an interpretation (about the Patriarch Abraham) for apologetic reasons, and then adding a second interpretation (about King David) for the same reason. Even in his commentary on the Pentateuch, signs of this intent are not lacking. Sometimes Rashi repeats arguments that already appeared in the Talmud and Midrash, because the contentions of both parties to the polemic had not changed over the generations.

Rashi's awareness of current problems is not limited to theological disputation alone. We may assume that some of his interpretations were written not merely to explain biblical verses, but also to educate and encourage his contemporaries in their hour of travail. In his commentary on the Pentateuch, he summarizes what he sees to be fundamental in the halakhic and midrashic tradition. In his commentary on

Proverbs, he writes at length against the heretics and inciters, and turns the book into a moral tract relevant to his day. In his commentary on the Prophets, he discusses in practical terms, as we shall see, the imminent redemption and the end-of-days.

Last but not least, Rashi transformed the 150 chapters in the book of Psalms into a new work that strengthens one's faith in time of persecutions. All of Jewish history through the four Exiles and until the redemption and the war of Gog and Magog is included in his commentary, along with a number of allusions to the most recent persecution, the decree of 1096. The great commentator wanted to assume for his generation a role similar to that of the rabbis of the Midrash and the famous *paytanim* (liturgical poets) who had preceded him. But since his forte was not in liturgical poetry, and the Jews of his generation had not yet learned to compose prose tracts dealing with faith, ethics, and polemics, he proceeded to unite himself and his generation with the written text, until the writer and the reader, from verse to verse, passed from the trauma of despair to a sense of confidence. And since it was not his intention to explain a specific text, but rather complete books—the entire book of Isaiah, the entire book of Psalms, etc.—he rejected messianic explanations in one place and ceated new messianic interpretations in others, not always from personal exegetical and apologetic considerations (which certainly were not lacking, and which the text required), but rather because of his understanding of the structure of the book in its entirety. Those who say that Rashi came to no decisions in these matters, or that in the main he tended to ignore them, are in error.

To understand the contemporary significance of Rashi's commentaries, one must also know the content of the anti-Jewish preachings to which Jewish ears were being subjected, as well as the interpretations and sermons of the Church Fathers and the summaries and revision based upon them in Rashi's generation. It is to be assumed that Rashi knew Latin and read these works assiduously. For example, in his commentary on Daniel, he intended to prove that most of the book spoke about the political events of the Second Temple period and not, as the Christians held, about the final redemption, which appear only in the last verses of the book. Rashi drew the relevant historical information for this from Josippon. Others, such as R. Sa'adiah Gaon, had preceded him in this approach. But the basic assumption must be that when Rashi wrote his commentary on Daniel, he had before him the book upon which the entire polemic hinges, namely, the commentary of Jerome, or a later Christian work based upon it.

One of the clearest allusions to the sorry events of 1096 is found, as already noted, in Rashi's commentary on Isaiah, chapters 52 and 53.

And his grave was set among the wicked—He surrendered himself to be buried wherever the wicked of the nations decreed, who would sentence him to death and an ignominious burial in the intestines of the dogs; *the wicked*—in the opinion of the wicked he resigned himself to be buried rather than renounce the living God; *And with the rich in his death*—and in the opinion of the ruler he surrendered himself to any sort of death decreed because he did not want to accept apostasy, to do evil like all of the gentiles among whom he lived; *and had spoken no falsehood*—to accept idolatry openly. (Isaiah 53.9)

Rashi evidently underscores something that he saw with his own eyes or that happened in his area, for the term he chooses for "ruler" *(moshel)* is found in his responsa and other contemporary Hebrew documents as a specific designation for the lord of a city and the lords of the land. In addition to the event alluded to, Rashi's words are especially significant because they express an attitude of martyrdom not found in such a form among his predecessors.

The turmoil of his time led Rashi to delve deeply into accepted points of view. He continues:

At the end of days the nations will recognize and admit, about Israel, that *it was our sickness that he was bearing*. . . . Now we see . . . that he was greatly tormented, for all the nations achieve atonement through Israel's torments; the illness that should have befallen us, he bore . . . *he was wounded because of our sins, crushed because of our iniquities*. . . . He suffered the torments of the peace that was ours, for which he was tormented, so that the entire world might have peace (53:4). *If he made himself an offering of guilt etc.* (53:10)—said the Holy One, blessed be He: "If his soul is given over and devoted to My Holiness, to return it to Me as a guilt offering for all that he has transgressed, I shall surely give him his reward."

Rashi adds an explanation in the legal terminology of his day: " 'Guilt offering' is the term for the restitution one makes to the person against whom one has sinned; in French: *amende*." Rashi was saying that by surrendering himself to death, a Jew acquires the world-to-come. He also earns this by his behavior and his integrity in life, in contrast to the lords and the other Christians of his time: "*Out of his anguish*—would he eat and be sated, and not rob nor pillage; *by his knowledge he justifies the righteous*—my servant would offer true judgment to all who come to judgment before him." Rashi speaks here not only of faith and apostasy, but of the differences in the social ethic of Jews and Christians.

* * *

In a number of instances we will not fully comprehend Rashi's intent unless we clearly distinguish between what he took from the Midrash and the new formulations which he added; and, finally, one must compare his innovations with contemporary Christian preachings and match them to the historical reality. Rashi's commentaries on Psalms 9 and 10 are an example of such a process. The comments of the sages collected in *The Midrash on Psalms*[3] already interpreted these Psalms as referring to the suffering of Israel, called "wretched" and "oppressed," "crushed" by his servitude to Edom, and surrendering his life in the sanctification of God's Name. The standard Christian interpretation explains the segment as referring to the sufferings which the Church must undergo in its war against the Antichrist and all the phenomena of the days of the unrevealed judgment which will precede the Final Day of Judgment.

Rashi opens his commentary: *"For the leader; al-mut labben*[4]—This psalm is about the distant future when the childhood and prime of Israel will become clear, their righteousness will be revealed, and their salvation will be near, when Esau and his seed will be blotted out." He continues with material found in the Midrash, with changes: *"You destroy the wicked*—that is, Esau . . . *ruins everlasting*—that enemy the ruins of whose hate are upon us forever, and that is Esau." The Psalm speaks of the judgment of the wicked Esau at the end of days, as Rashi notes in his commentary to verse 9.

Later, in Psalm 10,[5] Rashi finds further allusions to the activity of this wicked one:

They are caught by the schemes they devised—the lowly are caught by the schemes the wicked devise against them. *The wicked crows about his unbridled lusts*—for now the wicked Esau boasts that he achieves his unbridled lusts. *The grasping man reviles and scorns the Lord*—and the *robber* lauded himself saying that he reviled the Lord and he will remain at peace . . . *his eyes spy out the hapless*—the eyes of Esau lie in ambush for Israel who are Your army. . . . *He stoops, he crouches*—this is the way of the ambusher: he stoops, crouches, makes himself small so as not to be seen . . . *and the hapless fall prey to his might*—[to the might] of this wicked one, to his gestures and winks.

To be sure, "robber" is one interpretation of "grasping man," but Rashi's intention in his commentary on this psalm is explained in the light of the sermons of Augustine and his successors: "He compares the deeds of the Antichrist to the pattern of the robbers who hide themselves in order to kill the innocent;" and the representatives of the Antichrist are the heretics, the Jews, the dialecticians, and the philosophers.[6] Rashi thus describes in drastic colors the activity of the robbing, pillaging lord of his day who is the clear representative of Esau in his time.

We can also turn to Rashi's commentary on Isaiah 28:20:

The couch is too short for stretching out—I will bring upon you an enemy who will oppress you so that you cannot do his work adequately, and when he spreads his cover over you it will not be large enough . . . *and the cover too narrow*—for the prince that will rule over you, your place will be tight for him to enter.

In contradistinction, he describes the Messiah King of Israel: "Their king will not rob the poor nor smash the hapless and the weak" (Isaiah 42:3). But at this time, dominion is still in the hands of Esau: "*They divide my clothes among themselves, casting lots for my garments* (Ps. 22:19); and "*Let the faithless be disappointed, empty-handed*—the robbers and pillagers who leave the helpless bereft of their possessions" (Ps. 25:3). But Israel is told:

Do not be vexed by evil men—He admonishes Israel not to be vexed by the success of the wicked, to act as they . . . to do wrong as they. [Rather,] *trust in the Lord*—and do not say "If I do not rob and steal, or give to the poor, how will I make a living. . . . *The wicked man borrows and does not repay; the righteous*—but the Holy One, blessed be He, the Righteous One, *is generous*—with what is His, *and keeps giving*—to the one who lent to his fellow man that which he [the evil-doer] robs from him. . . . *The steps of a man are made firm by the Lord*—[that man] who is strong in the "fear of the Lord" (Ps. 37).

This last expression approaches the style of the later Ashkenazi Pietists.

These commentaries are, like that on Isaiah 53 cited above: "*Out of his anguish*—would he eat and be sated and did not rob nor pillage," covert or overt allusions that befit the historical reality as well as the historical-theological outlook of both Jews and Christians, except that each of the rival camps interpreted matters in its own manner.

In this regard, we must note that on occasion Rashi's terminology accords with and approaches expressions regularly used by the Christians. Rashi consistently interprets most of Psalm 45 to be "in honor of scholars," to disabuse the Christians who interpreted the entire Psalm as speaking of their Messiah and the Church *(Ecclesia)*. But at the end he returns to the words of the Midrash, "*Take heed, lass, and note*—Take heed, O congregation of Israel" and he adds on his own:

forget your people—the nations, for you are great among them . . . *O Tyrian lass, the wealthiest people will court your favor with gifts*—and as reward for this you will be privileged to have the wicked Esau bring you presents and gifts, for they are now the wealthiest people. *The royal princess . . . is led inside to the king*—That is what is meant by the verse (Isaiah 66:20) *And out of all the nations they shall bring all your brothers . . . as an offering*—those upon whom all glory depends, and they are the gathering of the King, who conducted themselves in humility.

Rashi uses the expression *knessiyah shel melekh*, the church of the king. The Hebrew term *knessiyah* means both assembly and church. Its use here may best be explained as a translation from the language used by the Christians—*ecclesia regis*.

Rashi also strays from the midrashic pattern in his commentary on Psalm 68, as he himself notes there at the end, and he interprets the entire Psalm in terms of Israel and Esau. We find there, *inter alia:*

> *God restores the lonely to their homes*—Israel who were scattered, He gathered each one of them together from dispersion and restored them to a complete gathering *(knessiyah)* . . . *the kings and their armies*—the gentiles, *are in headlong flight*—will wander and be cast out of the Land of Israel, and the congregation *(knesset)* of Israel who is *she that tarrieth at home, divides their spoils; even for those of you who lie among the sheepfolds*—if you lie within your borders and enjoy pleasures, this is My dove, My gathering.

One must remember that the lexicon of the sages recognizes the "gathering or congregation of Israel" *(knesset yisrael)* only as the collective personification of all of Israel *(klal yisrael)*, although not in such abstract language. In contrast, the Christians talk profusely of the relationship between the Messiah and his Church *(ecclesia)* as his mystic body, and they liken the Church to a home and a building in process of being built section by section.[7]

As we have already said, and as other scholars have noted, Rashi alludes to the mass persecutions of 1096 in a number of places in his commentary on Psalms. *"The great of the peoples*—who volunteered themselves for slaughter and to be killed in the sanctification of God's Name (47:10)." "When they gather together against me, I bribe them with money that *I have not stolen* from them" (69:5). "The legions of Esau who intend to turn me away from Thee" (140:10). In his commentary on Isaiah 26:16–18, he speaks of the hope of salvation tied to the year 1096 that was proven false: "We see constantly renewed troubles and believe that these are the harbingers of salvation and redemption . . . *"we were with child, we writhed—It is as though we had given birth,* as if we are about to be redeemed, yet there is no spirit and no salvation." This is also found in the tales of 1096: "For then we hoped for salvation and consolation . . . and it turned into sorrow and sighing." Like his confrères in the Rhine communities, Rashi interprets Psalm 83:13: *"who said*—those nations mentioned above, Edom and Ishmael and of all their cohorts, *Let us take the habitations of God as our possession*—the dwelling of God." But they did not succeed in their evil schemes to build the land. And on Isaiah 32:14 he wrote: *"For the palace shall be forsaken . . . My Temple shall be for dens*—shall be among ruins *for ever*—till the time of the end, *a stamping ground for wild asses*—for the lust of Ishmael *and a pasture*—for Edom and his troops."

Thus far, we have only one explicit testimony, in a letter of the Jews of Byzantium from the time of the First Crusade, of a messianic movement among Jews. From the Ashkenazi Jews, all that we have is the passing reference cited above. Yet we dare to suggest that a number of Rashi's writings dealing with the "end-of-days" can be interpreted as referring to the events of his day.[8] Indeed, it is understood that Rashi's interpretations of the biblical prophecies of redemption and the end-of-days are based upon an early or late midrashic tradition; however, even traditional material is explained in a fresh manner during a period of historic turmoil. Thus, on occasion even Rashi introduces something new into the customary formulation that cannot be entirely overlooked. His interpretation, for example, of Balaam's prophecy (Num. 24) about the end-of-days is well-known:

A victor issues from Jacob—and there will be yet another ruler from Jacob, *to wipe out what is left of the city*—the most important [city] of Edom [i.e., Rome], and it is of King Messiah that he is thus speaking . . . of whom it is said (v.24), *And ships from the hand of Kittim*—and the people of Kittim, who are the Romans, will pass over in big ships against Assyria . . . *and ships*—big ships, as is written (Isaiah 33:21) *mighty craft* etc.

It is certainly true that the Aramaic translations of the Bible already interpret the verse as referring to the final war of Rome against the great Oriental power, and that the two combatants, in the end, will submit to the King Messiah.[9] But who of Rashi's generation could read these words and ignore contemporary events?[10] After all, we do know that eschatological concepts were among the factors that motivated the deeds of the leaders of Christianity. Pope Gregory VII, who acted out of his belief in the imminent end-of-days was prepared from 1074 onward, to stand at the head of a large Christian army and help Eastern Rome defend itself against the Turks, as well as to cross the Mediterranean and capture the Holy Sepulchre in Jerusalem. Then came the First Crusade led by Pope Urban II, and it appeared that the long-accepted eschatological prophecies were being fulfilled. This was stated explicitly in the Pope's speech at the Council of Clermont, according to one of the versions transmitted in his name, and this version certainly contains a great measure of historical truth.

For the Jews of Rashi's generation, the First Crusade against the Turks and the Egyptians gave new life to the "final war" concept spoken of in the midrashim and the popular apocalyptic tales. At the center of the system is Esau-Edom and its city, Rome—the capital of the "pagan empire" of the midrashim, the renewed Christian Rome of the *Book of Josippon* (From which Rashi took a number of ideas, even where this is not specifically mentioned in his commentary), and the imperial Rome of Gregory VII and Urban II, which resumed its position of world leadership. Thus Rashi, in his commentary on Isaiah 27, with no compelling exegetical reason, introduces Rome alongside Egypt and Assyria as a third power:

In that day the Lord will punish . . . Leviathan the Elusive Serpent etc.—Targum Jonathan [the Aramaic translation of the Bible]: . . . and I say because these are three important nations, Egypt, Assyria, and Edom, therefore He said . . . *He will slay the dragon that is in the sea*—that is Tyre, the leader of the children of Esau, that dwells in the heart of the seas; and likewise, the Kittim, called the islands of the sea, and they are the Romans.

Every intelligent reader of that time could not help but find therein allusions to the wars that were then breaking out in the lands of the East between Fatimid Egypt, the Turks, and the Crusaders, and that were to end with the destruction of Rome, as also alluded to in Isaiah 27:10: "For the fortified city—of Esau will be *solitary, and the habitation—* will be *abandoned and forsaken, like the wilderness; there shall the calf feed—* Ephraim will inherit it." Rashi interprets all of the prophecies about Tyre (despite the hesitation in his comments on Isaiah 23:5) as uttered about Rome, Edom. On Isaiah 23:1ff. he wrote:

Howl, you ships of Tarshish!—they were becoming wealthy thanks to the merchants of Tyre who were bringing merchandise to Tyre on ships of Tarshish. Tarshish is the name of the sea [apparently Rashi means the Mediterranean], *For havoc has been wrought, not a house is left*—because it has been devastated from within, where you were used to stop . . . *from the land of Kittim*—they are the Romans *he was revealed to them*—the plunderer to the people of Tyre.

Another interpretation: From the land of Kittim the looting of Tyre was revealed to the people of Tarshish, for the people of Tyre fled to the Kittim [Rashi found similar interpretations in the *Book of Josippon*], and from there the word spread. Citing the Midrash, Rashi writes that the blows that befell Tyre are an example of the Ten Plagues of Egypt.

In his commentary on Isaiah 24:22, he alludes to the swords of the Messiah ben Joseph and the Messiah ben David, the war of Gog, and the last judgment of guilty Rome: "*They shall be gathered*—the nations *together*—which is to their disadvantage, *as prisoners*—to put them *into a dungeon*—prepared for those condemned to Gehinnom, to Gehinnom."

On Isaiah 25:2 Rashi writes: "*For you have turned*—the mountain of Esau, *from a city into a stone heap . . . the citadel of strangers into rubble—* the dwelling that they made in Your city that they destroyed." Or perhaps he meant the Crusaders' control of Jerusalem as he did in his commentary on Isaiah 25:26: "You will make of their citadel a ruin that *shall never be rebuilt*—upon the downfall of *all the nations*—that shall come to war on Jerusalem."

Commenting on Isaiah Chapter 26, he wrote of the redemption of Israel:

The *city* of Jerusalem that has ever been *for us a strength and salvation*, the Savior *will appoint its walls and bulwarks.* . . . *Open its gates and let a righteous nation enter that keeps faith*—that throughout its lengthy exile has kept its faith in God and its expectation that He will fulfill His promise . . . [a nation] that was close to God and strongly dependent upon Him, that did not budge from its faith for any fears or tortures. . . . *For he has brought low those who dwelt high up*—Tyre, Rome and Italy.

He writes in a similar vein in the following chapters, as well as on 32:19: "*And to the degradation*—to which Israel has been brought low till now, *shall the city descend*—the metropolis of Edom."

The prophet Ezekiel also speaks of the destruction of Tyre (Chapter 26 ff.), and Rashi comments:

Who dwell(s) at the gateway of the sea—at a harbor in which the vessels approach the walls and the gates . . . *who trade(s) with the peoples* (27:2)—It was their custom that merchants coming to it, some from the north and some from the south, were not allowed to trade with each other; the residents of the city bought from the one and sold to the other [i.e., acted as brokers].

Abraham Berliner [11] understood that Rashi was interpreting the situation in terms of medieval commercial rules and found an allusion here to the city of Troyes and the fairs of the Champagne region. But the text and its commentary speak of a large capital, a port city. Rashi was referring to Rome that, from the days of Gregory VII on, once again became the administrative-financial as well as commercial center of all Europe. Apparently he also introduced some elements of Venice, the mighty maritime power that assumed, along with her rivals Genoa and Pisa, a role of leadership in the Crusade and in the politics of Eastern Christianity. Apart from Rome, Venice is the only city that Rashi mentions by name—we cannot assume that he had been there, but he had heard of its greatness—and in an eschatological context (Isaiah 42:10): "*Sing unto the Lord a new song, His praise from the ends of the earth, you that go down to the sea*—who sail the sea *and all that is therein*—you who are settled in the sea, not on *the isles* but in the water, piling sand upon sand for houses and moving from house to house by boat like the city of Venice."

One cannot argue that the exigencies of interpretation compelled him to mention the city; rather, Rashi was reminded of it by a combination of concepts that were clear to the reader. Tyre is likened to a ship "because it was built on the sea and perished in the sea" (Rashi on Ezekiel 27:5); and likewise Rome, "*Your tacklings are loosed*—that pull the ship, guilty Rome" (on Isaiah 33:23); and on Ezekiel 27:32: "*Who was like Tyre when she was silenced in the midst of the sea?*—like Dumah, which is the name of the heads of Edom, as in the matter of *the Dumah pronouncement* [Isaiah 21:11]." In similar fashion, on Tyre (Zechariah 9:5), Rashi writes that "she was the head of the children of Esau." He then argues with the Christian commentators (vv. 9,10): "*Lo, your king is coming to you*—It cannot be interpreted except as referring to the King Messiah of whom it is said *And his rule shall extend from sea to sea*, and we find no such ruler in the days of the Second Temple." He continues in this vein to differentiate between what was said about the Hasmonean period (by Josippon) and the prophecies about the final redemption. Then he returns to the destruction of Rome (Zechariah 10:11): "*And over the sea affliction shall pass*—and affliction shall pass over Tyre that dwells in the sea and is head of Edom, *and shall stir up*—the Holy One, blessed be He, is the one who stirs up *waves in the sea*—to drown Tyre." [12]

Based upon the text, Rashi apparently had heard of some legend about Tyre having been drowned in the ocean, and this was transposed to Rome. [13] His commentaries on the prophecies about the destruction of Tyre, and his use of foreign (i.e. non-Hebrew, usually Old French) terms in this regard, reveal a great measure of interest—beyond that required by the commentary—in the nature of a commercial metropolis (such as Rome, in his opinion), and in the preparations of its enemies to besiege and conquer it. Perhaps he had also heard about the conquest of the port cities in Syria and in the Land of Israel, even though the real Tyre was to fall to the Crusaders after his death. All of this is merged by Rashi into a semi-legendary account of the destruction of Rome at the end-of-days and the "regime that will punish it with torments." *Justicia* (the non-Hebrew term used) will be meted out to it, in keeping with the terms of feudal law that Rashi likes to use, especially in such contexts. [14]

The subject touched upon by our random selections, though not new, still bears further investigation. Rashi's commentaries were written from his observation of the world around him, and the needs of his time. The relevance of his words to their period is the secret of their surviving to this day.

NOTES

1. See *Encyclopaedia Judaica* (Jerusalem: Keter, 1972), entries for Rashi, and other figures mentioned in this article.

2. See Solomon Zeitlin, "Rashi and the Rabbinate: the Struggle between Secular and Religious Forces for Leadership," *Jewish Quarterly Review* XXXI (1940). Yitzhak Baer takes issue with his views. Also see Salo W. Baron, *The Jewish Community*, 3 (Philadelphia: Jewish Publication Society, 1942), p. 538.

3. *The Midrash on Psalms*, translated from the Hebrew and Aramaic by Wil-

liam G. Braude, Yale Judaica Series, Vols. XIII:1, 2 (New Haven: Yale University Press, 1959).

4. Psalm 9:1. The phrase *al-mut labben* is obscure. Some scholars interpret it as referring to "the death of the son." Rashi reads it as *mitlaben* = clarify.

5. Rashi may have construed Psalms 9 and 10 as a single unit, as did the Christian commentators.

6. The author of these interpretations was Bruno Herbipolensis, the Bishop of Wurtzburg in the middle of the eleventh century.

7. See *New Testament: The Letter of Paul to the Ephesians,* 1:22–23, 2:19–22. 4:7–14 (here for the first time Ps. 68:19(18) is cited with a Christological interpretation), 5:22–30. In his commentary to *The Song of Songs* 1:8, Rashi also writes "my 'church' *(ecclesia)* and my congregation."

8. J. Sarachek, *The Doctrine of the Messiah in Mediaeval Jewish Literature* (New York: Hermon Press, 1968), pp. 46–51, does not mention such a possibility.

9. In the fourth century, "Kittim" was interpreted as the western islands near Italy; see Jerome's commentary on Isaiah 2:10 and chapter 23; Daniel, 11:30. " 'Kittim,' they are the Romans" is explicitly stated in *Josippon,* Chapter 1ff. (tenth century).

10. One of the apocalyptic segments undoubtedly written at the time of the First Crusade interprets *And ships from the hand of Kittim shall afflict Ashur* in connection with the wars of its time.

11. Abraham Berliner (1833–1915) prepared the first critical edition of Rashi's commentary on the Bible.

12. Commenting on Zech. 11:5, Rashi described the political situation of the Jews who were exiled and enslaved: *"whose buyers will slaughter them with impunity, whose seller will say, 'Praised be the Lord! I'll get rich,'*—The kings of the nations to which I shall exile them shall go unpunished; this one sells and the buyer kills, and no one feels any guilt over it at all; and the seller gloats, 'Praised be the Lord who has turned them over to me. I'll get rich,' and I am indeed wealthy."

13. Benjamin of Tudela (second half of the twelfth century) was a medieval Jewish traveller whose wanderings took him from Spain, through the northern port cities of the Mediterranean, and throughout the Near East. He writes: "A person who mounts the wall of the new Tyre sees the ancient Tyre which the sea has covered, a stone's throw from the new; and if he wants to arrive by ship, he will see the towers, marketplaces, streets, and palaces on the sea floor." Among the legends about the city of Rome that circulated among the Jews one must mention what Rashi writes (commenting on Talmud Bavli, *Avodah Zarah* 11b) regarding the scalp of Rabbi Ishmael, the High Priest, one of the Ten Martyrs: "and it still reposes in the treasuries of Rome." This is in keeping with the tradition that the graves of the Ten Martyrs are in Rome (after *Midrash Eileh Ezkerah* had earlier shifted the venue of their trial to that city).

14. See his commentary on Isaiah 32:7 and on Exodus 28:15.

* * *

For an English edition of Rashi's commentary on the Pentateuch, see *Pentateuch with Rashi's Commentary,* ed. A. M. Silbermann (London: Shapiro, Vallentine & Co., 1946).

8

GERALD J. BLIDSTEIN

Menaḥem Meiri's Attitude Toward Gentiles—Apologetics or Worldview?

Halakhic literature often seems to be completely immersed in the legal details of the observance of ritualistic and social-ethical precepts, hardly taking notice of current events and changes in the religious and social climate. Closer examination, however, reveals the dynamic elements in halakhic controversies and deliberations, sometimes reflecting opposing views concerning the relationships between Jews and non-Jews, or even basic differences in ethical world views. Such an example—a unique statement by the fourteenth-century halakhist in Provence, Rabbi Menaḥem ha-Meiri—is the subject of analysis here.

In his article "R. Menaḥem Ha'Meiri's Theory of Tolerance—Its Origin and Limits," E. E. Urbach drew attention once more to the status of the gentile in the halakhic-religious thought of this fourteenth-century Provençal scholar. While J. Katz argued the uniqueness of Meiri's tolerant stance and attributed it to the absorption of universalist-philosophic elements into his halakhic system, Urbach attempted to show that these were of no great significance and, indeed, were trivial.[1] Urbach's methodological guideline was halakhic; the extent to which a concept creates new halakhic practice, or leads to a legal decision that disputes prevailing opinion, makes the concept significant. Urbach pointed out that Meiri used the concept "peoples restricted by ways of religion" only as an *ex post facto* justification of various well-known exceptions to halakhic rule that had already been explained in other ways by scholars; Meiri refrained from utilizing this concept in order to demand a new halakhic reality, did not introduce it where it could

---

This paper was first published in *Zion* 51 (1985–86):153–66. The translation/adaptation is by Zippora Brody.

harm Jewish interests (as, for example, in the dispensation to take interest from gentiles), and did not apply it to sensitive religious areas, such as marriage law.

Katz also recognized the minor practical halakhic import of Meiri's concept, but nonetheless attributed cultural significance to its introduction. In his view, adherence to a new theoretical concept, with all its psychological and ethical weight and its novel categorizations, constitutes in and of itself a noteworthy phenomenon in the history of Jewish thought.

I would like once more to consider the concept discussed by these scholars, both by studying sources not previously mentioned in this context, and by reexamining several topics dealt with before. My interest lies not only in the practical conclusions Meiri drew, but in the halakhic techniques he adopted—based on the assumption that argumentation is instructive not only in its context, but in delineating its author's spiritual world as well.

WHO IS A "BROTHER"? THE SIGNIFICANCE OF ARGUMENTATION

Meiri obligated the Jew to return lost property to the peoples restricted by ways of religion, in contrast to the prevailing halakhic opinion which obligated only the return of property belonging to Jews. Utilizing this new category, he arrived at a novel halakhic decision. Although the exclusion of gentiles from this obligation had become embarrassing, and several of Meiri's predecessors, including Maimonides, had advised Jews to return lost property to gentiles in order to "sanctify the Holy Name,"[2] Meiri alone saw it as a categorical halakhic obligation towards the gentiles of his time—though it is doubtful whether this ruling had great historical-social significance. Nonetheless, Meiri's discussion of the theoretical aspect of the topic reveals how aware he was of the novelty of his view.

Now, Maimonides ruled: "The return of lost property to an Israelite is a positive commandment . . . *the lost property of a gentile may be kept, for Scripture says: 'Lost thing of thy brother.'* "[3] This homiletic-exegetical reasoning (the words "thy brother" are repeated several times in the biblical verses concerning return of lost property) is taken from a talmudic *baraita*.[4] Meiri, however, structured his argument differently, and therefore could draw his own conclusion.

A person is not obligated to search for lost property [of an idolater] in order to return it to him; moreover, even he who finds this lost property is not obligated to return it. For finding constitutes partial acquisition, and returning it is an act of supererogation[5] which we are not obligated to perform towards one who has no religion . . . *however anyone who belongs to peoples restricted by ways of religion and worshippers of God in any way, even if their belief is very different from our belief, are not included among these but are exactly like Jews in these matters, including [the obligation of] returning lost property and [the ban on] taking advantage of their mistake and all other things.*[6]

Meiri totally ignores the fact that (according to talmudic sources) the obligation to return lost property is directed only to "thy brother," and explains the exemption vis-à-vis gentiles on a substantive premise. The motive is clear: explaining the return of lost property as an act of super-erogation takes the teeth out of the attack on Judaism. Even more central is Meiri's intention to obligate the return of lost property to members of peoples restricted by ways of religion. For if the law extends only to "brothers," even the civilized nations are perforce excluded, since Meiri was not prepared to accept them as brothers. However, if idolaters were discriminated against on substantive grounds, one could distinguish between them and the peoples restricted by ways of religion, which is exactly what Meiri did, although only by ignoring talmudic and Maimonidean reasoning.

Meiri employed the category peoples restricted by ways of religion regarding another halakhic issue, that of defrauding the gentile. On this issue, Maimonides ruled: "A gentile cannot prefer charges of overreaching because it is said: 'his brother' (Lev. 25:17)."[7] Meiri, however, states:

Anyone who is restricted by ways of religion comes under the prohibition of overreaching; idolaters, however, are not within the category of fraternity [lit. brotherhood] which would prohibit overreaching in commercial dealings. The principle of the sages is: "Do not defraud your fellow—do not defraud those who share Torah and commandments with you."[8]

While there is a strong basis for the claim that the text is corrupt, as we shall see below, we must consider the possibility that it is not. In that case, we are to understand that according to Meiri, the laws of overreaching also apply to a gentile who is restricted by ways of religion—in opposition to prevailing halakhic opinion in the Middle Ages. While in this case (in contrast to his opinion concerning return of lost property), Meiri did not ignore the talmudic homiletic explanation, his opinion is that the category of fraternity excludes idolaters, but does not exclude the gentile who is restricted by ways of religion, for he is called a brother of the Jew!

This conclusion is quite farreaching. However, the text as we have it is not clear. The term "commercial" is superfluous for, according to the beginning of the statement, *no* idolaters came under the prohibition of overreaching. This problem can be solved if we assume that Meiri orig-

inally wrote, instead of "idolaters," gentiles. Then we would understand him to mean that gentiles who are restricted by ways of religion
are protected against exploitation, but that this refers to verbal offense,
for example, insults. However, the ban on commercial overreaching
applies only to a "brother" who "shares Torah and commandments
with you," and thus excludes any gentile, including one who is restricted by ways of religion. This emendation eliminates the textual
problem mentioned above, and even brings Meiri back to the fold of
prevailing rulings which applied the prohibition of overreaching to
Jews alone. We must accordingly assume that a copyist changed "gentile" to "idolater," a common change. We must also postulate that the
prohibition against verbal offense protects peoples restricted by ways
of religion, an opinion not found in the Talmud, although a basis can
be found in the sources.[9]

To sum up, if we adopt the proposed emendation, Meiri's statements on this issue have no major implications, although his extreme
consideration for peoples restricted by ways of religion is evident. If,
however, we accept the text as is, with all its textual and substantive
difficulties, Meiri seems to demand a halakhic change of serious social
and economic significance regarding the gentiles of his time. Moreover,
Meiri was prepared to term them brother, on the basis of an acknowledged ethical and religious common ground. We shall see that this is
not an isolated example, and that Meiri struggled with this value-laden
terminology and the problem it posed more than once. Perhaps Meiri
did not accept the interpretation of brother that excluded the gentile
from the prohibition of fraud, and his statement concerning the "fraternity" of the gentile bound by ways of religion was not meant to undermine the talmudic interpretation or narrow it. As we shall see, Meiri
stated elsewhere as well that the Jew has a relationship of fraternity
with the gentile who observes the seven Noahide commandments, although he is not his biblical brother. In any event, we must add to the
list of topics in which Meiri made novel halakhic use of the concept
peoples restricted by ways of religion that of overreaching, a subject of
extensive practical application.

FROM "RESIDENT ALIEN" TO "PEOPLE OF
RELIGION"—EXPANSION AND AMBIVALENCE

As both Katz and Urbach have pointed out, the concept people restricted by ways of religion is intimately connected with the halakhic
concept "resident alien." The consensus is that Meiri invented the first
term because the talmudic halakhic system did not allow for the extended application of the term resident alien. According to halakhic
opinion, as it crystallized in the Middle Ages, either a resident alien

could not be accepted into Judaism at that time (this is Maimonides' view), or one was not obligated to consider his needs any more than that of a gentile (*Rabad's* opinion), a view that Meiri accepted.

Maimonides made the acceptance of a resident alien conditional upon certain theological requirements and emphasized the lack of belief in the divine source of the commandments as the barrier to maintaining that status in his days, whereas Meiri saw the lack of formal acceptance of the commandments as the central issue in denying that status. Moreover, the halakhah assumed that a resident alien was an individual who formally and publicly took upon himself the seven Noahide commandments; Meiri, however, was interested in conferring a preferential status upon members of a certain culture in general, without a formal ceremonial requirement. For these and other reasons, Meiri could not extend the concept of resident alien, and the concept peoples restricted by ways of religion was designed to fill the vacuum created by the non-applicability of the talmudic category of resident alien in his day. Meiri also discerned another category of gentile in his study of Maimonidean law—one who did not worship idols, yet was not a resident alien, namely, the Muslim. This additional category proved that the concepts of resident alien and idolater were not an exhaustive description of the gentile. However, this new category posited by Maimonides was not equal in status to that of a resident alien and was insufficient for Meiri's needs; he therefore had to create the concept peoples restricted by ways of religion.

The creation of the new concept does not mean that Meiri neglected the old. The opposite was true. The spiritual and cultural drives that impelled him to classify his contemporaries and neighbors as peoples restricted by ways of religion, with all the implications thereof, provided a unique foundation for his attitude to the traditional category of resident alien. It becomes clear that the position of the resident alien was stronger in his eyes than that of peoples restricted by ways of religion, and that the former concept was the source of the latter. This is apparent in his special attitude to the resident alien in legal decisions (although primarily theoretical), in halakhic discussions, and in exegetical-legal deliberations. These seem to indicate that Meiri felt a spiritual need to find a more satisfactory way to define contemporary gentiles. Let us present several examples.

1. A striking illustration of Meiri's novel approach to the concept resident alien is found in his discussion of the laws of murder. The accepted opinion was that a Jew who murders a gentile, including a resident alien, was not punished by the court.[10] Maimonides apparently hinted that one who kills a resident alien, although exempt from punishment by the court, can be punished by the community's leaders or by government law.[11] Meiri's statement was more far-reaching:

A Jew [who murders a gentile], if the victim did not observe the seven Noahide laws, he is exempt, for he [the victim] is an idolater, nonetheless it is forbidden . . . but if he did observe the seven Noahide laws, he is considered to have a religion . . . and although the talmudic discussion here seems to indicate differently, be careful not to make a mistake and interpret it another way.[12]

Meiri hints strongly that a Jew who kills a gentile who observes the seven Noahide laws is liable for murder; he claims that only the murderer of an idolator is exempt, juxtaposing this case against the murder of an observer of the seven Noahide commandments. While Meiri did not spell out the murderer's penalty, he suggests that, in his opinion, a Jew is liable for killing a gentile. (From a terminological point of view, it is noteworthy that Meiri did not apply this halakhah solely to the resident alien—perhaps because he accepted the view that the classic resident alien did not exist in his day—but to all observers of the Noahide commandments who were also considered to have a religion. Here we see Meiri in the process of developing the new category peoples restricted by ways of religion.) Meiri's substantive lack of clarity here may reflect his awareness that the talmudic sources did not specify punishment in this case; but he himself was confident that the murderer was liable to severe penalty. Indeed, elsewhere he states explicitly that the killer of a non-Jew is to be punished. Discussing the issue of self-defense, Meiri concludes that the killer of a non-threatening intruder is liable: "He must be avenged (*yesh lo damim*) even if he were a gentile (*nokhri*).[13]

2. We earlier indicated that Meiri more than once considered the relationship between gentiles who observed some religion and the biblical and halakhic concept of "thy brother." We saw examples of this in the discussion concerning returning lost property and in the prohibition against defrauding peoples restricted by ways of religion. Similar deliberation occurs regarding the resident alien as well; Meiri, in essence, did not distinguish between these categories. In his commentary on Hullin 114b, Meiri discussed the dictum that it is preferable to give a carcass (which is forbidden for a Jew to eat) as a gift to a resident alien than to sell it to an idolatrous gentile.

It is a commandment to give a gift to the resident alien in preference to selling it to a gentile, for the resident alien, since he has come under the wings of the *Shekhinah*, is included in the principle of fraternity and one is commanded to sustain him, which is not the case with the gentile, for insofar as he is an idolater one is not commanded to sustain him.[14]

It is clear that the resident alien is considered as one who has come under the wings of the *Shekhinah*, a description generally reserved for true converts; moreover, Meiri did not question that he came under the category of fraternity. All of this is based on the commandment to sustain the resident alien. There is no doubt that the emotional-theological expansion of this law reflects Meiri's spiritual and cultural drives and is not an inevitable outcome of the halakhic dynamic.

Meiri's ruling is significant not only for the associative echoes of the phrase "comes under the wings of the *Shekhinah*," but for its surprising halakhic content. A resident alien is one who takes upon himself the seven Noahide laws (and no more), and these include, in terms of belief, only the prohibition against idolatry. There is no obligation to believe in God or worship Him. In the passage cited above, however, the resident alien is considered as one who comes under the wings of the *Shekhinah*, that is, one who has a positive relationship to God (and does not merely refrain from idolatry). Meiri apparently found it difficult to view the list of the seven Noahide laws as comprehensive, for he could not comprehend that a person would reject idolatry without accepting monotheism; he apparently did not consider atheism as a stage in the development of religion.

Moreover, in Meiri's commentary on the statement "he who rejects idolatry is as one who proclaims the truth of the entire Torah," he associated the first commandment, which calls (according to him) for a belief in God, with the prohibition against idolatry.[15] Meiri determined that "even the first commandment is an exhortation against idolatry, for rejection of God's existence and a belief in another constitutes idolatry." If we apply this principle consistently, it is apparent that Meiri maintained that the Noahides who are commanded to reject idolatry, are *ipso facto* also commanded to believe in God. Therefore, one who attains the status of resident alien, in the purely theological sense at least, comes under the wings of the Shekhinah. Meiri brought the resident alien closer to the world of Judaism in a positive and original manner, including him as part of the perfected and believing nations.

In contrast to this unequivocal statement, however, we also encounter sources indicating Meiri's ambivalence. We have already noted that Meiri included the peoples restricted by ways of religion in the laws of returning lost items, but only by suppressing the meaning of the biblical term thy brother—an indication that he did not view them as generally fitting this category. Indeed, elsewhere in his writings Meiri reveals the internal tension that accompanied this concept. Regarding the well-known dictum to sustain the resident alien, Meiri raises this difficulty:

Perhaps you may ask, how does one derive from "and thy brother shall live with thee" that one is commanded to sustain him [the resident alien], for only [thy brother] is mentioned? Perhaps the way it is written allows the reading "thy brothers" in the plural. [Translator's note: only the vocalization differs in the singular and the plural.] [Or perhaps because] he [the resident alien] is explicitly mentioned together with "thy brother" [Lev. 25:35], one can extend the law to include him as well, which is not the case with charging interest.[16]

According to Meiri, the term thy brother excludes not only an idolater but a resident alien as well, but he is prepared to weigh the possibility that thy brothers may include both Jewish brothers and gentiles. There seems to be no better example of the internal conflict which Meiri experienced on this issue. Although the statements occur as part of a technical halakhic deliberation, the context did not force this problem upon Meiri, for the second answer, based on the explicit mention of the resident alien in the verse, would have sufficed.

The material presented above leads us to an additional conclusion. H. Soloveitchik recently discussed the ways in which Jews in the Middle Ages refuted Christian claims that since Esau was Jacob's brother, it was forbidden to charge him interest. Soloveitchik indicates that this refutation was lip-service, devised for polemical-apologetic purposes alone. In their internal psyches, Jews needed no exegetical proofs that the Christian was not related to them. Soloveitchik claims that such essentially apologetic comments occur only in polemical or exegetical literature and leave no trace in the literature which served the internal needs of the nation, that is, halakhic literature.[17]

It seems, however, that Meiri was an exception to this generalization. First, his statements were made in a purely halakhic context. It was clear to Meiri that one charged gentiles interest, and that they were not considered brothers for this purpose. But he also dealt with the issue of the gentile's relationship to the Jew in other halakhic contexts; thus, the discussion quoted above indicates his hesitations on other halakhic topics. The problem, in Meiri's view, was not the identity of the Christian as Edom-Esau, Jacob's brother, but the status of the person who belonged to the category of peoples restricted by ways of religion or that of resident alien. This analysis indicates the systematic and non-polemical nature of his thought.

All this seems to lead to one of two conclusions: Either Meiri merely reacted to the polemical use to which these talmudic passages were put by Christians, or he internalized the question into his spiritual-intellectual consciousness and honestly demanded a response. This latter attitude led at times to the feeling that the gentile was actually a brother in certain senses and contexts, and that even in those circumstances where he could not be so termed (as in the case of returning lost property), one must deal with him to all intents and purposes as if he is included in that general category.

3. The consensus of those who have dealt with this topic is that Meiri did not use the term he created in a sweeping way, and that

there were areas in which this concept did not apply. I found no statement of principle in his work, but the boundaries that Meiri set himself are clear. To a certain extent, a similar problem exists in Maimonidean thought as well. Maimonides also based the prohibition against marriage to gentiles on their adherence to idolatry, but he gave no dispensation where the gentile was not an idolater.[18] We can nonetheless state that Meiri's readiness to distinguish between members of peoples restricted by ways of religion and the classic gentile is prompted by the concept of resident alien. In other words, Meiri eased prohibitions regarding peoples restricted by ways of religion only in those cases where there was no clear dictum enforcing that prohibition against a resident alien.

I did not find Meiri claiming a special status for peoples restricted by ways of religion in any case where the talmudic sources equated a resident alien with a gentile. The Mishnah gave permission to take interest from a resident alien as well as a gentile, so Meiri did not prohibit charging interest to the people restricted by ways of religion. He certainly did not apply the new concept to laws concerning marriage, where the halakhah perceived the resident alien as a gentile for all intents and purposes.

Is this equation necessary for the internal dynamics of the concepts? One can claim that members of the peoples restricted by ways of religion differ from the resident alien and are even superior. A resident alien is a gentile who observes the seven Noahide laws and does not practice idolatry, but who does not worship God. The members of the peoples restricted by ways of religion, on the other hand, "worship God . . . although their belief is far from ours," as we have seen. It is likely that Meiri took this superiority into account when he used the concept peoples restricted by ways of religion in those areas where the status of the resident alien is unclear, or where his predecessors, the medieval scholars, explicitly equated a resident alien to a gentile. However, where the talmud itself equated a resident alien to a gentile, Meiri was not prepared to accord any significance to the special status of peoples restricted by ways of religion as believers, and he did not overstep the boundaries which the halakhah had erected vis-á-vis the resident alien. In this way, Meiri remained within the talmudic framework and did not pursue the farreaching implications of the concept he coined.

On the other hand, if Meiri assumed that a resident alien was commanded to believe in God, as we suggested above, it is apparent that the religious signification of the term peoples restricted by ways of religion overlapped with that of resident alien, and it is unlikely that Meiri's definition of the talmudic resident alien emanated, among other factors, from his reaction to the cultural-social reality of his time.

GENTILES AND IDOLATORS

Meiri made limited halakhic use of the concept peoples restricted by ways of religion, and the details we have added admittedly do not constitute a turning point in the relationship between Jews and gentiles in practical halakhic terms—the basic idea already being found in polemical and disputational literature. Meiri's contribution is in his more generalized development of the concept and in putting it into the context of halakhic discourse. This is not insignificant, neither in terms of Meiri's intellectual-spiritual biography, nor regarding the history of halakhic (as well as social) thought. Actually, the concept peoples restricted by ways of religion is only one expression of Meiri's distinctive attitude to the gentile.

An additional expression of this distinctiveness, this time regarding gentiles in general with no reference to their status as resident aliens or peoples restricted by ways of religion, is found in Meiri's statement concerning moneylending. Medieval scholars differed on whether charging a gentile interest is a commandment, or is only permissible. They certainly did not view lending money to a gentile as a commandment or a positive value.[19] Meiri, however, writes:

However, concerning [lending money] to a gentile for profit [= interest], it has an aspect of commandment and morality, for one is forbidden to turn away emptyhanded one who comes to him, although one is certainly not commanded to give him a free loan . . . and this is what they said, "if thou shalt lend money to My nation,"—My nation and a gentile, My nation comes first . . . from this you learn that a gentile is also included by the Bible, although [giving] a free loan to a Jew takes priority over lending money to a gentile even for profit; a gentile has no priority, but he too is included as an aspect of commandment and morality.[20]

Meiri's thrust is not clear: Why does he attempt to derive a moral lesson here? Is there not an apologetic tone to this comment? It is clear that Jews had no need for spiritual encouragement to lend money to gentiles with interest! Did they need proofs that they did not thereby sin against the gentile? Or did Meiri, perhaps, feel a spiritual need to justify the norm?[21]

Let us turn now to the question of giving gifts to gentiles who were definitely idolaters. There were differing opinions among the sages on this subject: R. Judah forbade it, and R. Meiri permitted it. The concrete case involved giving a carcass (which was forbidden to the Jew) to an idolater. The law was usually decided according to R. Judah, and Maimonides rules accordingly. Additional substantiation for this position is found in a *baraita* which states: "Do not show them mercy—

do not give them gifts." [22] Meiri presents the topic in his own manner: "Do not give them gifts in order not to steal them from those to whom we owe more, such as the resident alien." [23] Meiri's artificial reasoning blurs the nature of the prohibition, in contrast to the unequivocal presentation in the Talmud.

The comment provides a suitable background for Meiri's statements on a similar topic. In explaining the *baraita* which determines that on the Sabbath "one places food before the dog in the courtyard . . . accordingly one gives food to the gentile in the courtyard," Meiri explained that the latter is permitted "for ways of peace, and moreover because one cannot compare people, even idolaters, to animals in this case." [24] In this way, Meiri attempted to solve a specific difficulty: how is it that one must make an effort on the Sabbath to feed someone for whom one is not obligated to provide? [25] Meiri was clearly offended by the comparison between the needs of man, any man, even an idolater, and that of a dog. In Meiri's statements on these subjects, we can detect then, the sensitivity which is expressed more openly in the passages dealing with the halakhic status of Noahides and peoples restricted by ways of religion.

In summation, one must pay attention not only to Meiri's categorical statements and decisions, but to his deliberations and equivocations, in order to sense his inner tension concerning the gentile of his times. Of course, one should not exaggerate: Meiri did not break (even in his use of the term peoples restricted by ways of religion) the mold of the talmudic concept of resident alien. His discussions of the law of prohibited foods, the Sabbath, forbidden relationships, do not reflect a unique attitude to the gentile—as Katz pointed out. In all issues concerning the direct relationship of man to his Maker, we get the impression that Meiri did not doubt the special status of Israel, along with all the social implications of this status. Moreover, his statements concerning issues of social interaction were directed in part to those halakhic topics that were the focus of the anti-talmudic attack characterizing Christian-Jewish polemics since the thirteenth century: returning a gentile's lost property, allowances regarding fraud and murder, and the prohibition against giving him gifts. [26] These accusations are not simply a general background for Meiri's activity; we have seen that he responded to them one by one. Nonetheless, one should not view Meiri's concern with the position of the gentile solely as an apologetic reaction, [27] for several reasons. Meiri extended the area of discussion beyond the topics which served the polemicists. He dealt, with originality, not only with the peoples restricted by ways of religion, but with the status of the resident alien, even (at least in one instance) with the general topic of idolaters.

The characteristics of Meiri's exegesis regarding these topics are singular among those who defended the halakhic tradition from outside attacks. Many times, Meiri hesitated and deliberated, qualities not characteristic of the apologeticist. Although this may reflect the embarrassment of an exegete who is forced to stray from the objective interpretation, it may also reflect an internalized confrontation with the question of the gentile's position in the spiritual legacy of the Jewish people.

NOTES

1. Jacob Katz, the prominent Israeli scholar of medieval Jewish social history, first explored Menaḥem Meiri's attitude to the gentile in his book *Exclusiveness and Tolerance* (Oxford: Oxford University Press, 1961), ch. 10. E. E. Urbach, known for his studies of halakhic thought, reexamined the subject in the article mentioned, published in *Studies in the History of Jewish Society in the Middle Ages and in the Modern Period Presented to Professor Jacob Katz* (Jerusalem: Magnes Press, 1980), 34–44 (Hebrew).

2. The *Great Book of Commandments* (*SMAG = Sefer Mitzvot Gadol,* a medieval Ashkenazic discussion of the 613 commandments), Positive Commandment 74. The concept of sanctification in this context is found in the Talmud and is mentioned by Maimonides, *Mishneh Torah, Robbery and Lost Property,* 11,3.

3. Maimonides, ibid, 11,1–3 (italics mine—GJB). All quotations of the *Mishneh Torah* are from the Yale Judaica Series translation with minor revision when necessary.

4. Bava Kamma 113b.

5. The distinction between an act of supererogation (which is not obligatory toward gentiles) and an act of justice (which is obligatory toward all people) is found in David Kimhi's twelfth-century commentary on Psalm 15:5, regarding taking interest from a gentile (although he admits that "I have expounded this at length in order to provide an answer to gentiles"). Naḥmanides' remarks on Deuteronomy 23:20 are based on Kimhi. Meiri expanded this category to include the issue of lost property. He also saw the potential of this argument to *obligate* appropriate behavior toward members of peoples restricted by ways of religion (in contrast to Kimhi and Naḥmanides, who saw it only as an *explanation* for discriminating against the gentile). Meiri may have based himself on the Maimonidean statement "We should treat resident aliens with the consideration and kindness due to a Jew" (*Kings and Wars,* 10,12). However, he did not use this argument to forbid taking interest from peoples restricted by ways of religion.

6. *Beit ha-Beḥira* to Bava Kamma, ed. Kalman Shlesinger (Jerusalem: 1961), 330. The phrase restricted by ways of religion is also used by Meiri to describe Judaism as perceived by the gentile (*Beit ha-Beḥira* to Ketubbot 11a, ed. Abraham Sofer (Jerusalem: 1947), 51). As my friend Prof. Carmi Horowitz pointed out to me, Meiri was even able to claim that the term "Israel," in the talmudic statement that "the stars have no control over Israel," applies to both the Jewish people and the nations restricted by the ways of religion (*Bet ha-Beḥira* to

Shabbat 156a, ed. Sofer (Jerusalem: 1965), 614–15). This assertion develops out of Meiri's understanding of the relationship of free will and astrology, where the restrictions of religion enable human free will to overcome astral influence. *Beit ha-Beḥira* is Meiri's halakhically-oriented work on the Talmud, written between 1287 and 1300.

7. *Maimonides, Sales,* 13,7. However, see Kimhi, "for it is forbidden to defraud or steal from a gentile as well."

8. *Beit ha-Beḥira* to Bava Mezia, ed. Nissan Alpert (New York: S. Goldman, 1949), 329.

9. In a previous statement (*Beit ha-Beḥira,* Bava Mezi'a, 328), Meiri differentiates between verbal fraud and commercial overreaching, applying the statement "one who defrauds the convert" to verbal fraud (like Rashi's commentary on Bava Mezi'a, 59b). The sages apparently had similar differences of opinion regarding the identity of thy brother, to whom the prohibition of taking interest applies. In contrast to the Mishnah, which understands thy brother to mean a Jew, and therefore permits taking interest from the resident alien, several other sources (Tractate Converts 3,3, and compare *Sifra* to Lev. 25:35–36) prohibit taking interest from a resident alien, apparently interpreting thy brother to include him.

10. Maimonides, *Murderers,* 2, 10–11.

11. See Karo's commentary *ad loc,* and compare Maimonides, *Murderers,* 2, 1–4.

12. *Beit ha-Beḥira* to Sanhedrin 57b, ed. Abraham Sofer (Jerusalem: 1965), 226–27. See as well the material cited by Urbach, 39. While some earlier Ashkenazic scholars included gentiles in the prohibition against murder, their statements did not deal with the punishment meted out to the murderer, nor did they distinguish between a resident alien and other gentiles. Note that Meiri also determined that it is forbidden to murder an idolater.

13. *Beit ha-Beḥira* to Sanhedrin 72a, (267).

14. *Beit ha-Beḥira* to Ḥullin (New York: Massorah, 1945 [no ed.]:) 475; (my emphasis—GJB).

15. *Beit ha-Beḥira* to Horayot 8a, ed. Sofer (Jerusalem: Sinai, 1958), 265. Maimonides also viewed idolatry as a denial of God, as implied by his use of the term "heretics" to signify idolaters. This may have influenced Meiri's views on the subject. (I thank Rabbi Aaron Adler who pointed this out to me.) As is well-known, Maimonides made the status of a resident alien conditional upon his acceptance of the fact that the commandments were divine and revealed at Sinai (*M. T. Kings and Wars,* 8, 11), which of course presupposes belief in the existence of God and the truth of Moses' prophecy. I do not find, however, that Meiri adopts this position. See S. Schwarzschild, "Do Noahides Have to Believe in Revelation?" *JOR* LIII (1962–1963): 38–40. For other aspects of this topic, see my *Political Concepts in Maimonidean Halakhah* (Ramat Gan: Bar Ilan University Press, 1983), 227, 240–41 (Hebrew).

16. *Beit ha-Beḥira* to Bava Mezi'a, (401).

17. H. Soloveitchik, *Pawnbroking, A Study in the Inter-Relationship between Halakhah, Economic Activity and Communal Self-Image* (Jerusalem: Magnes Press, 1985, 17–21 (Hebrew). Meiri certainly was aware of this polemical literature, which was written partly in Provence in the thirteenth-fourteenth centuries.

See for instance: S. Stein, "A Disputation in Moneylending in . . . Meir b. Simeon's *Milḥemeth Misvah,*" *JJS* 10, 1–2 (1959):45–62. Another debate, not necessarily connected to the above, centered around the brotherhood status of a Jew who converted to Christianity. See my article: "Who is Not a Jew?—The Medieval Discussion," *Israel Law Review* 3 (July 1976):378–82, 384–88.

18. See Maimonides' *Book of Commandments,* Prohibition 52. For the use of the term heretics, see ibid., Prohibition 39, 46, 48, 51, 58. From Maimonides' statement in *Forbidden Intercourse,* 12,1, it emerges that the prohibition of marriage applies to any gentile without distinction.

19. Maimonides, *Creditors and Debtors,* 5,1, and *Rabad ad loc;* Naḥmanides' critique of Maimonides' *Book of Commandments,* Sixth Principle, and his commentary on the Bible, Deut. 15:3, etc. According to Maimonides (*Book of Commandments,* Positive Commandment 198), permission to lend money to a gentile is contingent (!) upon charging him interest, for otherwise the loan would constitute helping a gentile, which is forbidden.

20. *Beit ha-Beḥira* to Bava Mezi'a 71a, (400). His statement is doubly significant when juxtaposed against that of Maimonides.

21. Meiri indicates that he is not the first scholar to take this position: "There are those who explain that the sages referred to this [the commandment to lend money to gentiles] when they said: 'Lend money with interest to the gentile': this is a positive commandment." However, I have not been able to identify Meiri's reference to "those who explain." Concerning Meiri's involvement in moneylending to gentiles on a fairly large scale, see R. Emery, *The Jews of Perpignan in the Thirteenth Century* (New York: Columbia University Press, 1959), 28. This was one of the principal occupations of local Jews.

22. Avodah Zarah 20a. See as well, Pesaḥim 21b; Ḥullin 114b; Maimonides, *Idolaters,* 10,4.

23. *Beit ha-Beḥira* to Avodah Zarah 20a (46).

24. *Beit ha-Beḥira* to Shabbat 155b, ed. Y. S. Lange (Jerusalem, 1965), 613. See as well his comments on 19a: "There is an aspect of commandment in sustaining them" (ibid, 76).

25. See for example, *Tosafot,* Shabbat 19a, which rests content with the reason "for ways of peace" alone. In *Beit ha-Beḥira* to Bezah 21b, ed. Lange (117–18). Meiri also used this explanation. See the continuation there, regarding inviting a gentile on the Sabbath and holidays; there seems to be a contemporary flavor to his statements, particularly in his extensive discussion. Two points are of particular importance from a social perspective: 1) The description of a Jew who invites a gentile to his home: "When we invite the gentile . . . we do so voluntarily, and since we feel kindly towards him, our thoughts center around him so that we cook mainly for the gentile." 2) Maimonides ruled: "One may invite a heathen guest on the Sabbath, but not on a festival, lest one should prepare more food especially for him. If, however, a heathen guest arrives uninvited, he may be permitted to join in the meal, for everything is then already prepared" (*Repose on Festivals,* 1,13). Meiri stated: "One does not invite a gentile on a holiday . . . but if one says to him when he enters, 'I invite you to partake of what is prepared' . . . it is permissible." (ibid, 116). It is clear that Meiri attempted to provide a halakhic solution in the context of an existing social situation.

26. Katz points to these accusations as the background for Meiri's activity (see *Exclusiveness and Tolerance*). Concerning misleading the gentile, see L. Loeb, "La Controverse de 1240 sur le Talmud," *REJ* II (1881): 266–68. For a more extensive discussion of the topic, see J. Cohen, *The Friars and the Jews* (Ithaca: Cornell University Press, 1982).

27. See Jonathan of Lunel's statement: "To answer the heretics we can say that the Mishnah spoke only of the seven nations whose blood was permitted." (Commentary on B. T. Bava Kamma, ed. Sh. Friedman [Jerusalem: Feldheim, 1969], 106). According to the editor, (51), R. Jonathan composed his commentary between 1165–75, an indication that this talmudic law was the subject of controversy as early as the twelfth century (compare Cohen's book, *The Friars and the Jews*). It is generally agreed that this phenomenon was common by the thirteenth century, and Meiri's innovations can be viewed as parallel to the turn which the Church's accusations took.

9

YORAM JACOBSON

The Image of God as the Source of Man's Evil, According to the Maharal of Prague

Rabbi Judah Loew of Prague, known by the acronym Maharal, was one of the greatest Jewish thinkers of the sixteenth century. In over a score of volumes, edited in various formats, he wrote a comprehensive commentary on the talmudic legends, using the ancient rabbinic traditions to develop a highly original worldview. He derived many terms and ideas from Jewish medieval rationalistic philosophy, and some impact of kabbalistic mysticism may also be discerned in his writings, yet, as a whole, his theology is original and unique. His thought had tremendous impact on subsequent generations, including the hasidic movement and the twentieth-century thinker Rabbi Kook. This study is a presentation of Maharal's theology concerning the key issue of God's responsibility for evil in the human realm.

The concept of the "image of God" appears numerous times in the Maharal's extensive writings. However, it is not defined with any precision. The Maharal's philosophy is an original system whose components coalesce into a unified, comprehensive, and consistent approach excelling in its dialectic sharpness. Within this system, the key concepts used by the Maharal recur in various forms and frequently acquire significance differing from their original meaning. Thus, the precise definition of these concepts is a precondition for any attempt to comprehend his doctrine and its orientation. However, the Maharal's language is cumbersome and often vague, and despite his frequent repetitions that seek to achieve precision in meaning and intent, his

This article was first published in *Da'at, Journal of Jewish Philosophy and Kabbalah* 1 (1987):103–36. The article was translated and adapted by Zev Kahanov and Priscilla Fishman.

concepts often remain initially unclear. Only an exacting textual and philosophical analysis may lead to their precise clarification.

This comment is also applicable to the concept of the image of God. Despite its great import—both for man in general and for the way of life and conduct of the Jew in particular—this concept has not been granted appropriate attention by scholars. One may also note that an important factor contributing to the concept's obscurity has been its significance in kabbalistic thought.

It should be stated, at this point, that the kabbalistic nature of the Maharal's philosophy remains to be clarified. To what extent did kabbalah penetrate the deepest levels of his thought and help to focus its direction? Although we do not know which kabbalistic books the Maharal possessed, nor the scope of his familiarity with the sources, it is clear he was well acquainted with kabbalistic tenets and symbols, which he frequently employed. Furthermore, he loved kabbalah, respected and admired its spiritual achievements, and viewed it as an ally in his battle with philosophy. Despite this, or perhaps because of it, he effected a policy of intentionally concealing kabbalistic ideas, disguising and only hinting at them.

In the context of considering the image of God, we must emphasize that the Maharal is not to be perceived as a kabbalist in the normal sense of accepting kabbalistic ideas and permitting them to fashion his philosophy. He assimilates the kabbalah into his own thinking and employs its ideas in his own way. The Maharal is not a theosophist who deals with the mysteries of the Divine Presence; he is not even inclined to consider the classical queries of medieval theology. His central interest is focused on man's essence, his relationship with God, and his place in the world—both in terms of the individual's ethical-religious conduct and of man within history. To the extent that the kabbalah (like philosophy) is present in the Maharal's thinking, it undergoes a far-reaching transformation. Its notions and symbols no longer appear in their original context, but are employed to express his concept of man. This transformation helps to explain the Maharal's influence over the later hasidism of the Ba'al Shem Tov.

THE IMAGE OF GOD

The starting point for the Maharal's discussion of the concept image of God obviously rests on the familiar understanding of the term "image" as the form of man's body, organs, and the likeness of his face. At the same time, it is apparent that the phrase as a whole rejects the sole or central significance of this initial notion and seeks to reveal the divine dimension of human existence. The image is not bodily, but divine. The Maharal discusses this concept more than once; but perhaps the principal discussion is to be found in his commentary to Tractate Avot: "Beloved is the man created in the image: More love is ascribed to the one created in the image because the verse says, 'and God created man in His own image.' " It is apparent that the Maharal's interest is focused on the religious-ethical meaning of man's image and not on the anthropomorphic kabbalistic myth of the divine image. At the same time, one cannot deal with the image in isolation from its metaphysical significance and its link to the divine dimension. In this context, it is clear that the image is not a bodily representation, for "one can in no way ascribe a bodily form and name to God, blessed be He," and one may not employ a material or human term in this regard. The Maharal also rejects Maimonides' interpretation that the image is the "human intelligence," for the Mishnah testifies that man created in His image is "even more beloved than the angels" who, as pure spiritual beings, possess knowledge and wisdom.

Man is unique in combining elements of natural beings with the pure intellect of the angels. The image alludes in a material sense to what may be found in God, who is immaterial, for man can certainly portray the separate spiritual entity that is present in what is corporeal. The meaning of the expression is not that God has an image and form, but that the manifestations of material reality reflect or allude to "what is within God."[1] In this understanding of the image, the Maharal adhered to the basic principle of kabbalistic symbolism, but he did not follow its mythical content. This material world, he explains, is separate. Just as the clothed person is perceived by the clothing he wears yet his attire does not constitute his true nature, so God is perceived by the material world in material terms, for the finite world is limited in its conceptual ability.

The Maharal explains the difference between Moses who prophesied through the "clear glass" (Yevamot 49b), and other prophets. Moses' prophecy ascended to the heights of pure spirituality where there is neither image nor form; the other prophets neither soared to this level nor were totally detached from material reality. Moses knew that "man shall not see Me" (Ex. 33:20) "for this is no material representation of what God, blessed be He is like—and seeing Him is impossible, for He is distinguished from everything." God exists beyond the capacity of sight which remains forever limited to visible reality even when man's eyes are turned to the transcendental. Isaiah (and, by implication, the other prophets) saw God in a material force, called a "dim glass;" he viewed God through the physical world, which is but the clothing that lends appearance to the one who wears it.

The Maharal's writings contain a number of allusions to the kabbalistic division of the divine system to the right, the left, and the line of uprightness in the middle. In this context, the image is expressed in man's upright bearing. He explains that when man comes to depict God, who reigns over all and there is nothing beyond Him in reality, he draws an upright figure—though one is definitely not to represent, Heaven forfend, God Himself. Whatever is to be found in the Holy One is represented in material man who was created upright, unlike animals which walk bent over. For the creature walking bent over declares that there is a master ruling over it, but God has no such master. Through an important analogy, the image is revealed as the essence of man's uniqueness among all that exists and as determining his relationship with God. "Just as the Holy One, blessed be He, reigns over all that exists, and all the world's creatures are subordinate to Him, man is king over the creatures in the lower world, and there is none over him in the lower spheres."[2]

It is apparent that the image of God present in man is worthy of honor and is the source of the fear felt by all other creatures, even by those that are harmful. Man's divine dimension justifies the important injunction not to shed his blood or humiliate him, for destroying the image of God in man nullifies the honor of the image. The honor of the image is independent of external conditions and expresses man's nobility and true essence; one might term this the divine dimension that is not extinguished even upon man's demise. It will return and be revealed in the supreme perfection of the resurrection that will be achieved by man through the image that is inherent within him as his unique essence and the basis of man's sanctity.

The Maharal considers the image at great length, in order to determine the extent of man's uniqueness in the world and to emphasize his superiority, even in relation to the angels. The image is not form or representation, but the divine radiance which inheres in man. The Maharal's words deserve to be presented at length.

The expression "image" appears in the description of man's creation [Gen. 1:26] . . . Everything that possesses an image and a form is imbued with radiance which constitutes its essence . . . as·it is written, . . . "and the form of his face changes."[3] Thus, ". . . let us make man in our image . . ." [Gen. 1:26] implies that a heavenly spark and radiance adhered to [Adam's] face, and this is the image of God. In this, man is distinguished from all the other creatures. This radiance is not a material one at all, but rather a separate, divine radiance and light which adhered to man, . . . for God, blessed be He, is called light, for . . . light is altogether incorporeal. . . . This is the concept of the image . . . material man has something totally separate and immaterial clinging to him—the brilliance of God's image. Just as man acquires an exalted soul together with his corporeality, so does he acquire this supreme spark and radiance. When this light is stripped of everything material, it is God's image entirely. (*Derekh Hayyim*, p. 143)

The Maharal adds that the image is the "separate supreme spark" granted to Adam "and its traces are like those of the sun" which is "the supreme radiance."

From this passage we learn several of the Maharal's basic ideas:

1. The image and the soul of man are not identical. In fact, the image may be found in all creatures, for they, too, are God's creations: "All creatures possess the divine element which adhered to them at their creation—the glory and magnificence which is immaterial."[4] Nonetheless, only in man may this be called the image of God, for he is "more God-like."

2. Glory and beauty constitute the divine radiance inherent in creatures. Beauty cannot be ascribed to the material realm which, in itself, is foul and ugly. Only the spiritual is comely in its clarity and purity. However, the divine radiance manifests itself in varying intensities; different realms of reality reflect a dimmed glory and a diminished spiritual beauty. Only the image of God (e.g., man) is the perfect reflection and manifestation of the supreme divine grace on earth.

3. The glory and splendor embodied in all creatures also reflect their position in the overall divine order of reality. Their harmonious coming together within this order manifests the glory and perfection of the act of creation, and their integration within the divine order brings them out of the dark abyss and chaos of the material realm. It purifies their matter and elevates them to a perfect spiritual existence, to the point that they acquire their divine "form" and sparkle in the beauty of their spirituality and the splendor of holiness. Order, which is attractive in its harmonious perfection and coordination, is the principle of form.

4. One may describe the image as a coat of radiance that was not entirely taken away from man when it changed into a coat of skin. In that coat of light, man's material existence glows even after he has sinned—but only after removing the material clothing will the perfect image of God be revealed. The image signifies the holy tie of man to the transcendental layer of reality—not only through the purity of his spiritual existence, but also in his earthly, God-like entity. When this tie is perfect, at the time when man is "disrobed of the earthly," the spiritual beauty will shine through, and he will become a "total image of God."

The Maharal determines that the constituent parts of man, the body and the soul, together comprise the image of God. This combination is the hallmark of human existence, linking heaven and earth, the lower and upper spheres.[5]

The essence of humanity which includes both body and soul constitutes a third element evolving from them, like a house whose constitutent parts are wood and stone, with the form of the house, a third element, being created by the two. From the terminology and analogy employed by the Maharal, we may conclude that the body and soul have a material status, while the image revealed in their coalescence is the form of man, the manifestation of his unique being. However, it is apparent that the image exists in the body, just as the Torah "exists in material entities" despite its "supremacy over all." The Maharal stresses that although man's image is manifested in the material, matter is not an essential revelation of is existence, and his status as a human being is exhibited in his form. Indeed, "the image of man *is* man." It is the essence of man that provides his unique position among all creatures.

The Maharal repeatedly depicts the image of God as man's loftiest attribute. The purpose of the Torah is "entirely to serve as a commentary on how man should attain this level, so as to be entirely in the image of God." The actualization of God's image is an act of exaltation and sanctification, as man transcends material reality. God's image in man provides the opportunity to reach the state of coming close and cleaving to God. It is man's meeting ground with the transcendental, the realm of spiritualizing the earthly, the sphere of divine revelation in a concrete reality.

The image of God exists at different levels among all human beings and in all nations, but its clearest manifestation is apparent in the people of Israel. The divine quality of the image was inherited from Adam by Jacob, who attained a similar spiritual beauty, a "coat of light." In contrast, Esau, who was immersed in the worldly sphere, acquired only the "quality of clothing," which grants authority in material reality. Esau's legacy had nothing of the separate and divine.

The nations manifest the materialism that increased after Adam sinned, whereas Israel embodies and reflects the purity of human existence before it became defective and material. Only the people of Israel have a unique spiritual quality, and within their hearts one finds awakening devotion and yearning to return to the Golden Age of mankind, as well as the potential to extricate themselves from the material world and to be elevated to the point of being linked to the divine experience. The image is prepared to reveal itself in its fully glory within Israel who have been granted a "final form." Upon reaching the level of the "total image of God," the all-embracing unity will reveal itself. However, this special quality will only be revealed in the future, for perfection and form manifests itself only at the end. "Just as man was created after all the creatures . . . for man is governed by form which comes last . . . all the nations were created before Israel, as there were 70 nations in existence in the generation of Babel . . . for Israel is governed by form which comes last" (*Tiferet Israel*, ch. 12, p. 42).

THE "IMAGE" AS FORM

The Maharal tends to deal extensively with the image in terms of form, and the implications of this association should be considered.

The terms "material" and form are clearly the legacy of medieval philosophy with which the Maharal was well acquainted. He was aware of their Aristotelian significance but he used them in a fundamentally different way. They no longer are philosophical terms applied to apparent reality, but rather are principles of contradictory values describing, within a theological context, man's conduct in God's world.

Matter, or the material, is deficient in that it lacks form. "Matter is common to all things," whereas form is "the manner of recognizing an entity." Contrary to matter, form is perfect; it is a "complete entity," shaped and crystallized in its own identifiable existence, where the principle of universal order is revealed. In a certain sense, one may say that the form expresses the active divine principle, while matter represents the passive and continuous principle. Form signifies will, strength, and authority. God is the supreme formative principle of reality, the source of the world's order and form, and the purpose of its perfection through His expanding holiness. Form is the "worker and king," molding reality, subjugating matter, and maintaining it within the visible framework.

This determination is significant for the realm of ethics. Material life is marked by its subordination to demands, needs, and desires. Form, on the other hand, expresses spiritual elevation, with man being liberated from the grasp of the material as he transcends it to the point of attaining a refined and pure form separate from the material, that is, a divine holiness, which is the metaphysical form of the concrete world and its transcendental order. It is apparent that man, "in his perfect form, deserves to reign over material things, namely the non-speaking animals at the material level that is ruled by form."

One who is merely concerned with the natural world (primarily in the sense of psychological existence) and only acts to fulfill himself in his own sphere, with the exclusive aim to extract benefit and advantage, lowers himself to the depths of the lesser and defective material reality. Such a person does not succeed in achieving a spiritual life adhering to a separate divine reality. It is in this context that the Maharal explains the talmudic saying, "The best among doctors will go to Gehenna" (Kiddushin 82a). Man is permitted to consult doctors but should "place his trust in God to be his healer beyond the natural sphere. . . . He who is a physician but does not also study God's Torah is concerned with the material and is, therefore, bound for Gehenna." In contrast to the person who is solely immersed in the material, we find the "adherent of the Torah" who is elevated by it to the transcendental order embodied within it. Contrary to matter, which is evil because it is inherently deficient, form embodies good, which is separate from the material, soars above its deficiencies and purifies its inclinations. Form extricates the world, both physically and ethically, from the chaos of reality and imposes a divine order over it. Thus, form is the perfecting principle. In this sense, it comes "at the end," and matter precedes it in the realm of the deficient and the void. Matter is the reality of subjugation, slavery and exile, while form is a state of redemption—the revelation of the wondrous order of God's will and His supreme wisdom. Matter is akin to darkness, while form is the divine light revealing the metaphysical order that reigns over the world.

The image is "the simple form which is totally separate." Having emanated from God, it reunites with Him "like the spark uniting with the candle," except that is has a material mantle. The image is the "form of man" and the "mode of his recognition."[6] The Maharal does not refer to man's visage, but rather to his inner being which is reflected in his countenance as it is shaped by his ethical judgments: "When man is righteous in his deeds he is in God's image, and if he is evil he is likened to cattle. The righteousness or evil of his deeds may be seen in the organs of his body, which are his image for better or worse."

The image, therefore, has a physiognomic aspect: man's body testifies about man. In his body, one can perceive the psycho-physiological reality in which man is immersed, relative to God's world—whether he has endeavored to cling to Him and sanctify himself, to achieve a full revelation of the image within him, or whether he has been tempted by his desires to sink into chaotic matter and be submerged in its turbulence. Because man was created in the image of God, he is the "principal form" of creation, and thus he was created last, complements reality and, in an orderly fashion, brings light into the chaotic darkness. In the image of God, man imposes his authority over material reality, effecting a process of elevation and sanctity and revealing the metaphysical order of the world.

We may better understand God's image as a supreme, divine, and separate radiance, which shines upon man and clings to him. This radiance manifests the spiritual dimension in man's existence, that is to say, the dimension of form, which is simple, separate, clear, pure, and divine. It is clear, however, that this depiction negates any possibility of perceiving the image as man's astral body. In some of his writings, the Maharal links the spiritual light of the image with the world-to-come. Its perfect actualization, the utter release from its latency in material reality, until man's body would glow as did Adam's, is linked to the effort of transcending the world and reaching the separate divine reality, discovering its perfect spiritual order, the supreme intellectual manifestation of the Creator among His creatures below. The endeavor to reveal the image of God signifies man's knocking at the gates of the world-to-come, which is worthy of achieving only because of the image of God within him. The person respecting the image and endeavoring to reveal it ascends in the process and, consequently, adheres to God; while he who humiliates his friend extinguishes and loses the light of the image and, therefore, has no part in the world-to-come.[7] The image, man's supreme virtue and the goal of his perfection, expresses the ascendancy to perfect spiritual life—the life of the world-to-come.

MAN IN RELATION TO THE ANGELS

The Maharal also determines man's special quality relative to the angels. In a rather polemical tone, he argues against the claim that angels excel and are superior to man because they are separate spiritual entities. Although the "loftiest level" is not fully and perfectly present in man, because of his very nature, he is "special enough" to have the glory of God shine upon him. The angels do incorporate the highest level within themselves, but they do not receive God's glory to the same degree that man does. Because of the divine glory within man, which is "the main element in the world," all the angels were created to serve him.

The Maharal also explains that the angel is a separate entity of pure spiritual being which exists beyond earthly reality, and in this sense is at a higher level than man who is, after all, but a material being. Yet, for this very reason, man enjoys an advantage: man is basically material, but being a recipient of the separate divine force, that is, the image, he may elevate himself with a supreme effort to a much higher degree of spirituality in the process of seeking perfection. Thus, man's limitation is the source of his superiority! Angels are, indeed, separate from the material sphere, but they cannot attain actual attachment to the divine existence, whereas man may achieve release from his worldly imprisonment, ascend beyond it, grasp the Throne of Glory and cling to its holiness. The quality of man's form is so superior that he is more beloved than the angels who have no material body.

The difference between man and the angels becomes apparent in the context of their standing relative to the Throne of Glory.[8] The angels surround Him as they serve Him, while man, created in His image, "has his place under the Holy Throne itself" and is thus unique in his direct line to the divine world. The Maharal clarifies the difference: Ezekiel's famous vision (1:26) indicates that man's form belongs to the Throne itself, which it grasps. Therefore, "man's position under the

Throne . . . is more elevated than that of the angels," who merely "surround the Throne of His glory." The angels also surround man who grasps the Throne of Glory and are at his service. Indeed, all of reality rotates around man as the embodiment of its supreme form and final purpose.

Finally, despite the angels being distinguished from earthly matter, their status is elevated only in the context of the cosmic hierarchy. The creation of man in God's image, however, is in a sense an inherent preparation for the world-to-come, a world of a purely divine spirituality and sanctity, which is man's true place. God's image will be fully revealed only with the fulfillment of the eschatological vision. Only in the future will the radiance break through and unfold in its great intensity. At that time, man's body will become unblemished and clear, and he will again wear garments of light, as at the beginning.

No less important in this context is the hidden spiritual potential of the image, namely the superlative cleaving to God that is nearly mystic in nature. Unlike Adam, who manifests complex human existence at its point of source, Jacob denotes the peak of human spirituality in supreme sanctification and adherence to God. "Adam was named after the earth *(adamah)*, for the image of God clung to matter . . . but Jacob was separate from the inferior matter, and therefore was named Israel, for the glory and authority of God *(El)* which are distinguished from inferior matter" *G'vurot Hashem*, ch. 67, pp. 312–13). Jacob adhered to the Throne of Glory, and God's glory was revealed to him and through him in the sparkle of the supreme light.

In describing the relationship between Adam and Jacob, the Maharal employs a surprising style. He states that matter was dominant in Adam to the point of obliterating form, whereas Jacob was elevated to such holiness that form obliterated matter. Thus, he attained the "perfect image of God." The sages commented that "Jacob's form is engraved on the Throne of Glory . . . for the quality of Jacob's form is in harmony and adherence with the Throne. Things that are in total unison and harmony with one another are rendered as having one form, by virtue of the adherence. . . . These are very deep issues and should not be expanded upon." (ibid.) The experience alluded to in this extraordinary description is obviously not *unio mystica*. However, despite the linguistic restraint employed, there is evidence of exaltation toward the deepest, essentially intimate, attachment between man and the divine experience associated with the Throne of Glory.

Man's "totally separate force" is one of extreme exaltation and inordinate attachment. It signifies both spiritual strength and the capacity for spiritual elevation and bonding on a transcendental plane. This force is so exalted that it can be revealed only in the bearer who embodies the material basis of its full manifestation. "There is no doubt that a force which is separate has a bearer." Such a bearer is the human body, and the force revealed in it is the image.

The Maharal draws a parallel between the image and the Torah: "Just as man stands in the lower sphere with a supreme soul hewn from underneath in Throne of Glory, the commandments of the Torah, though they are earthly in nature, possess an inner secret which is of the higher world." The nature of this parallelism is further clarified:

Just as man has attained the highest quality, having been created in the image of God which is placed within a material body, so the Torah, which is exalted above all, is dependent on material things—the practical commandments. . . . Angels do not possess the divine image which man has . . . for such an image, by virtue of its supreme state, requires a bearer, namely, the human body. . . . Likewise, the Torah, being an elevated intellect, requires an earthly bearer, namely, man. For the commandments, which are exceedingly intellectual, do not stand by themselves; they require a material bearer like man who was created in the image of God. (*Tiferet Israel*, ch. 24, p. 74)

This concept reveals a definite dialectical dimension: In this world, a pure spiritual being can only reveal itself through a material being, and because of its elevated degree and the great delicacy of its spiritual nature, the image can reveal itself only in a bearer of a lower worldly rank. In this respect, the Maharal had a guiding rule: "Everything that is entirely of the upper sphere requires a receptacle that is material." The assumption is that the divine is never manifest in this world except in a material form and is apparent only as a dim reflection of concrete actuality. The Maharal seeks to teach man the path to self-elevation and sanctification, to the point of having the divine form of the world reveal itself even in the lower sphere, and the unifying metaphysical order prevail in reality and unite all its creatures.

THE RELATIONSHIP OF THE "IMAGE" AND THE BODY

We must now consider the interrelationship between the body as a "bearer" or receptacle and the image. We have already noted that the image is revealed in man's exterior, that is, in his upright bearing. The Maharal repeatedly emphasizes as well that the essence of the image is apparent in man's face, which reflects what is within him, that is, his ethical nature. Man is "identified and considered separate" by his face, which is "the very form of man," and by which he is made known to people. Accordingly, the face is less covered than other parts of the human body. Man's uniqueness, both his external appearance and his inner spiritual features, is expressed in his visible features. The face indicates the reality of the individual—for visibility is reality and, therefore, has a dimension of form or, in the Maharal's terminology, a relationship and a likeness to form. In other words, only that which is revealed, that has undergone a formative shaping, is considered a discernible reality and rises above the chaotic disorder of matter.

At one point, the Maharal distinguishes between man's face (in its literal and metaphoric senses) and man's rear. The face is to be understood as the world-to-come, toward which man is to direct all his material and spiritual being. This is indicated by the fact that all man's movements are forward and not to the rear. The Maharal contrasts the face and the leg, especially the thigh. While the face is visible, the thigh is concealed in a dark place, as it is matter that has no actual reality and "exists in darkness and hiding." The angel injured Jacob in the thigh, for there, even in Jacob, form was obliterated by matter. It is impossible for man, as an earthly creature, not to have some deficiency, and this is manifested in his leg and thigh, which are devoid of the image of God. Man's heels are at "the lower end" of the divine image, whereas man's face possesses a higher and separate quality, since it exhibits his particular nature and essence, and reveals the radiant holiness of his image. When Moses was united with the Torah, the supreme divine intellect, "he acquired some of the brilliance and the light . . . as it is written, 'Man's wisdom will make his face shine.' Therefore, the face of Moses acquired light and brilliance." (*Tiferet Israel*, ch. 46, p. 143)

While the image shines forth in man's face in particular and in its features, it is, obviously, also present in all the 248 organs of the body, and "although they are material . . . the image is separate and entirely incorporeal, and is, therefore, called the image of God" (*Commentaries to the Legends of the Talmud*, III [Jerusalem, 1996], p. 193). In this connection, the Maharal holds that physicians are mistaken in thinking that man's organs are as natural as those of other animals. By employing medicine, which relies on the study of nature and its processes, these doctors are "witch doctors" who "do not know the true nature of man and his organs, for he is entirely divine. . . . Through his organs, which are 248, like the commandments, he was created in the image of God" (*Tiferet Israel*, ch. 4, p. 16).

The Maharal repeatedly states that in order to attain the highest degree of the divine dimension that is in man, he must embrace the Lord and fulfill the 248 commandments which parallel his organs in number. Only when man acquires the intellectual Torah and totally adheres, with his 248 organs, to the metaphysical order that is contained within its 248 commandments, will he bring forth his divine image from the darkness of its material hiding place into the light of the world. Through divine intellectual actions, man is sanctified by the commandments, that is, is separate from the material, transcending it until the supreme radiance of the divine features illuminates his bodily existence. Only then will he be a complete man.

Adam's great failure is to be ascribed to his inability to maintain a suitable equilibrium between body and soul. Because of his superlative state as one created in the image of God, neither Adam, nor the following generations who were close to this highest level, developed a commensurate foundation; they were like a tree whose branches are more numerous than its roots, such additions being a deficiency. What is this "foundation" that, only when it is strong enough, permits man to attain the highest state and strengthen himself in the image of God that is within his inner self? It is man's body, which is considered the essence and the foundation of man and draws everything after it. It is only when this foundation is stripped of its inferiority, that it may soar until it achieves the supreme level. This is akin to the tree that grows increasingly strong and tall from its roots. However, when its quality is not derived from the roots but only from its loftiness, it usually is deficient. Similarly, it is only when man removes the materialism from his body and seeks to make it pure, that the radiance of the image shines from within him. The essence of the image as the possibility of man's adherence to the transcendental plane of being, and the existence of the image within the body, are very closely linked. Man acquires his image through the sanctification and spiritual elevation of the body, not through being removed from it! Hence, the surprising conclusion: the image was, indeed, initially revealed in Adam and shone brightly in him. However, it first achieved an enduring existence in Abraham.

Abraham was the first to understand that only through struggling with his body, attempting to sanctify and purify it, would he attain the enduring state of the image. He was the first to comprehend that "the greatness of intellect, which is the Torah, requires a material bearer, for the intellect emerges from the material" and becomes a form. The crucial turning point in man's development occurred in Abraham; it was revealed through man's progress towards the King of the universe and towards the image of God which inheres in his inner self.

Delving more deeply into the concept of the image, the Maharal distinguishes three states: the image, the veracity of form (or form, in brief) of man as a speaking creature, and the body. This is the general distinction between separate spiritual strength, spiritual strength imprinted in the body, and the body itself. The image denotes man's attachment to that which is beyond him—his ascending to a separate reality by virtue of being detached from himself. The veracity of form denotes man's perfectibility within the framework of reality. In other words, the image signifies the divine in man, and the veracity of form represents his humanity—which separates him from the animals that do not speak, but is unable to make him transcend nature in true spiritual devotion. Man's veracity of form discloses the philosophical dimension of his intellectual activity, while his image reveals the mystic dimension of the supreme vision.

THE IDENTITY OF LIGHT AND EXISTENCE

In various writings, the Maharal refers to the subject of "light," and to the significance of the image as light. "Light grants reality," he states, "and darkness is its opposite, for that which was light exists and is visible" (*Derekh Hayyim*, p. 144). Light is the only medium by which an entity is seen and examined. It is the productive principle of the divine existence that sustains and influences life. Darkness, on the other hand, is a state of chaos, in which everything totally disappears and in which nothing is known. Darkness, in which the boundaries of reality disappear, is identified with matter, the ancient metaphysical principle that stands in contrast to the divine existence. The latter grants reality, and implements it in an actual order, whereas the former is the anti-divine principle of eliminating actuality and subsistence. Light has more than a metaphoric significance; it is a non-material quality distinguished from matter.

The Maharal further maintains that all the entities that do not emit light are earthly, while the non-corporeal world-to-come, the "separate world," is distinguished by its glowing brilliance. At its supreme level, reality, which by its very nature is organized, is ruled by the formative divine principle and is entirely distinguished from the primordial, chaotic, and dark state of matter. For this reason, the faces of those elevated to the highest spiritual state are radiant.

As a pure spiritual entity, light is good and expresses the perfection of the world. Light is, obviously, also present in the lower levels of the world in various degrees, but anything that is material cannot shine purely because the material eliminates the light. Thus, the more material an entity is, the darker and murkier it is in contrast to the "wheels" whose matter is so clear and delicate that it is almost not considered matter. The elements of fire and air are not as delicate and do not shine as much: the element of water is still heavier and more material, and earth, whose matter is thicker and coarser, is total darkness. The light created during the six days of creation is the purest light, and for this reason it is kept in hiding, for the righteous in the world-to-come. When the world will be redeemed from its earthliness, and is "totally distinguished from the material," the light of creation will again play its role as at the beginning, and to an even more wondrous degree.[9]

The identity of "light" and "reality" is of eminent significance for the deeper study of the concept of the image. Because light indicates reality, one may state that the image of man is the light of man's reality in

God's image. Man has more reality than all else save God, but he does not possess absolute reality, for he is subject to another authority. However, man is sovereign over the lower spheres and possesses absolute reality there, although he is subject to God's authority: "The heavens are the Lord's and the earth was given to man" (Psalm 115:6).

The hierarchical classification of the levels of reality in the general order is determined by their relationship and likeness to the absolute or "complete" reality that emanates from itself and is not dependent on anything beyond it. Anyone existing under the authority of someone else is dependent, since his reality is acquired by virtue of that other entity and is dependent on its will. "Man, created in the image, is sovereign in the lower spheres with only God over him; therefore, he has more of the light of reality than even the angels" (*Derekh Hayyim*, p. 144).

Reality describes that which is most distinct from the material, such as intelligence: that which is material has less reality. It is God who shapes reality in its metaphysical order, and man, who is the reflection of God in the world, is the form of the world and its sovereign. Form is the compelling, shaping, principle in relation to matter; it signifies the unique essence of an entity. Matter in itself has no form. In the realm of reality, whose distinct expression is in the existence of form, man is particularly close to God and superior to all other beings, including the angels, through his essential attachment as a form to the Creator of forms.

In summation, the Maharal employs the term image as referring to "recognition of the reality of an entity." Man, whose reality is apparent and separate from all those in the lower spheres, was created in the image of God. God alone has true, compelling reality, by which He is distinguished from all others and is absolutely transcendental. Similarly, in the lower spheres, man is separate from all the lower beings, and his creation in the image of God denotes the divine in man's existence.

ISRAEL AND THE NATIONS

An important element in the Maharal's discussion of the image of God concerns the relationship between Israel and the nations of the world. He states unequivocally that the image of God is an integral part of all mankind, both Israel and the nations, and that they are all beloved for having been created in the image of God. Nevertheless, they are distinguished from one another in the extent to which the form is manifest in them. "Just as man is distinguished from the rest of the animals in having intellect while animals do not, there are also differences among the nations, some being more inclined toward the material. In contrast, even the lowest quality in Israel exhibits intellect."[10] The highest essence of man's form is found only in Israel and is absent in the nations, but there are also animals which are in between man and the rest of the animals, such as the monkey; in the same way, there is a man who is not perfectly a man.

Who, then, is the "perfect man," and how can he be recognized? The response to this query discloses the two contradictory meanings of the term image. In the primary sense, as an exterior form, the image denotes the "countenance" of mankind, who are all equal. But an immeasurably important significance is attributed to the image as perceived on the spiritual plane: namely, the spiritual form of man in which the divine dimension of his existence is embodied and revealed. In this plane, the crucial substantial differences between men find their expression, for some have more of the divine dimension than others. This world is the world of the natural, and "what is natural deserves to be equally distributed among mankind . . . but the divine element is not found equally within it." (*Tiferet Israel*, ch. 1, pp: 8–9). And so, the perfect man is the one who actualizes the image of God that is in him, who uproots himself from the material plane of existence and soars to the transcendental quality that is within him.

This potential, the Maharal explains, is the form of God's image, and is present only among the people of Israel; they are fully "man," without material inclination, whereas the nations possess "a little of the quality of man." The decline of the nations into the material reality is so great that they grow akin to the animals of the forest in that their ears are not ready to listen to the voice of God emanating from beyond the world, and their eyes do not seek the image of God within them. It is no wonder that this world is the world of the nations, the arena of their historical activity and civilization. Israel, on the other hand, lives in the world in a state of exile that is the result of its very appearance on the historical stage and is its characteristic trait, up to the moment of revealing the magnificent order of the world-to-come, in which the image of God will become known in its perfection.

The Maharal often repeats this dichotomy, which is crucial with regard to the fate of Israel and its historical status. Frequently, he expresses this notion in an extreme manner, comparing the relationship between the nations and Israel to that between the animals which do not speak and mankind. Israel is the essential essence of reality in this world: this reality alone is perfect and true. God is Israel's true form or final form, as a result of their devotion and cleaving to Him as the only cause of existence. The meaning of Jewish existence on the individual, as well as on the collective national, plane rests on the absolute attachment to the transcendent, through a tremendous effort of becoming a form. This attachment is inherent in the Jewish nation. Beginning with the Patriarchs and onward throughout its history, Israel's reality was acquired in a process of liberation from strangers and oppressors. Its link to the absolute imparts a meta-historical significance to its historical existence. By virtue of this devotion, the people of Israel can remove themselves from the limits of the natural world and, by fulfilling the will of God, that is, by sanctifying themselves through linking their 248 organs with the 248 portions of the divine Torah, they ascend toward the state of the perfect image of God, the prevalence of absolute sanctity on earth, the world-to-come in the sense of the reformation of this world.

Is the diminished image among the nations an a priori fact, or is it the result of a process, in the course of which the image is gradually diminished? On the one hand, the Maharal writes that "After God selected Israel, the 'image' became diminished among the nations" (*Netzah Israel*, ch. 11, pp. 73–74). However, an analysis of his writings leads to the conclusion that the lesser image of the nations is not the result of an ongoing process, but of the division of the inheritance of Adam between Jacob and Esau, between the emissaries and subordinates of the divine essence, and the nations of the world who are the faithful sons of earthly history. From the very beginning, the image has not been present in the nations in its divine radiance, but rather exists in their external beauty and in the respect and authority they attain in the natural world. The struggle between Israel and the nations is the historical manifestation of the metaphysical dichotomy between form and matter, the crucial battle between the divine and the natural, the spiritual and the material. Within man himself this is the dichotomy between the inner image of God and the image that man makes for himself.

THE IMAGE AS THE SOURCE OF EVIL IN MAN

An interesting conclusion arising from all these issues relates to the extent of the manifestation of God's image in man. First and foremost, the image signifies the potential for great sanctification in human life. To express the image of God is man's great purpose. Only when he attains this image completely can he ascend to the level of the uppermost, separate world, the world-to-come, which is the origin and purpose of the image of God in man, or of man as God's image. The Maharal does not detach the world-to-come from concrete reality. His writings follow the kabbalistic (rather than the philosophical) tradition, which claims that the world-to-come is not purely spiritual, but a world that will assume form and be revealed within earthly experience, that will grow clear and pure with the resurrection of the dead.

Here we perceive a dialectic turnabout in the Maharal's thinking.

The image of God expresses man's highest perfection; but at the same time, it is also the source of defects in his ethical-religious conduct and the root of his pains and woes.

As one created in the image of God, man has

the prerogative to do what he wishes . . . and if God sees man intending to commit a sin, He does not prevent him from doing it, since the right to choose is his . . . . for man was created in the image of God . . . This choice is not available to the angels, who do not have this choice and perform as God commands them . . . but man who was created in the image of God possesses the quality of being his own master, like God, who acts as He wishes. (*Derekh Ḥayyim*, pp. 147–48)

Man's having been created in the image of God grants him complete autonomy and absolute freedom to choose either good or evil, as he wishes. Thus, man's special quality, namely, the image of God within him, is both the source of his great perfection and the root of his immense deficiency—the danger of becoming detached from God, when his unqualified autonomy expands.

Instead of being totally under the jurisdiction of the First Cause and absolutely devoted to Him, man might act on his own authority, as if there is none above him. It is clear that in creating man who possesses the quality of form, God intended him, by virtue of his link to the transcendental, to praise and more perfectly glorify the Creator through that spiritual form and the principle of harmonious order which it reveals. However, the form in man can be an immense source of danger if man turns inward toward himself and grows mighty in the consciousness of having unique independence in the lower spheres. Then he becomes arrogant, saying: I shall be sovereign. The Maharal holds, however, that man is not granted freedom of choice in order to use it, but rather in order to annul and transcend it as he turns to God and adheres only to Him in total devotion.

This is the most important principle in the Maharal's ethical philosophy, and the cornerstone of the religious-ethical conduct of a Jew: his major responsibility is to repeatedly discover his state of being only an effect and recognize that everything of necessity comes only from God, and nothing from himself, for the one who is an effect receives from the First Cause. God exercises absolute sovereignty over the world; the world is utterly dependent on Him and could not exist by itself if it did not turn to God. The world's cleaving to God expresses the subordinate's constant dependence on the superior. It manifests God's oneness, and makes known His unequivocal uniqueness, sovereignty, and absolute perfection in which the metaphysical cosmic order is maintained. This encompassing order must also be expressed in man's religious-ethical conduct; through the acknowledgment of this absolute dependence, God becomes known as the only ruler of the universe: "All that exists needs Him and depends on Him, to the point that all is God's" (*Netivot Olam, Netiv Ha-Avodah*, ch. 3, p. 82).

These statements seek to explain both the very existence of the world and the significance of its existence. The perfection of its existence lies in its Creator, and there is neither significance nor perfection in the world except through the absolute order that is revealed in it when man cleaves totally to God. Therefore, despite man's upright bearing and his status as ruler of the lower spheres, he must accept God fully, bow before Him, and accept the yoke of the heavenly kingdom. This is the shield against the danger inherent within him. Particularly because man rules in the lower spheres, he must accept "the heavenly decree." "Without this yoke of divine government man would, Heaven forfend, be God himself." This applies to all mankind and is part of the seven Noahide commandments.

The Maharal likens God's sovereignty to that of a great king, which exists precisely when the rulers and princes of the world whose armies are large and powerful submit to him. How can sovereignty be great if it is only exercised over a land whose subjects are few and weak? Furthermore, accepting the yoke of sovereignty is possible only by one who is himself a ruler and who understands the nature of sovereignty and knows its taste. Man is to diminish himself to the point of being likened to "formless flesh"—form being that which grants man his essence. "When man likens himself to formless flesh he is considered as nothing. . . . However, if he considers himself somewhat . . . even as grass [that is, if he achieves even a modicum of value], he has a form which gives each entity its characteristics." Each entity is defined by its individual existence and value stance, as expressed within its limitations and through the reflection of its awareness. Then, it is not an "absolute effect but a creature in its own right" [11] (*Netivot Olam, Netiv Ha-Avodah*, ch. 6, p. 92).

The coarse person who thinks highly of himself exists in a material reality that is limited: "Man limits himself by saying that he is great to such and such an extent." According to the Maharal, modesty is a distinct "intellectual" quality; the modest person thinks nothing of himself and soars to the pure separate state that is beyond the coarseness and density of the material. Then the Torah, which is "pure intellect" may be revealed in him in its endless scintillations. It is clear that while man is an entity unto himself, and supposedly his own cause and not an absolute subordinate, it is stated (according to Sotah 5a) that man's prayer does not deserve to be heard unless he views himself as a nonentity. This understanding constitutes the crucial central value of man's life and determines his conduct relative to God and other people.

The Maharal distinguishes between man's essence by virtue of his creation when the purity of man's essence prevailed prior to his sinning, and "by virtue of being created in the image of God." Adam did not merit to be like God who is capable of distinguishing between good and evil, for man is subordinate and should cleave to God who is goodness itself. Then he is removed from the state of knowing evil.

The supreme "goodness" of the First Cause embraces the knowledge of ethical perfection in its most comprehensive sense, namely, knowledge of the divine order that links all creatures and joins them in wonderful wholeness. Man attains this supreme understanding of the order of reality when it is an expression of his perfected state and his integration into the divine order. Such knowledge means the realization of its goal, for the understanding of supreme good means execution of this supreme good.

From allusions contained in writings of the Maharal, we may formulate a picture of Adam's perfection prior to his sin. He was immersed in continuing contemplative activity, knowing only God, and sharing in the supreme good. At that time, man did not enjoy free choice; the dichotomy of good and evil as objects of understanding and options of choice had not yet undermined his soul or weakened his adherence to God. Knowing good and evil is unnecessary for man "since knowledge of evil was the cause of death in man." According to the Maharal, man should be "eternally innocent." Such a person is satisfied with what God has given him and does not attempt to achieve more knowledge; such a man is neither independent nor governed by his mind that pretends to be wise in its considerations—he is only with God.[12]

The understanding of good and evil is "comprehensive" wisdom that encompasses the contradictions of existence. Attaining such a state is a considerable achievement, but for that very reason it is an impediment to man. The capacity for choice turns man into an individual who is sovereign over himself and separate from God, his cause. Only God is not harmed by this all-embracing wisdom, since He is the absolute reality, which integrates within itself all the contradictions, both good and evil.

At the same time, however, because man was created in the image of God, he "certainly deserves to be capable of distinguishing between good and evil." Although his devotion to God renders him *capable* of "knowing good and evil, when he turns away from his God, as was the case after he sinned, he achieves knowledge of good and evil" (*Derekh Ḥayyim*, p. 148). In other words, man created in the image of God may turn away from God and become mighty in his own sovereignty. He becomes fortified in his own independence and knows both God and himself as an individual. Such a man knows good and evil, for whatever is other than God is evil. Freedom of will, often described by the Maharal as the elevated quality that distinguishes man from both the natural creatures and the angels who are separate in their pure intellectual state, is thus a stumbling block for man and the source of his great failure.

Particularly because man has freedom of choice to effect his wishes, he should be directed in his deeds, for otherwise his choice renders him master of himself and lacking divine order and ties to God. Thus, the image of God within man contains the pre-eminent danger of man being an individual, separate from God and master in the lower spheres, just as God is Lord of the upper spheres. The fact that man was born free and in the image of God, and was not subjugated to any external or internal order, may explain why he succumbed to the snake's invitation to eat of the Tree of Knowledge, an act contrary to God's instructions not to eat thereof. It is because man has something of God's essence, being created in the image of God, that the snake said: "you shall be as God, knowing good and evil." The Maharal explains this statement not as a promise to understand good and evil, but rather as a promise of supreme status, the condition for its attainment being the knowledge of good and evil and the realization of the freedom contained therein.

The snake's efforts to lead man astray were aimed at strengthening the negative disposition of God's image, by virtue of which man would turn away from God, become self-centered and independent. In other words, the snake endeavored to activate the potential of man who was created in the image, so as to oppose God and, so to speak, to be like Him. The snake's promise is that one who acquires knowledge of good and evil and, thus, expresses the inner image of God and achieves independence, would be "totally like God, who has none over Him."

The best summation is made by the Maharal himself:

It becomes clear that the knowledge of good and evil emanates from man's independence and his not turning to God, who is the good. . . . The authority to choose is given to man by virtue of his having been created in the image of God, being unique in the lower spheres, and this causes him to know good and evil, like God who understands good and evil. This is, however, not to man's benefit, for it is better to be subordinate to God and to have no choice that enables one to do evil. (*Derekh Ḥayyim*, pp. 148–49)

NOTES

The following are the sources for the vast majority of the quotes appearing in this text (all from Hebrew sources): *Netivot Olam* (Jerusalem 1971), *Netzaḥ Israel* (Jerusalem 1971), *G'vurot Hashem* (Jerusalem 1971), *Derekh Ḥayyim* (Jerusalem 1971), *Tiferet Israel* (Jerusalem: L. Honig and Sons, 1970).

1. In *Be'er haGolah*, the Maharal (c. 1525–1609) explains that if man sought

"to do something that would signify God who reigns over all, he would do an upright action, as an indication that God who rules over him is divine, omnipotent and upright. . . . This is called the image of God." The significance of man's upright bearing is two-fold: it indicates God's absolute rule as King of kings, and man's attachment to the divine existence. The Maharal said that "the image of man embodies the drawing near to God." In this statement, the phrase "image of God" was not accidentally replaced by "image of man."

2. The Maharal writes: "God is above all, and all is created for His sake and glory. Similarly man is supreme in the lower sphere and all the creatures are there to serve him. Thus, man has six extremities: his head points heavenward as though attached to heaven; his legs point to the earth; his body to the four points of the compass; and in this man is all."

3. The verse from Daniel refers to Nebuchadnezzar who was filled with fury. This is an example of the Maharal's homiletical method of basing his ideas on biblical verses.

4. "The entire world is God's, for He created all, and all that is God's is holy. . . . Through the creatures and the act of their creation, one may witness the glory of His deeds , and therefore, all is holy to God." *(Netivot Olam).*

5. *Netivot Olam* distinguishes between the three parts of man, in hierarchical order: the image, the soul, and the body.

6. In *Netivot Olam*, the Maharal develops, in extravagant language, a mystical notion whose importance is particularly significant, in light of the scarcity of such texts among his writings. Man is made in the "image of the Divine Presence . . . and because of this resemblance unites with the Divine Presence which influenced this form." The Maharal links this to the importance of welcoming visitors, an action that, in the sages' opinion, is superior to the welcoming of the Divine Presence. He emphasizes that the term "visitor" pertains to someone who has not previously visited with the host and is unknown to him. When a person is introduced to his guest and welcomes him for the first time, he "welcomes the essence of his image" or "unites with the essence," that is, becomes attached to the form by which a man is known, and has just been revealed and made known to him. From this we deduce that the form does not denote man's external features and countenance, but a person's essence. Welcoming a visitor establishes a spiritual link with the source of his form, and implies that the true encounter between two people constitutes a renewal of divine abundance, to the point that the meeting becomes a clearly theurgic act which may even have a symbolic significance.

7. In this context, the Maharal explains the metaphoric significance of bloodshed: the humiliation of a person constitutes bloodshed in the "inner sense." The Hebrew phrase for humiliation is "to cause one's face to turn pale." Thus, "he who humiliates his friend extinguishes the light of his face," as though extinguishing a candle, and may be called shedding man's blood. In his writings, the Maharal refers to the denigration of the image through an act of humiliation as the "annulment of man," crushing the bearer and embodiment of divine sanctity.

8. Based upon Gen. 41:40, the Maharal explains that "the Throne is effectively the Kingship," a notion signifying the special relationship between the Jews and their God. Israel is "under the Throne of Kingship and He is called

the King of Israel, for they follow all His sovereign commandments." The Kingship is the manifestation of God in the lower beings, for God alone judges them and their evil. Hence, God instructed Moses, in his dispute with the angels: "Hold the throne of My glory . . . for His sovereignty protects the righteous" (Shabbat 81b). These words undoubtedly incorporate kabbalistic overtones.

9. An important interpretation of this concept appears in a sermon given by the Maharal on the Sabbath of Repentance: "When man keeps himself holy, pure, and free of inferiority, a candle is alight on his head and by its means he looks at the world from one end to the other." This shining candle emanates from the heavenly light and radiance, and is distinguished from what is material. It is said that a fetus in its mother's womb has a lit candle over its head . . . for a spark from heaven affects it, and through it, it "sees what it sees." Whatever vision a man has is due to a heavenly spark that shows him what he sees. We also learn that man who is satisfied with his lot, merits a heavenly spark, just as the fetus, which lacks for nothing in its mother's womb and craves nothing, has a candle lit over it. Man should be exceedingly wise and lack nothing, and thus be a perfect man, as he ought to be (*The Maharal's Sermons*, 741).

The principle significance of this homiletic interpretation lies in its directive regarding man's ethical-religious conduct. Man is to aspire toward a pure and unblemished existence which is liberated from bodily demands and desires. It is not a tangible deficiency that bars man from fulfilling his aspiration for perfection, but a deficiency in his consciousness. This deficiency is man's dependence on others, which means that his reality is defective and wanting. Only when man transcends the deficiency and the dependence and is "exceedingly wise," enjoys the fruits of his labor and is content with his lot, does he soar to a reality of pure form, and become the "perfect man" worthy of the world-to-come.

The "heavenly spark" is a perception of the spiritual state. The Maharal may even be hinting at the vision of divine existence but because he would consider that too daring, he did not elucidate, and used the term "he sees what he sees." It may be, however, that his intention was much simpler and closer to the literal meaning of the passage, namely, that when man purifies himself of the material, he is no longer bound by the visual limits of flesh and blood. The Maharal certainly does not refer to the type of esoteric vision described by the kabbalists.

10. "Intellect" refers to the quality of stubbornness which is of the unchanging intellect, a formative state that is stable and constant. By contrast, the nations are inclined to repent, testifying to the prevalence of the material that is easily changeable, for any matter can be altered with ease.

11. The use of the term "form" here seems to contradict the quality of form toward whose full realization man is to strive, as the perfection of his religious-ethical conduct. One must, therefore, clarify the numerous meanings of this term. In one of its aspects form is the principle of individualization, indicating the entity that is immersed within itself. Man is to sunder himself from his material being to the point of being liberated from his form which separates him from God and limits him to his individual state. Only then can the "spiri-

tual form" of the image of God be revealed in him. Only one who liberates himself from his own form can prepare himself for the revelation of God's image within him. On the other hand, form is also a spiritual essence that is above matter, and the more elevated it is, the more it is beyond the possibility of individualization, a capacity that exists only in matter.

12. The Maharal explains that "as long as Adam was innocent, he was alive," for in his righteousness he was absolutely devoted to God. The devotion of the subordinate to the First Cause is the source of human existence; defective man has no existence except through God and his relationship with Him. The Maharal elucidates further that when Adam was created, "he was *distinguished from all by his intellect*, and he was also innocent." The meaning of the highlighted phrase is equivocal: a) from the very beginning, Adam was distinct and distinguished from all the creatures by virtue of his intellect; b) his mind was neither concerned with the rest of the creatures around him, nor did he view them as objects of learning. He made no major efforts to define and classify them in an intellectual order, based upon the criteria of beneficial or harmful, good or bad. His intellect was directed to one object alone—to the Divine One.

10

MORDECHAI PACHTER

Kabbalistic Ethical Literature in Sixteenth-Century Safed

The cultural center established in Safed in the sixteenth century produced some of the most meaningful spiritual phenomena in early modern Judaism. The jurists, mystics, and scholars of Safed opened the door to new practices in halakhah, in kabbalah, and in Jewish ethical and homiletical literature. This study describes the early fusion between the Jewish tradition in ethics and the new kabbalah that developed in Safed, a process that began a new chapter in the history of Jewish popular spirituality.

The kabbalistic ethical literature produced in sixteenth-century Safed represents a new phenomenon in the history of Jewish ethical literature, as well as in that of kabbalistic literature.[1] While scattered ethical works of a kabbalistic bent had appeared before that time, they do not constitute a coherent entity meriting the designation of "kabbalistic ethical literature."[2] Entirely lacking in these works is the awareness of constituting an independent genre and a sense of the genre's necessity.[3] This is not true of the kabbalistic ethical works composed in Safed in the sixteenth century. That entire century bears the mark of an increasing awareness that the historic hour had arrived for the kabbalah to break out of its self-imposed confinement,[4] a recognition which attained its fullest expression in Safed, where it became a principal motivation for the creation of kabbalistic ethical literature. This literature was designed from its outset to spread kabbalistic concepts among all strata of the Jewish people and to shape their beliefs and observances

This article was first published in *Culture and History*, Ino Sciaky Memorial Volume, ed. Joseph Dan (Jerusalem: Misgav Yerushalayim, 1987). The translation/adaptation is by Joseph Gindsberg.

in the spirit of Jewish mysticism. Thus, this literature is clearly distinct from what had preceded it, both in the goals and tasks that it had set for itself from the start, as well as in its well-developed self-awareness, its deep sense of overriding urgency, and its creative drive.

If, therefore, we wish to investigate the beginnings of kabbalistic ethical literature in Safed, we must track down the first expressions of this self-awareness and conviction. In my opinion, early traces may be found in certain ideational developments within the *havurot* (societies or circles) of mystics and hasidim of Safed.[5] It appears that the origin of kabbalistic ethical literature may be attributed to these groups.

In order to establish this, we must first clarify the nature of the ideas emerging in these *havurot,* and then seek to disclose the connections between these circles and kabbalistic ethical literature. These links would be proof that the first appearance of kabbalistic ethical literature is indeed traceable to the mystic-hasidic *havurot* of sixteenth-century Safed.

THE MYSTIC-HASIDIC HAVUROT OF SAFED AND THEIR RULES OF CONDUCT

Important historical records concerning the mystics of Safed in the sixteenth century have come down to us in the form of compendia of regulations *(takkanot)* and religious rules *(hanhagot)* of the Safed rabbis. These are contained in various manuscripts, such as those published by Solomon Schechter and by Jacob Moses Toledano.[6] These writings have been analyzed by David Tamar, a historian of the Jews of Eretz Israel, for the light they shed on the various hasidic *havurot* in Safed. The earliest was, almost certainly, that of Rabbi Solomon ben Moses ha-Levi Alkabez and Rabbi Moses ben Jacob Cordovero (the *Ramak,* 1522–1590); it is, in any event, the first one of which we have any detailed knowledge.[7] Tamar bases his analysis primarily on the rules of Cordovero, being careful to note that they were not necessarily written either by him or by Alkabez; the 36 rules attributed to Cordovero simply delineate the lifestyle of those belonging to the circle over which he presided. It is thus conceivable that these regulations were set down as the outcome of a consensus reached among the members. Tamar even raises the possibility that the regulations were intended not only for the members of this circle, but for the Safed community as a whole. That these conjectures of Tamar's are indeed correct can be verified by careful study of the various compendia at our disposal.

As we embark upon this study, it should be stated that, with regard to the ideational ethical character of the written records that have come down to us, their contents are consistent with one another. They all display general agreement concerning the details of the principal religious practices and rules, and it may be said that they reflect a uniform life pattern. Yet, precisely against this background of a shared common denominator, certain differences stand out sharply—between the Cordovero list of rules and all the others; and between the four compendia published by Schechter and the two published by Toledano.

The first of these two distinctions consists primarily of differences in style. In the Cordovero rules, the dominant style is typical of rabbinical rules, namely, instructions and commands;[8] the remaining records are chiefly of a descriptive nature, rather than guides of conduct. At least insofar as their wording is concerned, they are descriptions of an existing situation.[9] This distinction is of major importance. For even if we accept Tamar's assumption that the Cordovero regulations reflect the lifestyle adopted by the membership of the Alkabez-Cordovero circle, we cannot disregard the fact that they were written down not in order to record an existing reality, but for the purpose of establishing it firmly. Indeed, their phraseology clearly proves that they were meant to guide, direct, establish norms, and regulate conduct.[10] Most of the other lists of *takkanot* are quite different; while they, too, were intended to serve as guides and to establish standards of conduct, nevertheless, as their style shows, their authors aimed to achieve this by describing what they saw as an exemplary way of life.[11] It would be futile to question the extent to which these sources present a realistic image of the actual conduct and customs of the Safed community, inasmuch as the very essence of these sources was the concern with the presentation of these customs as an ideal.[12] In short: whereas Cordovero's list of rules permits us only to conjecture that they reflect the actual lifestyle of a particular and defined circle, all the other sources indicate, with a large measure of certainty, that they do reflect the religious-ethical reality for the great majority of the Safed community.[13]

Moreover, inasmuch as the totality of the available records presents a uniform picture of patterns of conduct, we may regard those compendia which are of a descriptive nature as conclusive evidence that the rules bearing Cordovero's name, in addition to defining the way of life within the circle of ḥasidim and kabbalists, went far beyond those confines in imprinting their unmistakeable mark upon the reality of life in Safed as a whole.[14]

And now for the chronological aspect. True , we do not know when the Cordovero rules were composed, nor when the other three lists published by Schechter were written; yet it is almost certain that the Cordovero rules antedate the other rules and guides of conduct. Moreover, these lists do not depict a static situation, but rather a developing process. This process starts with the fashioning of a lifestyle within the circle itself and culminates in this lifestyle moving beyond its confines, eventually becoming an organic part of the community at large.

This chronological-developmental point of view is also corroborated by another distinction between the four sources published by Schechter, and the two published by Toledano. The latter two are distinguished by the fact that they can be dated accurately, the second list explicitly stating that it was sent out in 5337 (1576–1577). We may assume that the first list, which is related to the second, was sent somewhat earlier. It is clear, in any event, that both were composed some time close to 5337. This does not mean that they were necessarily later than the lists of practices prepared by Rabbi Abraham ben Mordecai Galante, R. Abraham ben Eliezer ha-Levi Berukhim, or R. Moses of Liria. What is quite certain, however, is that they are later than the Cordovero list of rules; for even if those were not written in his own hand, they were certainly recorded in his lifetime, that is, before 5330 (1570). It follows then, that the six lists in our possession trace the progressive development of a norm of living extending over a period of at least seven years.

The importance of this development lay in the extension of the rules and practices beyond the kabbalist circles and their conversion into regulating forces in the life of the entire Jewish community of Safed. The two lists published by Toledano provide an additional dimension to this development—and therein lies their chief distinction vis-á-vis the other sources; they bear clear and explicit testimony to yet another phase in the development we have traced, namely the spread of the kabbalistic rules and practices outside of Safed. The first of these two compendia, sent from Safed to Jewish communities abroad, reads:

"These are the words of the covenant" [Deut. 28:69] of the twenty-four regulations sent forth by men of action,[15] a holy community, in the holy city of Safed (may she be speedily rebuilt in our days), unto every holy congregation outside of our land, which they have sent to them so that they may live in accordance therewith, and render glory to their Creator, to cleave unto the Lord, and each of them shall gird his loins to act accordingly. (*Ozar Genazim*, p. 48)

We are thus provided with direct historical evidence of the recognition attained by the "men of action" in Safed; their rules and customs merit emulation not only by all within their own community, but by all Jewish communities wherever they may be. In other words, they felt that the time had come to disseminate among the masses of the Jews in every land the rules of conduct of the ḥasidim, rules founded on kabbalistic views.[16]

This determination within the *ḥavurot* of kabbalistic mystics in Safed necessarily affected the character of these groups. No longer are we dealing with closed groups bent upon preserving their esoteric views and customs; on the contrary, these circles now seek to spread the ideals they cherish, especially their religious lifestyle, and have them adopted by the entire Jewish people.

We find additional evidence for this in the two *havurot* founded by R. Eleazer ben Moses Azikri (Azkari), namely the *haverim makshivim* (hearkening companions [Song of Songs 8: 13]) and the *sukkat shalom* (tabernacle of peace). Rabbi Azikri had founded them as instruments for influencing the public, and their principal purpose was the promotion of a mass movement of repentance. Moreover, their activity provides the clearest testimony regarding the initial development of kabbalistic ethical literature within the ethos of these circles of hasidim and mystics. Rabbi Azikri wrote his treatise *Haredim* as an expression of the concern of his *havurot* with repentance and as an appeal to the general public to join this movement. The writing of his book is organically linked with R. Eleazer Azikri's activities within his mystic circles.

The *havurot* we have discussed so far were organically linked with the Cordovero school in Safed, and everything we have brought to light applies, in fact, only to the circle of Cordovero (and Alkabez) and to the circles of their main disciples.[17] This is of great significance to our investigation, and we shall return to this point later on.

We must now turn our attention to the *havurot* linked to the school of Rabbi Isaac ben Solomon Ashkenazi Luria (the *Ari*[18]), namely the circle of disciples who were devoted followers of the Ari until his death (5332/1572), and to the group of his disciples who, in the well-known "contract of loyalty" signed in 5335/1575, accepted the authority of R. Hayyim ben Joseph Vital. The outstanding characteristic of these two circles—or, one might say, of these two permutations of the circle of the Ari's disciples—is their exclusiveness. As is known, the disciples,[19] evidently at Luria's explicit instruction, insisted upon maintaining a tight esoteric wall around their circle. After his death, however, this wall was breached to some extent (evidently by R. Joseph ibn Tabul). But, precisely for this reason, the contract of loyalty imposed even greater stringency regarding the esoteric rule.

In this respect, without a doubt, the circle of the followers of the Ari is radically different from those we have dealt with before; nevertheless, this circle also seems to confirm the general rule we posited for the *havurot* in sixteenth-century Safed. While it is true that we are dealing here with a tightly closed and exclusive group, we must not overlook the fact that its esotericism applied only to the teachings of the Ari and not to anything connected with his personality or his practices. Indeed, the legend of the Ari sprang mainly from this circle, and in spreading the legend, the circle also spread the practices of the Ari which had become interwoven with it. These practices became known in widespread Jewish communities, long before the teachings of the Ari reached there. Thus the circles of the Ari are no exception in regard to the obligation assumed by all ḥasidic circles to exert an influence on the Jewish public by propagating practices based upon their own life-style.

It may thus be said that the endeavor to propagate their worldview and, more importantly, their way of life, became the primary distin-guishing characteristic of the ḥasidic and kabbalistic circles in Safed; in their influence on the total Jewish community, these circles did indeed realize this goal, either directly or by means of the rules and guides of conduct that were disseminated within the community and even sent abroad. Moreover, this endeavor found yet another channel for its full realization, namely, kabbalistic ethical literature that, we suggest, origi-nated within these circles. To substantiate this, however, we must first demonstrate with certainty the connections existing between kabbalis-tic ethical literature and the ḥasidic-mystic circles.

THE EMERGENCE OF KABBALISTIC ETHICAL LITERATURE

The links between kabbalistic ethical literature and the ḥasidic circles in sixteenth-century Safed manifest themselves first and foremost on the literary-philosophical plane. We have already seen that the bulk of our information on the nature, practice, and ideals of these circles is provided by the lists of rules and religious practices. These documents constitute the burgeoning of an independent branch within kabbalistic ethical literature. While the lists of practices do not occupy a pre-emi-nent place in the kabbalistic ethical literature of sixteenth-century Safed, they eventually develop into one of the major branches of Jew-ish ethical literature. Even in its initial stages, this genre is the literary expression of the norms prevalent within the *ḥavurot*. It thus illustrates the emergence of kabbalistic ethical literature out of the life experience of the ḥasidic *ḥavurot*.

The foremost evidence for this may be found in the book *Totze'ot Ḥayyim* (the issues of life, [Prov. 4:23]) by R. Elijah ben Moses de Vidas. This work, contrary to widely-held opinion, is not a shortened version of his other book, *Reshit Ḥokhmah* (discussed below), even though the two works are clearly related. Mainly a compendium of practices, *Totze'ot Ḥayyim* has two main themes: repentance and prayer. Because of its narrow thematic scope, the book does not reflect the totality of rules and practices which governed the *ḥavurah* of Alka-bez and Cordovero. Nevertheless, the close connection between this work and the ambiance of the *ḥavurah* is beyond all question. In his book, de Vidas presents rules and practices ordained by Alkabez for his *ḥavurah*, as well as one of the Cordovero rules for that circle. In addition, he includes a good number of rules and practices attributed simply to the members, and these turn out to be none other than rules and practices found in the Cordovero list discussed above. We conclude from this that the book constitutes a compendium of rules reflecting life as experienced in the Alkabez-Cordovero circle. Rabbi Elijah de Vidas, Cordovero's outstanding disciple, presumably belonged to his master's circle and, influenced by its spiritual environment, was inspired to compose this book of conduct. We may assume that his longer work, *Reshit Ḥokhmah*, was also written in response to the recognition within this circle of the need to create a kabbalistic ethical literature.

Another Cordovero disciple and member of his *ḥavurah*, R. Abraham ben Eliezer ha-Levi Berukhim, authored one of the lists of practices published by Solomon Schechter. He also wrote a pamphlet on Sabbath practices entitled *Tikkunei Shabbat* and was known for his zeal in preserving the sanctity of the Sabbath in full conformity with the law.[20] In this pamphlet, he set down rules and practices based on predominantly kabbalistic concepts, accompanied by outspokenly kabbalistic interpretations. Inasmuch as we are dealing with a pamphlet concerned with one single topic, we cannot expect it to display very many connecting links with the lifestyle of the circle in which Berukhim was active, but as far as the Sabbath is concerned, his pamphlet reflects the life and ethos of his circle, a mode of life he endeavored to hold up as a model for all Jews.

The common feature of these two books of conduct, *Totze'ot Ḥayyim* and *Tikkunei Shabbat*, is their limitation to one or two defined topics. A different picture presents itself in regard to the third book of conduct which we shall discuss: *Sedar ha-Yom* by Rabbi Moses ben Makhir. The title page of the book (printed in Venice, 5359/1599) identifies the author as the head of the yeshiva in the village of Ein Zeitun near Safed. While nothing definite is known regarding his relations with the scholars of Safed, his book allows us to infer that he was in contact with the Cordovero school.[21] The book treats the detailed "order of the day" (*seder ha-yom*) of the Jew for every day of the year: weekdays, Sabbaths, and the various festivals. It is intended to provide the Jewish public with a fixed order of the day that, when followed faithfully, would ensure that their time is not spent uselessly.

The book bears a pronouncedly kabbalistic stamp. This is evidenced by the sources cited for the various practices,[22] as well as by the numerous interpretations given for the prayers, and the *kavvanot* (devotional thought patterns) that are to accompany the prayers. It should be noted that the book does not show the slightest trace of the kabbalah of the Ari; in fact, it never transcends the bounds of possible influence by the kabbalistic method of Cordovero. However, the salient evidence for the close links between this book and the Cordovero school lies in the fact that the work is the most extensive literary collection of prac-tices and regulations traceable to the ḥavurot of Cordovero and his dis-ciples. Many of the practices which we have found in the lists of direc-tives of these circles are detailed and interpreted in R. Moses ben Makhir's book[23] in a manner that is in keeping with the intended pop-ular appeal of the work; for the book is meant to serve as a guide for all Jews everywhere. We may thus state that *Seder ha-Yom* constitutes a full and comprehensive literary expression of the goal set by the ḥasi-dim and kabbalists of Safed: to regulate the mode of life of the entire Jewish people in accordance with the existing mores and lifestyle that had developed in Safed.[24]

From the books of behavior that emerged within the circles of Cor-dovero and his disciples, we move on to conduct literature that was developed in the school of R. Isaac Luria, the Ari, and became wide-spread in the seventeenth century. We shall, however, focus upon the beginnings of this literature in the circles of the Ari's followers in the sixteenth century, rather than on the later developments.

The first rules of practice which found their way outside these circles are concerned primarily with repentance. Our principal source is the book *Marpe la-Nefesh* (cure for the soul [based on Prov. 16:24]) by R. Abraham ben Isaac Zahalon (Venice 5355/1595). It contains the Ari's rules for repentance, embellished by R. Abraham's own commentary. He explains in the preface:

And thus, to pave a smooth road, for one who comes to purify himself, I have set a table of purification and potions of healing, so that he who is sick of soul may drink it, and, though it be bitter, "his life shall be given him as a spoil" [Jer. 21:9], and he "be thoroughly healed" [Ex. 21:19]. And I, not through any great wisdom of mine, did compose this book to light the path of souls seeking the right path. . . .

Indeed, I have dipped the tip of my strong desire and deep longing into some of the sweet nectar of that "righteous one, flourishing like the palm-tree" [Ps. 92:13], the godly kabbalist, our master and teacher, R. Isaac Luria Ashken-azi, of blessed memory. My two eyes lit up; such mysteries had not been re-vealed since the days of R. Simeon bar Yoḥai, his memory be blessed. And in order to benefit the public, I undertook to publish them, and so I arose and began to gather up the gleanings, forgotten sheaves and corners [based on Lev. 19:9–10; Deut. 14:19] from the words of our sages, may their memory be blessed—for when I groped among all my [own] goods [based on Gen. 31:37] I found me no wealth [based on Hos. 12:9]—and to tie them all together, lest "anything be lacking therein" [Deut. 8:9]. . . .

As this quotation shows, R. Zahalon did not himself write down the practices of the Ari regarding repentance. These he received as a fin-ished literary product; he merely intended to publish them, with additional comments of his own. From the little we know of R. Abraham's life, we can state with certainty that he did not personally study under the Ari and therefore could not have directly recorded the words of the great kabbalist.[25] It follows that his practices concerning repentance were recorded and styled in literary form by his disciples, members of his circle (whose identities in this instance are not known to us), who then disseminated them in manuscript form.

This is borne out by the words of R. Menaḥem Azariah Fano, in the preface to his formulation of the rules of repentance of the Ari. The preface contains valuable information about the initial stages in the development of the Lurianic literature of conduct and the manner in which it was disseminated.

I bear witness that, oftentimes, beloved friends from near and far have pressed me to clarify obscurities in the rules of repentance faithfully reported in the name of the Ari (his saintly memory be blessed), one volume of which has already been published, but with gross errors, as is well known. And last year, an erudite and trustworthy man, by name R. Jacob ben R. Ḥayyim, reported to me that many of the ḥasidim of Germany[26] gather together large groups in their cities in order to fulfill all the requirements of these rules, and that they are in great need to be informed on many of the particulars which are not sufficiently clear. And "great is repentance for it brings closer the redemption" (Yoma 86b). Yet I did not rush to accede to his request, in order not to trespass on ground that is not mine for I knew not who the saintly person was who had written that volume which, having been copied time and again, did not escape the errors of unskilled copyists. For although the book gave credit to the name of the Ari, yet he [the unknown author] labored and searched the marvels of supreme wisdom—happy the eye that saw and the ear that heard and understood it! From the course of the exposition, and how it is [logically] tied together . . . it is clear that the rules of repentance explain themselves quite naturally, "and are sweeter than honey and the honeycomb" [Ps. 19:11], not senseless precepts, as they might appear to one who reads them out of context without knowledge of their origin and ramifications; "for it is not the many that are wise." [Job 32:9]

These words, first of all, openly voice an explicit criticism regarding the first version of the repentance rules of the Ari as published by Rabbi Zahalon, with emphasis placed on the fact that these rules were not written by the Ari himself but had passed through many hands. We find here, at the same time, explicit evidence for the spread of these rules among the Jews of Germany, indicating the wide distribution which the Lurianic conduct literature had achieved outside Palestine. And, lastly, R. Menaḥem Azariah Fano acknowledges that he does not presume to present us with an authentic original text of the repentance rules; indeed, his words imply that such a text did not exist. He is therefore careful in designating "repentance rules expounded by the disciples of the Ari in his name." This final point is of major significance: it provides us with the conclusive evidence that the Lurianic conduct literature was codified by the disciples of the Ari who disseminated it in pamphlet form. Rabbi Menahem Azariah did indeed have a number of such pamphlets at his disposal, as he continues to relate:

I say, "my sons have defeated me" [Bava Metzia 59b], they enticed me and I was enticed [based on Jer. 20:7], and I hasten to send to them, out of what is in my possession, governed by my judgment, one certain pamphlet; not the [original] words, and not in their [original] order, but rather in satisfaction of my own understanding of them, after having drawn upon other pamphlets in which the matters were arranged more suitably; for I went over the intended meaning that arises from them. (*Tikkunei ha-Teshuvah mi-Ha-Ari*, Venice 5360/ 1600, pp. 1a–b)

Here R. Menahem Azariah acknowledges that the wording of the repentance rules, as found in his book, is his own, based on various pamphlets in his possession. This indicates that different versions and traditions of the Ari's repentance rules existed at the end of the sixteenth century, probably disseminated by his disciples, the members of his *havurah*. In this context, it must be stressed that the followers of the Ari also set down and circulated the master's general practices.[27]

In summary, in the promulgation and dissemination of conduct literature, the *havurot* of R. Isaac Luria's disciples are not different from those associated with the school of R. Moses Cordovero. Both groups strove to spread their practices and regulations among all strata of the Jewish population, and both accomplished their aim in two ways: through direct dissemination of the lists of regulations and practices which were even sent abroad, and through the creation of a conduct literature that is, in fact, the extended literary crystallization of the former writings. We conclude, then, that the conduct literature did indeed spring from the very midst of the Safed *havurot* attached to the school of Cordovero or of the Ari.

In addition to the conduct books, systematic ethical treatises sprang from the lifestyles and the ethical and religious atmosphere prevailing in the *havurot*. The first such treatise is *Tomer Devorah* (palm-tree of Devorah, [Judges 4:5]) by Cordovero. While the circumstances and date of its composition are not known,[28] it seems to display traces of the religious and ethical ambience which characterized the Alkabez-Cordovero *havurah*. Another book by Cordovero, *Gerushin*, is a diary of the visions and new Torah insights which he and Alkabez experienced during their "banishments" (*gerushin*), that is, their mystic excursions outside Safed, apparently in the company of the entire *havurah*. Reference to the practice of banishments, engaged in by this *havurah*, is also found in *Tomer Devorah*, "and this precept is observed in the manner of 'ye that walk by the way, tell of it' [Judges 5:10], being those who have banished themselves from their homes to occupy themselves with Torah, causing those left in the home to occupy themselves with the affairs of state [worldly affairs]." (*Tomer Devorah*, Bnei-Brak: Fisher, 1965, p. 40)

Furthermore, *Tomer Devorah* turns this practice into an ethical-religious obligation:

Let him be exiled from place to place for the sake of Heaven, thus creating a *merkavah* [chariot] for the exiled *Shekhinah* [Divine Presence] . . . and let him humble his heart in his exile and bind himself to the Torah; then the *Shekhinah* will be with him. And let him engage in *gerushin* and banish himself always from his domestic tranquility as R. Simeon [bar Yoḥai] and his fellows would banish themselves to occupy themselves with Torah (p. 50).

This text recalls the style of Cordovero's rules, but whereas those rules were intended to govern the mystic-religious life of the circle, the present prescription intends to regulate the life of each and every Jew in light of the model offered by the mystic circle. This is not to deny the possibility that originally this rule also served the needs of the *ḥavurah*.

This possibility fits in with other matters in *Tomer Devorah*. We may reasonably assume that uppermost in Cordovero's mind was the obligation of each member of the *ḥavurah* to care for the welfare of his fellows, in line with the maxim stated in his book: "Just as the Wisdom [God] thinks for the benefit of all that exists, so must each person think for the benefit of his fellow members [*ḥaverim*]." In other words, the book was composed against the background of the *ḥavurah* and emanated from it. If this assumption is correct, major importance must also be attributed to what immediately follows the previous quotation.

Let him take good council with God and with his people, the individuals and the community as a whole [*perat u-khlal*] and he who has strayed from the good practice will be led by him to the just practice, and he should serve him like intellect and thought, to guide him and lead him to acts of goodness and justness, as the Supreme Thought which makes just the superior man [*adam elyon*].[29]

This means that a member of the Cordovero circle is enjoined to be responsible not only for his fellow members, but for the entire community of Israel. We thus encounter precisely the same phenomenon that we faced in the rules and customs recorded in the name of Cordovero or his disciples, the members of his *ḥavurah*: the same refusal to settle for the religious-ethical improvement of the self alone, and the insistence upon the religious-ethical improvement of the entire people. We see, then, how the state of mind that characterized the Safed *ḥavurot* also comes to the fore in *Tomer Devorah*.

These links, though few in number, between *Tomer Devorah* and the *ḥavurah* headed by Cordovero, offer sufficient support for the assumption that the entire book reflects the religious-ethical atmosphere prevailing in that circle. For it is unlikely that Cordovero would enjoin certain details of the teachings or established practices of his *ḥavurah*—and these were not necessarily the most lenient of his rulings—while in other cases he might enjoin otherwise. It is much more reasonable to assume that just as the book reflects the religious and ethical reality of his circle in some details, this is also true of the remainder, even where those links are not evident. The entire book reflects the religious-ethical life of the *ḥavurah*, whether it was written *after* the spiritual image of the circle was already fully delineated, or whether it was written *before*, and in furtherance of that delineation. This applies not just to certain portions of the book, but to the entire ethical picture that emerges from it. It is to be assumed that the ethos of the book, which incorporates the ideal of *imitatio dei* as adapted to the kabbalistic concept of the divinity, was the ethos of the circle headed by Cordovero.

A similar statement could be made, perhaps with even greater emphasis, regarding *Reshit Ḥokhmah* (beginning of wisdom, [Ps. 111:10]; printed in Venice 5339/1579) by R. Elijah de Vidas. However, it is most difficult to unravel the threads that link this book to the lifestyle and practices of the *ḥavurah*, because this is a systematic treatise with but a few references to modes of conduct. At the same time, when R. Elijah cites, for instance, a prayer for sustenance instituted by R. Solomon Alkabez, we may be justified in assuming that an environment did exist in which Alkabez's rules were followed and his prayers recited. But for our purposes, it is of even greater importance that de Vidas distinguished clearly between the system of ethics and the realm of practice, and that he devoted a separate book to each. We have already shown that his conduct book, *Totze'ot Ḥayyim*, reflects the practices of his circle, while, at the same time, it is strongly related to his ethical treatise, *Reshit Ḥokhmah*. Thus, we have sound reason to assume that the latter book, too, mirrors the ethical-religious atmosphere of the *ḥavurah*.

In *Reshit Ḥokhmah*, moreover, we find the most explicit expression of the need for a kabbalistic ethical literature, together with a clear exposition of its main goals and tasks. These, de Vidas formulated most clearly and explicitly; and by explicating them exhaustively and in detail in his book, he developed fully what his preeminent teacher, Cordovero, had briefly outlined in the treatise *Tomer Devorah*. This is borne out by the obviously formative influence which Cordovero and his *Tomer Devorah* exercised on *Reshit Ḥokhmah*, both in the structure and purpose of the book, and in the religious-ethical worldview expressed therein. Based on this, one is justified in concluding that *Reshit Ḥokhmah* embodies the mind-frame of the Alkabez-Cordovero *ḥavurot* and school regarding all aspects of kabbalistic ethical literature. If this be so, it must also be the most extensive and comprehensive systematic embodiment of the ethos which guided the lives of the Alkabez-Cordovero *ḥavurot* and of the circles linked to their school.

But the work which most clearly testifies both to the circumstances of its composition and to the lifestyle and worldview of several Safed *ḥavurot* is, without doubt, R. Eleazer Azikri's *Ḥaredim* (they that tremble at [God's] word [Isaiah 66:5]; printed in Venice, 5361/1601). In the preface, the author discloses that the book grew out of the activities of the two *ḥavurot* over which he presided, *Ḥaverim Makshivim* and *Sukkat Shalom*:

Says the author: when we, hearkening companions, were near the tombstone of Rabbi Simeon bar Yoḥai, occupying ourselves with his sayings, his pure sayings, as is our way, several times a year, from one day to the same hour the next day, "from one self-examination to the next," [30] "there we sat down, yea we wept" [Ps. 137:1] in bitter sorrow . . . "we trembled and were sore afraid" [based on Job 32:6] for our souls and said—woe to us on the day of judgment, woe to us on the day of reproof: how can we enter the world-to-come in disgrace? Such would happen to us time and again, and when returning to town [pulled by] the cords of time, our hearts would be confounded by our troubles, for "our sighs were many" [based on Lam. 1:22] and "the sea grew more and more tempestuous" [Jonah 1:11] toward us. Then the day came to pass when we said—"it is time to labor for the Lord" [Ps. 119:126], for our God has assured us that "he who comes to be cleansed will receive help" [Shab. 104a] . . . and we also "turned many away from iniquity" [based on Mal. 2:6] as He has commanded us. Here in Safed we have founded a holy society; we have named it *Sukkat Shalom* (tabernacle of peace) and many come together to repent with all their hearts . . . also one association of companions hearkening [*Ḥaverim Makshivim*] [meet] together on weekdays to [learn] secret matters concerning Torah and worship that roar like the sea. I say—"the heavenly royalty is like the earthly" [Berakhot 58a, in reversed order], and so "books must be sent" [Esther 3:13] concerning the glory of the Holy King who is without equal, "and the children shall come trembling from the west" [Hosea 11:3], from the ends of the earth shall they come trembling, to return unto Him in repentance from their iniquity, and to be firm in the performance of His commandments. For He said—"Cry out, spare not, lift up thy voice like a horn" [Isaiah 58:1], "and all the people shall hear and fear" [Deut. 17:13]. This have I started to do in the name of the God of Israel.

Furthermore, a goodly portion of the book was composed in the course of R. Eleazer Azikri's activities within these *ḥavurot*. I have shown elsewhere that his personal experiences, which he recorded in his mystical diary, underwent a process of objectivization, as evidenced in his ethical manual *Milei di-Shemaya* (heavenly words) which was used as a compendium of directives and rules for his two circles. I have also shown that many sections of *Milei di-Shemaya* were adapted and formed the most important chapter on ethics in his book *Ḥaredim*. Not only did that book emerge within the framework of the *Sukkat Shalom* and *Ḥaverim Makshivim ḥavurot*, but significant portions of it were written expressly for their use. This means that *Ḥaredim* is in every respect the direct outcome of R. Eleazar Azikri's involvement with the two *ḥavurot* which he had established.

Still another book, R. Ḥayyim ben Joseph Vital's *Sha'arei Kedushah* (gates of holiness; printed in Constantinople, 5494/1734) has such a circle as its background.[31] This we learn from the author's preface:

I have seen those who seek the ascent, and they are few, and they long to rise up; but the ladder is hidden from their eyes. So they immersed themselves in the ancient books, to seek and to find the path of life, "the way wherein they must walk and the work they must do" [Ex. 18:20] so as to raise up their soul to God, its supreme Source, "and to cleave unto Him" [Deut. 11:22], for He is the eternal perfection *[shelemut]*; this is the manner of the prophets who in all their days cleaved unto their Maker, and by virtue of this cleaving *[devekut, communion]*, the holy spirit descended upon them.

This book, then, was meant for "those who seek the ascent," who wished to attain the very highest levels of *devekut*, that is, the level of prophecy. Rabbi Ḥayyim Vital planned the character of his book with this purpose in mind, as he explicitly states further on in the preface:

Therefore, "the spirit within me constraineth me" [Job 32:18] to release the seclusive ones *(perushim)*, to give them support, to show them "the way wherein they must walk" [Ex. 18:12]. And therefore have I composed this work, poor in quality and great in quantity [should read: small in quantity and great in quality] for "those that are wise and will shine" [Dan. 12:3], and I have named it *Sha'arei Kedushah* [gates of holiness], and in it I shall explain things hidden, that could not have been imagined by those who came before us; for I have received them from a saintly person, a "messenger of the Lord of hosts" [Mal. 2:7], my teacher, the godly Rabbi Isaac Luria, of blessed memory. But inasmuch as they are "mysteries of the universe and dark secrets" [from the Yom Kippur *Amidah* prayer], I shall uncover a handbreadth while covering up two thousand cubits, and shall reluctantly open the gates of holiness "like a fine needle" [Eruvin 53a], and whoever is worthy will be privileged to enter the very inner sanctuary [or Holy of Holies, Yoma 61a]. And the good Lord "will no good thing withhold from them that walk uprightly" [Ps. 84:12].

The goal which R. Ḥayyim Vital has set for himself in *Sha'arei Kedushah* is to show the "seclusive ones" and the "wise" the way leading upward to the heights of prophecy and divine inspiration. He therefore does not refrain from disclosing secrets from the teachings of his master, the Ari. It follows that the book was not originally intended for the broad masses, but for a restricted circle of ḥasidim and mystics to whose needs he addresses himself. But the printers of his book thought otherwise. Omitting what is befitting only the most saintly, they presented the rest to the Jews at large.[32] Here we see how a book originally intended for the circle of the mystics can eventually breach the framework of that group and became a classic kabbalistic ethical text available to the entire Jewish public.[33] Thus, *Sha'arei Kedushah* also verifies our conclusion that the kabbalistic ethical works written in Safed sprang from the fertile soil of the mystic *ḥavurot*.

Before concluding, we should turn our attention to two additional aspects of our general subject. The first is chronological. Essentially all the kabbalistic-ethical literary output of Safed was created in the last thirty years of the sixteenth century.[34] This period coincides with the years of major activity in most of the *ḥavurot* we have discussed.[35] It is clear that in this period, we witness the ultimate crystallization of the determination to carry the religious-ethical message of these mystic *ḥavurot* beyond the confines of their membership. This chronological overlap is, of course, not a matter of coincidence, especially in light of the fact that all the authors of the kabbalistic ethical literature belonged to those circles.

The second aspect is that of the personalities involved in this ethical literature. As we pointed out before, the great majority of the *ḥavurot* were closely connected to the Cordovero school. Similarly, it can be stated that the principal originators of the kabbalistic ethical literature of sixteenth-century Safed were Cordovero and his outstanding disciples. Indeed, these creative thinkers were not only products of this school, but were the leaders or active members of the mystic *ḥavurot* associated with it. The authors of the Lurianic ethical literature were also members of the same *ḥavurot* or those of followers of the Ari, foremost among them R. Ḥayyim Vital. Thus, we find that all the writers of the kabbalistic ethical literature in Safed, in its various forms and nuances, belonged without exception to the *ḥavurot* of ḥasidim and kabbalists.

The authors, dates of publication and, above all, the literary and philosophical content of the works reveal the close links between the kabbalistic ethical literature created in sixteenth-century Safed and the *ḥavurot* of ḥasidim and kabbalists which were founded and which flourished in that great spiritual center and, to a large extent, shaped its unique character. These ties clearly prove that the roots of kabbalistic ethical literature are firmly planted in the soil of those circles, and it is on that soil that it originated, flourished, and spread.

NOTES

1. See G. Scholem, *Major Trends in Jewish Mysticism* (New York: Schocken, 1954), 250–51; G. Scholem, *Kabbalah* (Jerusalem: Magnes, 1974), 73.

2. See M. Harris, "Marriage as Metaphysics: a Study of the Iggeret Ha-kodesh," *HUCA* 33 (1962): 197–220; H. G. Enelow, *Menorat Ha-Maor by R. Israel ibn Al-Nakawa,* vol. 3 (New York: Bloch, 1931), 29–34; G. Scholem, *Kabbalah,* 66.

3. This is true even in regard to such works as *Sefer ha-Musar* by R. Judah Kalez, published by R. Moses Kalez in 1537 in Constantinople. Rabbi Moses included a considerable amount of kabbalistic material in this book, most of it quotations from the *Zohar,* and he explains this in the preface by citing the need to explicate the reasons for the commandments *(ta'amei ha-mitzvot),* and to make the practices rooted in the kabbalistic worldview known to the general Jewish public. These remarks do indeed imply a recognition of the need to propagate the kabbalah, perhaps even in the framework of ethical literature; yet they do not in any way indicate a full awareness of a kabbalistic ethical literature as such.

4. See G. Scholem, *Major Trends in Jewish Mysticism,* 244–47; G. Scholem, *Kabbalah,* 67–68, 72; G. Scholem, *Sabbatai Sevi, the Mystical Messiah—1626–1676* (Princeton: Princeton University Press, 1973), 18–22.

5. The term ḥasidim, "pietists," has been applied to individuals as well as to members of various movements—notably the Ḥasidei Ashkenaz who flourished in Germany in the twelfth and thirteenth centuries and the movement (Ḥasidism) that emerged in Eastern Europe in the eighteenth century. These are, of course, quite distinct from the mystics of sixteenth-century Safed (most of whom were of Sephardic origin), despite certain shared concerns and concepts and despite the settlement in Safed of Polish ḥasidim 200 years later.

6. Appendix A in S. Schechter, *Studies in Judaism, vol. 2* (Philadelphia: Jewish Publication Society, 1908) (Hebrew) lists the moral precepts of R. Moses ben Jacob Cordovero, R. Abraham Galante, R. Moses of Liria, and R. Abraham ha-Levi Berukhim. The volume also contains an essay, "Safed in the Sixteenth Century" (292–301).

J. M. Toledano was a rabbi, historian, and Minister of Religious Affairs in the State of Israel. The relevant publication is his book *Ozar Genazim* (Jerusalem: Mossad Ha-Rav Kook, 1960) which contains two lists of rules. All these were translated into English by Lawrence Fine and may be found in his book *Safed Spirituality* (New York: Paulist Press, 1984).

7. Earlier ḥavurot might have existed in Safed, such as the "Companions Hearkening to the Voice of the Lord" which is mentioned by R. Moses ben Joseph Trani (the *Mabit,* 1500–1580) in the preface to his book *Iggeret Derekh ha-Shem,* but it is not clear if, indeed, it was a ḥavurah in that same sense.

8. Typically, these instructions start with a negative formulation: let him not swear . . . , let him not ponder . . . , let him not establish . . . , etc. When positive language is used, the formulation is: let him take heed to pray . . . , . . . to say grace after meals . . . , . . . to associate with one of the companions . . . , or the like.

9. A typical formulation here uses the third person plural in describing the desired conduct ("they put on prayer shawl and *tefillin* [phylacteries] during

the afternoon prayer . . ."), and sometimes the practitioners are identified ("some Torah scholars study [all day ?] every Friday . . ." or, "certain ḥasidim and men of action require . . .").

10. We quote the following typical rules: "Let one associate with one of the companions every day, in order to discourse with him earnestly on matters of worship" (Schechter, *Studies in Judaism*, 292); "One should sit every night on the ground and lament the destruction [of the Temple] . . . " (294), and similarly in all the other regulations.

11. This is confirmed, for example, by the opening phrases of R. Galante's list of practices: "These are the things 'which man shall do to live by them' [Lev. 18:5]" (ibid., 294).

12. This is also confirmed by the titles of these lists. Rabbi Abraham Galante's list is entitled: "Good and holy customs practiced in Eretz Israel, copied from a manuscript by the perfect scholar, our teacher and Rabbi, R. Abraham Galante, long may he live, who resides in Safed, may she be speedily rebuilt in our days for those who fear God" (ibid.). The list of R. Abraham ha-Levi Berukhim begins: "These are other pious customs practiced in Safed" (ibid., 297).

13. This is not to say that the entire Safed community observed all the practices specified in these lists. We merely assert that these writings include practices accepted by various segments of the community, so that, as a whole, they do embrace all strata of the Jewish population of Safed.

14. This is illustrated by the custom to wear a prayer shawl and phylacteries during the afternoon service *[minḥah]*. This practice is couched in the Cordovero rules in the form of an instruction and a warning: "To take heed to say the afternoon prayer with prayer shawl and phylacteries, also during the repetition [of the *Amidah*] (Schechter, *Studies in Judaism*, 293). In contrast, R. Abraham Galante states: "One wears prayer shawl and phylacteries during every afternoon prayer, just as during the morning prayer *(shaḥarit),* and this custom has spread among all the people" (ibid., 294). We have here explicit evidence for the spread of a ḥasidic rule, originating in a ḥasidic *ḥavurah,* into the entire community. It is no accident that this practice is found in all the lists without exception.

15. On the term "(ḥasidim and) men of action," see *Encyclopaedia Judaica,* 7:1384.

16. The kabbalistic character of most of the practices and rules is not evident from their wording. At the same time, one cannot deny that most of them originated in the world of kabbalah. Explicit proof for this is offered by the lists of practices recorded by R. Moses of Liria, which are accompanied by brief glosses on the origin of and reason for each practice. These explanations indicate clearly that the conceptual bases of these practices are firmly rooted in the kabbalistic worldview.

17. R. Abraham Galante, R. Abraham ha-Levi Berukhim, and R. Moses of Liria, the authors of the lists of rules and practices, in addition to R. Eleazar Azikri, were the disciples of Cordovero (Schechter, *Studies in Judaism*, 294–301).

18. The acronym *ha-Ari* is based on Rabbi Luria's honorific title *ha-Elohi Rabbi Yitzḥak,* "the divine Rabbi Isaac."

19. The disciples of the Ari are often referred to as "the lion cubs"—a word play based on the meaning of *ari* "lion."

20. *Tikkunei Shabbat* was printed in Venice, 5360 (1600), together with the abbreviated version of *Reshit Hokhmah* prepared by R. Jacob Poito. The title page carries the following note: "These are the rules for the Sabbath expounded by a sage and hasid, namely R. Abraham ha-Levi the Elder, one of the scholars who were masters of the *Pardes* ("paradise" or marvelous garden, a mnemonic for the four methods of Torah exegesis: *peshat*—the plain meaning of the text; *remez*—hint, or allusion; *derash*—homiletical interpretation; *sod*—mystery), with delectable additions which he heard from the Ari, both of blessed memory." Below this notation, R. Abraham ha-Levi Berukhim is further described as follows: "All his life, he was a great guardian over the Sabbath, ever proclaiming warnings for all Israel, men and women, concerning its observance."

21. Extremely little is known of the life of R. Moses ibn Makhir. Two editions of his *Seder ha-Yom* were printed during his lifetime, in 5359 (1599) and in 5365 (1605); in the second edition, his name is still followed by the formula wishing him long life. We know, moreover, that in 5362 (1602), in the village of Buki'a, he added his signature to a halakhic decision of R. Joseph ben Moses Trani (the *Maharit*, 1568–1639), together with the great Safed authorities of the day. Both editions of *Seder ha-Yom* were published in Venice by the author's son-in-law, R. Solomon Mor David, who spent time in Italy on behalf of the yeshivah of Ein Zeitun. The information regarding the ties of R. Moses ibn Makhir with the school of Cordovero in Safed is derived mainly from his book.

22. For example, the custom to study Torah at night; the posture of *nefilat appayim* (prostrating oneself) assumed during the *tahanun* (petition) prayers; the rule to recite, at the conclusion of the Sabbath, Psalm 119 together with the 15 Songs of Ascents (Psalms 120 through 134); and other practices.

23. For instance, the practice of wearing prayer shawl and phylacteries during the *minhah* service, the custom of going outside the house, or even outside the town, to welcome the Sabbath, or the practice of spending the entire night on the eve of the Shavuot festival occupied in Torah study. These practices appear in the lists of R. Abraham Galante and R. Abraham ha-Levi Berukhim.

24. There are a great number of instructions and rules which show that the book was intended for a broad strata of the people. Some instructions are concerned with a man's labor and livelihood, and indicate a positive attitude toward gainful work, despite its possible interference with the pursuit of Torah study. Others concern the public sermon on the Sabbath; these are addressed specifically to two groups—those engaged in Torah instruction for the public, and those likely to attend the Sabbath discourse. Yet another class of instructions involves the ten days of penitence from Rosh ha-Shanah to Yom Kippur: "And if he cannot stay up until dawn during all these nights of the watches, then let him make every effort to stand on his post from the time he rises for *selihot* [the penitential prayers said at night] until he recites the morning prayer, and let him not turn his thoughts to any matters other than prayers and supplications, or the study of Torah and commandments. . . . And as for study on these days, it behooves him who understands *the path of truth* [i.e., the kabbalah] to occupy himself with it, putting all other study aside; for it [the

path of truth] keeps man on the right path, and he merits to cleave to the tree of life. And so his repentance will be more acceptable, for it rises upwards to the highest level and he who cannot master this, let him occupy himself with the study of Mishnah which also aids greatly in bringing man close to his Father in Heaven and is the base and mainstay of the Oral Law . . . and if he cannot study this, then let him occupy himself with such study as is most pleasing to him, with matters that draw his soul close to the service of God."

25. R. Abraham Zahalon was almost certainly born in Safed, for his father, R. Isaac Zahalon, was a resident of the town and this is how R. Abraham refers to him at the beginning of the preface to his commentary on the Book of Esther, *Yesha Elohim* (salvation of God [Ps. 50:23]). R. Abraham wrote the book in Baghdad in 5353 (1593) when he was 24 years of age; the book was printed in Venice two years later. It follows that at the death of the Ari in 5332 (1572), he was a three-year-old child. He also relates, in the same preface, that since his youth he had been footloose, wandering "from city to city and from province to province" [based on Esther 9:28]. He gives a similar report in the preface to his book *Yad Harutzim* (the hand of the diligent [Prov. 10:4, 12:24]), printed in Venice, 5355 (1595). It appears then that he cannot actually be counted among the sages of Safed, and, indeed, he never refers to himself as a Safed resident.

26. R. Menaḥem Azariah uses the term *ḥasidei Ashkenaz*, probably intending this to mean "pious men of Germany." But perhaps he wants to see in them a revitalization of the earlier movement.

27. See Méir Benayahu's study of the Ari's biography, *Sefer Toledot ha-Ari* (Jerusalem: Ben-Zvi Institute, 1967), 309–14.

28. *Tomer Devorah* was first published in Venice, in 5349 (1589), by R. Moses Basola (II), from a manuscript that had been in the possession of R. Menaḥem Azariah Fano. Neither the book itself nor any notations by R. Moses offer any hints as to the time or the circumstances of its composition.

29. See "Adam Kadmon," *Encyclopaedia Judaica* 2:248–49.

30. In the Mishnah (Niddah 1,1), the term refers to successive examinations a woman performs to check on the onset of her menstrual period.

31. I am assuming that *Sha'arei Kedushah* was written at the end of the sixteenth century. In that case we are clearly not dealing with the circle of Ari disciples we had discussed above but, rather, with a *ḥavurah* of disciples and followers of R. Ḥayyim Vital that was almost certainly established in Damascus. In principle, however, this historical fact has little bearing on our subject.

32. This is indicated by the following printer's note found near the end of the book, after the opening of Part 4: "Says the printer: This fourth part should not be copied and should not be printed, inasmuch as it is all [holy] Names and combinations [of letters] and hidden mysteries which it is improper to make public."

33. This is to some extent reminiscent of the phenomenon encountered in R. Joseph Caro's book *Maggid Mesharim* (declarer of right things, cf. Isaiah 45:19—"I declare things that are right"). Here, the editors or printers set aside a section at the beginning of the book for instructions and exercises of an ethical nature. These, originally intended for the exclusive use of R. Joseph Caro himself, were thus made available to the broad Jewish public.

34. The exception is *Tomer Devorah*, which Cordovero wrote before 5330 (1570), perhaps *Sha'arei Kedushah* which I believe was written after 5350–5353 (1590–1593) and possibly at the beginning of the seventeenth century. The composition of the remaining books fall within the final 30 years of the sixteenth century: *Reshit Hokhmah* was written between 5330 and 5335 (1570–1575); *Haredim* in 5348 (1588); *Seder ha-Yom* not long before 5359 (1599), when it was printed in Venice by R. Solomon Mor David; *Totze'ot Hayyim* was written some years after 5335 (1575), when *Reshit Hokhmah* was completed, and before 5350 to 5353 (1590 to 1593), when R. Elijah de Vidas died. My conjucture is that *Tikkunei Shabbat*, by R. Abraham ha-Levi, and *Tikkunei Teshuvah*, by the Ari, in the version by R. Menaḥem Azariah da Fano, were written before 5360 (1600), the year in which R. Jacob Poito's shortened *Reshit Hokhmah* was printed. The book *Marpe la-Nefesh* was written not long before its printing in 5355 (1595).

35. The exception is the *ḥavurah* of Alkabez and Cordovero that was founded many years before 5330 (1570), the year in which the latter died.

11

JACOB ELBAUM

The Influence of Spanish-Jewish Culture on the Jews of Ashkenaz and Poland in the Fifteenth–Seventeenth Centuries

In modern times, the culture of the Jews of Spanish descent and that of Ashkenazi Jewry are regarded as separate phenomena, for historical developments tended to drive these two great segments of Judaism apart. In earlier periods, however, closer ties existed between the two. This study describes the main outlines of the contacts between these two cultures from the fifteenth through the seventeenth centuries. The rich heritage of Spanish Jewry, in rationalistic philosophy, in the classical works of the kabbalah, and the great systematic compositions of the halakhah, were available to the Jews in Poland in this period, and many of the characteristics of East-European Jewish culture were determined by the choices made concerning their utilization.

As surprising as it may seem, the cultural life of the Jews of Ashkenaz has received little attention from historians and students of Hebrew literature. Research in history, literature, and other areas tends to focus on key periods and issues. The cultural and creative life of Ashkenaz Jewry has not generally been considered to be of critical importance, and cultural life between the ḥasidism of Ashkenaz in the thirteenth century and the modern ḥasidism of the eighteenth century, has remained quite unknown.

Although this subject has been partially investigated (many of the works are still in manuscript form), research has focused on the history of halakhah, with reference to the development of institutions of the *kehillah*. A major breakthrough was made by H. H. Ben Sasson who

This article was first published in *Culture and History*, Ino Sciaky Memorial Vol., ed. Joseph Dan (Jerusalem: Misgav Yerushalayim, 1987). The translation/adaptation is by Sam Friedman.

studied the social issues that were dealt with. One should not be surprised by the attention paid to these questions; it is natural that
the problems that disturb the scholar in his own life determine the
issues that become the subjects of his academic, historical investigations.

Within the framework of this article, I cannot be expected to give a
full description of the culture and creative life of Ashkenaz Jewry in
the designated period. I will deal with only one topic—that delineated
in the title—but I must emphasize that this issue is not a marginal one;
quite the opposite. The "Spanish" influence on the literature of the
Jews of Ashkenaz and Poland was critically significant, perhaps even
revolutionary, at least during the sixteenth century. I shall attempt to
substantiate this claim by following three routes. First, I will focus on
bibliographical and bio-bibliographical particulars. Second, I will briefly
discuss the literary forms in use during that period. Finally, I will discuss one issue in the realm of moral literature. In this way, I hope to
arrive at a comprehensive description of the topic.

TENDENCIES OF SECLUSION

Jewish literature of the fifteenth century, on any topic, is essentially
"closed," that is, it derives primarily from its internal sources. This is
the case regarding all forms of halakhic literature, and it is certainly
true of literature dealing with *minhagim* (customs) that is generally seen
as the dominant literary genre of that period (though I question that
conclusion). This literature includes several known works, such as *Sefer
ha-Minhagim* (The Book of Customs) of R. Abraham Klausner (died
1408), the book of customs of R. Isaac of Turnau (1380/5–1421), *Hilkhot
u-Minhagei Maharash* (R. Shalom Neustadt; died after 1415), and later
works such as *Sefer Maharil* and *Leket Yosher*.[1]

My claim about the internal autarchic nature of halakhic literature
also holds true for the rather extensive responsa literature of the fifteenth century to which many of the great rabbis of the period devoted
their energy,[2] for the literature of *pesakim* (judgments) that, in my esti-
mation, is the dominant form of halakhic work in this period,[3] and for
the literature of *nimmukim* (reasons) which are distillations of the responsa and the *pesakim*, the great majority of which remain in manuscript form in libraries throughout the world.[4] The halakhic monographs of the period, which focus primarily on three subjects—laws of
ritual slaughter and examination of meat for purposes of *kashrut*, laws
of *issur veheter* (ritual laws), and laws of marriage, divorce and *halit-
zah*—as well as the literature of annotations, commentaries, and
abridgements, all rely on internal traditions.

In sum, in the works of these different genres (with but few exceptions), there is virtually no mention of authors outside Ashkenaz except for such well-known Sephardic scholars as Maimonides, the *Rif* (R. Isaac ben Jacob Alfasi), the *Rosh* (R. Asher ben Jehiel), and the *Tur* (R. Jacob ben Asher), and even these four are mentioned relatively infrequently. For example, Moellin says that his teacher the *Maharash* was not wont to study *Arba'ah Turim*. Moellin himself, according to what is told in *Sefer Maharil*, "was accustomed to take the book *Arba'ah Turim* with him when he went to the synagogue, and he would study the book whenever the cantor was embellishing the prayers with his singing, or when the *kedushah* or *kaddish* were being recited" (*Leket Yosher*, ed. I. Freimann, *Oraḥ Ḥayyim*, p. 121). However even his relationship to that work was ambivalent—not because of its source, but because he was opposed to halakhic rulings *(pesikah)* based on books by halakhic authorities *(posekim)*, also rejecting such popular books as *Sha'arei Dura, Mordechai* and *Sefer Mitzvot Gadol*. I will illustrate this by way of a quotation which also has significance for another issue, namely, Yiddish literature. In a response that appears in *She'elot u'Teshuvot Maharil haHadashot* (New Responsa of Maharil) he writes:

I hasten to answer my dear friend Rabbi Ḥaim, may he have long life. I was very surprised to see that you have put your mind to writing in the language of Ashkenaz [Yiddish]. . . . Many laymen who know no more than to read Rashi's commentary, the Bible or the Maḥzor, or who learned the system of the Tosafot in their childhood and have discontinued their learning since then, many never having studied seriously, read the works of our sages such as *Sha'arei Dura, Semak [Sefer Mitzvot Katan]* and *Turim* and issue halakhic rulings based on these works . . . And despite all this you wish to add to our troubles and disseminate knowledge to the wooly-minded and to idle women, and give them the means to learn and to instruct others, on the basis of your works in the language of Ashkenaz, on matters of personal purity which occupied our earlier and later scholars. There will be no end to such things. It has been unheard of since the time of your forefathers.

It was not until the time of Isserlein (mid-fifteenth century) that the *Arba'ah Turim* became an influential book and the subject of annotations; *Leket Yosher* (Joseph b. Moses) is, apparently, the first book in Ashkenaz to be modelled on its format.

Even based upon these abbreviated remarks, it is apparent that acceptance of the *Arba'ah Turim* was slow. Indeed, the question of the relationship of the sages of Ashkenaz to the work of this Ashkenazi-Sephardi author as reflected in the writings of that period, remains for historians of halakhah to answer.

Nonetheless, one can find occasional signs of a degree of openness. It is, however, important to stress that such references should not be considered to reflect external influences. In this respect, a difficult question (to which I have no answer) exists regarding the phenomenon of hair-splitting argumentation and casuistry *(pilpul)* which was a prevalent form of scholarship and learning in the fifteenth century. The question is whether the ascendency of this form of learning was an inherent development or was influenced by Maimonides' *Guide of the Perplexed*. Even if the methodology and basic concept of *pilpul* stemmed from outside influences, we would still be justified in saying that the world of Ashkenaz Jewry was quite closed and reveals only small beginnings of openness throughout this period. This is evident when we turn to other areas of creative output of the sages of the fifteenth century.

First, a short comment about biblical commentaries. There was some activity in this field even though the contribution made by the sages of that period was not of great significance. In *Hilkhot u-Minhagei haRosh* by Asher ben Jehiel, one finds several passages of exegesis based mainly on Rashi's commentary. One of the students of the *Rosh*, R. Dosa ha-Yevani, a Bulgarian scholar, compiled a collection of commentaries on Rashi heard from his teacher and others. Other books of commentaries appeared as well, but none of these works compare, either in form or in content, with the innovative annotations of the Tosafists. On the whole, the works of Ashkenaz are reformulations (at times imperfect) of those scholars. One finds therein almost nothing other than homiletical interpretations based on systems of numerology and acrostics. Needless to say, there are exceptions to the generalization I have been making. For instance, in the work of R. Menaḥem Zioni of Cologne (late fourteenth–fifteenth century), one finds traces of both Sephardic and Ashkenazic mysticism. This is also true of the writings of R. Avigdor Kara of Prague. We now sense a more definite tendency toward openness, reflected in the growing interest in mysticism and in philosophy.[5]

How deep and far-reaching was this development? Most of the sages who displayed this openness were active, as far as we know, in Prague, after a sage from Provence, R. Solomon ben Judah haNasi, wrote a commentary on the *Guide of the Perplexed* that influenced many of his contemporaries. One may, however, query whether this change really extended beyond the boundaries of Prague, and whether the interest in philosophy actually led Jewish scholars in Ashkenaz much beyond the study of the *Guide of the Perplexed* and its commentaries. This is indeed the case in the literary works of R. Menaḥem Agler but, on the whole, there are no signs of an openness to what was being written in Spain and Provence from the mid-fourteenth century until their day. Nevertheless, one cannot deny the existence of more than a hint of a desire to move beyond the confines that were characteristic of the literature of Ashkenaz until then.

We find something similar when we look at the attitude of the fifteenth-century scholars in Ashkenaz to kabbalah. There is the occasional reference to mystical matters based on the writings of the sages
of Spain and its settlements, but the kabbalah is not a significant element in their world.[6] Nonetheless, it is noteworthy that references to
the kabbalah also appear in explicitly halakhic works, and in the responsa of sages (such as R. Moses Mintz and R. Israel Bruna) who
do not identify themselves as kabbalists. R. Israel Isserlein writes in
Leket Yosher:

> He who is a kabbalist directs his prayer to the divine names that emerge from
> the prayer and to the attribute which is alluded to; this is the essence of prayer.
> But those who are not initiates fulfill their obligations by thinking of the simple
> meaning of the prayer. What is essential is the intent, for the prayers are com-
> posed and based upon the 'secret,' as it is said, "He brought me to the house
> of wine" [Song of Songs 2:4], and it is said [Eruvin 65a] "when wine goes in,
> counsel departs," and this alludes to the secret of the prayers. Our rabbis, of
> blessed memory, said: "A song of praise is sung only over wine" [Berakhot
> 35a].

The term "secret" here has a double meaning: First, the ordinary sense
as understood by the sages of Ashkenaz; but Isserlein also speaks of
the "attribute," which is an allusion to kabbalistic symbols. It is said
that from the first of Elul until after the Day of Atonement, Isserlein
periodically studied kabbalah behind closed doors.

The most interesting evidence of the attitude toward kabbalah is to
be found in *Sefer Maharil.* There R. Zalman of Sankt Goar quotes a sage
by the name of R. Zelmlin of Erfort who reported that *Maharil* Segal
(Jacob ben Moses Moellin) would recite prayers with kabbalistic significance, and that he also said, toward the end of his life, that if the
Lord prolonged his days he would like "to change many expressions
in the accepted Rosh Hashanah and Yom Kippur prayers." This could
not have been a facile statement for one who studied, analyzed, and
preserved the traditions accepted by his generation. Segal had always
declared that he was careful to act "in the customary ways determined
by our great rabbis." I believe that this change was connected to Segal's
increasing exposure to kabbalah, which led him to deviate from the
traditions of ḥasidei Ashkenaz concerning the secrets of prayer. Here
and there, one finds other signs of this tendency.[7]

The conclusion to be drawn is that while fifteenth-century literature
in Ashkenaz remains almost exclusively within the traditional framework, the influences of other writings are occasionally evident. While
these influences are not yet strong enough to change the basic forms,
they indicate the potential for change in Ashkenazic literature, as the

above example indicates. (An equally interesting question is the attitude of Sephardic rabbis to the works of the rabbis of Ashkenaz.)

Support for my claim can also be found when we look at other aspects of the creative output of that period. The literature of the fifteenth century is devoid of explicitly philosophical works. Perhaps this claim should be qualified somewhat, since we do possess such works by R. Yom Tov Lipmann Muelhausen and by his contemporaries in Prague. However, this provides no real evidence to the contrary because, as I have already suggested, Prague was somewhat of an exception. Moreover, these occasional examples do not display the degree of perfection in form and content found in the philosophical (and kabbalistic) literature that had been written outside the borders of Ashkenaz. Moreover, even the homiletical works that for generations were to serve as the means by which Ashkenazim expressed their views were as yet nonexistent. It is true that traces of the homiletic form can be found in the writings of the important sages of that period, but these works were merely collections of parables and illusory ideas expressed by means of the homiletical techniques already in use by the tosafists and the ḥasidim of Ashkenaz, for example, acronyms using initial letters or final letters of words, acrostics and numerology in every conceivable form.[8] An examination of the conceptual and ethical issues dealt with in these writings also indicates occasional traces of absorption of Sephardic traditions, although the extent of this is minimal.

The question arises: How did these currents of Sephardic creativity reach Ashkenaz? The answer is not easy to identify. Historical circumstances and personal motives certainly led sages to move from place to place. Migration was one of the many aftermaths of the bubonic plague; apparently this was what motivated R. Solomon ben Judah to move his household (from Provence?) to Bohemia (via Italy?). One must also examine the extent to which the various expulsions of Jews, including the great expulsion from France, influenced the culture of Ashkenazic Jewry. R. Naphtali Herz Trèves (Drifzan)—whom I shall refer to later—was the great-grandson of R. Joseph Trèves (died in Italy in 1429), and the latter was the son of R. Mattathias ben Joseph, the chief Rabbi of Paris, who was educated in Spain by R. Nissim b. Reuben Gerondi (the *Ran*) and others. R. Mattathias is mentioned in the responsa of the *Ribash* (R. Isaac ben Sheshet Perfet). It should therefore be clear that the borders were not closed to physical movement nor to cultural influences.

Certainly, Italy constituted one channel of communication. A large Ashkenazic community was forming in northern Italy, and there is no doubt that it served as a cultural bridge to the regions further to the north. While the Ashkenazic Jews in that vicinity were more closely tied to their place of origin, at least until the mid-sixteenth century, there is no doubt that they were not entirely cut off from the local environment, and that there was contact between them and the "Italiani"—the Jews who had lived in Italy since the beginning of the Christian era. We have definite information about these contacts in the sixteenth century, and they can be traced back to the fifteenth century.

One must not exaggerate the extent to which the sages of the fifteenth century had knowledge about material and cultural life outside their own localities. We have not found in the writings of the aforementioned scholars any information about, or responses to, the fateful events which befell Spanish Jewry from 1391 onwards. However, the channels of influence that have been proposed (from the west and from the south) do not exhaust all possibilities. One cannot exclude influences from the east. Reports about the activities of R. Moses "Hagoleh" of Kiev (who travelled widely to many Jewish communities), and the information presented by S. Ettinger in his discussion on the cultural life of East European Jewry, indicate that even in the most remote areas of Ashkenazic settlement, there were Jews who were receptive to cultural influences other than those of their own traditions.[9]

Even if the possibility that Central European Jewry was influenced by Sephardic literature as a result of contact with the Jews of Poland and Lithuania is but a remote hypotheses, it may nonetheless serve as one explanation of the willingness of the Jews of Poland and Lithuania in the sixteenth century to adopt, virtually unconditionally, areas of cultural activity that were foreign to their Ashkenazic predecessors, yet generally known among their Sephardic brethren.

TRENDS OF OPENNESS

The above presentation ends with the final decades of the fifteenth century. I shall skip over a period of about seventy years, but it must be emphasized that these were not years of creative stagnancy. There was literary activity in every form of Ashkenazic culture, and in the realm of intellectual thought there were increasingly clear signs of the absorption of philosophical theories and kabbalistic views of Sephardic origin. These found expression in the prayer book of R. Naphtali Herz Trèves, in *Siddur Thuengen* (Thuengen, 1560) and a supercommentary on the commentary of Baḥya (Heddernheim, 1546; later printed under the title *Naftulei Elohim*, Ferrara, 1556, and Cracow, 1593). The writings of R. Naphtali reveal a massive penetration of Sephardic kabbalistic literature alongside the traditions of ḥasidei Ashkenaz.[10] In contrast, R. Joseph of Rosheim chose to rely on the writings of the philosophers, more precisely on the work of R. Abraham Bibago (in *Derekh Emunah*

[The Way of Belief], Constantinople, 1522). Nonetheless, one may still maintain that the literary scene described above remained basically unchanged.

This is certainly no longer the case when we turn to Ashkenazic creative activity in the sixteenth century, which was centered at that time in Poland; such writing included theoretical treatises, books of sermons, and hundreds of other works. What is common to them all is that they openly rely on writings of earlier and later writers who were not necessarily local. Even though we have yet to examine all the works that were available to the sixteenth-century Ashkenazic scholar, it is clear that my generalization stands, namely, that at this point there was definite acceptance of every aspect of creative activity throughout the entire Jewish Diaspora.

We find an example in the testimony of R. Mano'ah Handil ben Shemaryah (died 1611). This scholar wrote a commentary on *Hovot ha-Levavot* (*Mano'ah haLevavot*, Lublin, 1596), and mentions his other writings in the introduction. He writes that in his commentaries he took great pains to understand and explain, in accordance with "the good and generous hand of God," first—all the books of the Bible in brief according to their meaning and language. He then lists other works he had written—on the *Arba'ah Turim*, the Mishnah and Talmud, the philosophy of Maimonides, grammar, kabbalah, anatomy, surgery, engineering, mathematics, geometry, astronomy, and astrology! (A few of his works have survived in manuscripts, but have not yet been examined.) From this introduction, we learn something about the areas of interest and activity of one of the lesser-known scholars of the period.

This testimony has far-reaching implications. Careful examination reveals that there was hardly a sage of that period, whether of greater or lesser stature, who did not try his hand at commenting on works in those areas and others too numerous to mention. For example, R. Moses Isserles (1530[?]–1572) and R. Mordecai ben Abraham Jaffe *(Maharam* Yaffe; 1530–1612) wrote annotations to Maimonides' *Guide of the Perplexed*. Interest in this work did not wane, and in 1612 a commentary on it, *Giv'at ha-Moreh* was published in Prague by R. Joseph b. R. Isaac Halevi, and enjoyed the imprimatur of the best-known Ashkenazic scholars of the time. *Sefer ha-Ikkarim* by R. Joseph Albo was also very popular and is mentioned in almost all the writings of the sages of that period.[11] Commentaries were written on the popular book *Ruah Hen* attributed to R. Judah ibn Tibbon, and frequent reference was made to *Behinat 'Olam* by Bedersi, with R. Yom Tov Lipmann Heller adding a commentary to the Prague 1598 edition of that work. R. Abraham Horowitz composed commentaries on Maimonides' *Shmonah Pera-*

kim and on R. Samuel ibn Tibbon's preface to that work. This list is not exhaustive.

We also find commentaries on kabbalistic works: R. Mattahias Delacrut, a Lithuanian sage who lived in Italy and returned to his country of origin after his books were condemned, wrote on *Sha'arei Ora;* the aforementioned *Maharam* Yaffe and Solomon b. Jehiel Luria each wrote a commentary on Recanati; and many commentaries were written on the *Zohar*. There were also other areas of commentary: on the halakhah, the *Arba'ah Turim*, the *Beit Yosef*, the *Shulḥan Arukh*, etc. More than twenty books dealing with Rashi's commentary on the Talmud were written in this generation alone. The commentary of the *Re'em* was printed in Cracow (1595), and R. Isaac ben Naphtali Hacohen of Ostrog composed an abridgment of it (Prague, 1604). Needless to say, in a century in which hundreds of books were written, many literary works dealt with the Bible, and these, too, alluded to the main works of Sephardic sages such as R. Isaac Arama, R. Isaac Caro, R. Abraham Saba, R. Isaac Abrabanel, and others.

A marginal question—though important in its own right—concerns the wide distribution of such works of exegesis, and the reason for their dominant place in literary activities. The sages of this period preferred to comment on existing books rather than create works of independent thought. Perhaps this points to some weakness, fearfulness, or wariness of independent self-expression—but we should not jump to any rash conclusion. We know from the tradition of commentary literature that very often the commentator, even while attached to the text he is explaining, manages to express himself and his own views quite well. This technique was very common in the literary tradition of Ashkenaz.

When we examine the commentaries in other areas—on *Tractate Avot*, on aggadah, etc.—we find that the works of various scholars seem to be solely compilations containing a pronounced component of "Sephardic" material.[12] However some works, without a doubt, reflect their author's confrontations with and assimilation of such material. Examples of these are *Derash Moshe* by R. Moses of Poznitz on 256 aggadot of the Talmud (Cracow, 1589–1590), *Ḥiddushei Aggadot* by R. Samuel Eliezer ben Judah haLevi Edels (Maharsha; printed in Cracow, 1632, i.e., after the period under consideration). Needless to say, many of the writings of the Maharal of Prague belong to this genre or to the closely related genre of *perush* that was completely different from sermons of the previous century. (In fact, this specific type of work was non-existent in the fifteenth century.) Not only did the conceptual sources expand and increase immeasurably, but the literary forms were modified beyond recognition. They were now modeled after Sephardic paradigms, under the influence of *Akedat Yitzhak* (by R. Isaac ben Moses Arama), and similar works.

In summation, I believe that what I have said thus far supports the conclusion that the Ashkenazic writers of that period, as well as their descendants and successors, were familiar with classic Sephardic literature. Moreover, large numbers of books by earlier and later sages were printed during that period in Prague, Cracow, and Lublin. In the area of ethical literature examples are: *Kad haKemach* and *Shulhan Shel Arba* by R. Bahya ben Asher, all the books of R. Jonah Gerondi, *Sefer ha-Yashar* attributed to Rabbenu Tam, *Menorat Hama'or* by Israel al-Nakawa, and *Sefer haMusar* by R. Yehuda Kaletz that became one of the most influential works of that generation and even entered Yiddish literature. (It was the basis of *Lev Tov* by R. Isaac ben Eliakim of Posen.) [13]

The impression that arises from these details is that classic Sephardic literature was accessible to everyone. We can learn about its impact in one area from the words of Isserles who justifies his attempt to deal with the mysteries of the world. He writes in *Torat ha-Olah:* part 3, ch. 84.

Many of the masses are eager to learn the kabbalah for it is so alluring, especially [the works of] latter-day writers who have clearly explained their meanings, and especially since books of kabbalah such as the *Zohar,* the Recanati and *Sha'arei Orah* have been printed. Anyone who wishes to can consult them. Many believe they understand, even though they do not truly understand . . . Many laymen who do not know their left from their right jump at the chance of learning kabbalah and this leads the generation to decline and be sinful . . . Anyone with the slightest inkling of [kabbalah] is proud and speaks about it in public, and will be held accountable in the future.

But the battle was a lost cause.

It appears there was only one sage who attempted to turn back the hands of time, namely, Rabbi Joseph Ashkenazi. He opposed the philosophers, especially Maimonides whom he calls a complete heretic, because "there is not a single chapter in the *Guide of the Perplexed* which is devoid of heresy." Other philosophers and kabbalists were also unacceptable to him, and he "cursed, reviled, and cast scorn on many of the great sages of Israel" because some had dealt in philosophy and biblical criticism, and others had analyzed and interpreted legends from the Talmud—as reported in a pamphlet probably written by his adversary, R. Abraham Horowitz, who noted that he had arguments with Ashkenazi when they both lived in Prague, and that the latter had not learned from his failure there. It would certainly be very difficult to find any person who would be judged worthy in the eyes of one who claimed that even the Bible "should not be studied too much by any Jew." An interesting historical question is whether this obscurantist—whom R. Abraham Horowitz labelled an "imbecile," an "ox," a "fool," and a "contaminated brain"—was an isolated individual in his views. It seems that there were others like R. Joseph Ashkenazi, and that in Posen he found followers and sympathizers, including his father-in-law, R. Aharon Land, who was the rabbi of the Posen region. The author of the aforementioned pamphlet called R. Land "the great ass who publicly shamed his education," quoting Land's explanation that "sorcery had decreased because Asmodeus, king of the devils, had died."

There were others who followed the traditionalist position (whose most eminent exponent was the thirteenth-century sage R. Moses Taku), and who took an active, even militant, role in a war against all that they considered to be inconsistent with the old, authentic, Jewish traditions. From the list of those whom they called "deviants," one can learn to what extent the phenomenon which these individuals were resisting had spread. From the negative references one learns about the on-going process, but one also learns that it did not necessarily lead to openness. In this case, it led to the opposite result—a pronounced desire to immure oneself. The penetration of new ideas is likely to lead to a breach of frames of reference that, in turn, is liable to lead the conservative personality to confine himself still further and withdraw, rationalizing this by an appropriate ideology.

What had changed in this century, leading to what may be called, without exaggeration, a revolution in the creative thinking of the Jews in Poland and Ashkenaz? There is no doubt that a primary factor was the activity of printers and printing presses. As one example, we may point to the rapid spread of the *Shulḥan Arukh* (The Set Table) by R. Joseph Caro, first printed in Venice in 1565 and immediately available in Poland. R. Moses Isserles was able to complete his commentary on it, entitled *HaMappah* (The Tablecloth) before his death in 1572. Thus, the *Shulḥan Arukh* became the primary book of halakhic rulings for Polish and Ashkenazic Jewry. The *Beit Yosef* also spread quickly throughout Poland and Ashkenaz; the great scholars of that generation began to refer to it immediately following its printing (Venice, 1550–1551). This did not happen by chance; printers and booksellers took the initiative in the rapid distribution of books. For example, Samuel Judah Katzenellenbogen, when writing to Isserles, noted that a Jew in his community had purchased a complete edition of the *Rif*, which had been printed in Savionta in 1554–55. The volumes are "very beautiful, and I think that he will sell them for 4½ of our sondo for each book." He then asks whether Isserles would like him to send fifty copies.

No less important is the direct contact between the sages of Poland

and Ashkenaz, and sages whose intellectual background included areas of knowledge which were not initially available to the former rabbis. Again, I return to the Italian connection. Italy was visited by various rabbis of Ashkenaz and Poland—including (probably) R. Yisrael the father of Isserles; R. David Darshan, a younger contemporary who recorded the latter's responsa and the responsa of his brother-in-law R. Joseph Katz (resided in Italy in 1557); R. Mattathias Delkrut; the Prague sage R. Isaac Hayyot, who reported that he visited Italy in 1565. *Maharam* Yaffe, the author of *Levushim*, lived in Italy for several years, and the *Rema* of Fano reported that Polish rabbis came to his house of study and were among those who urged him to print his book *Pelekh haRimon*.

There was also movement in the opposite direction. Italian sages, including rabbis of the Heilborn, Rappaport, Katzenellenbogen families and others, came to Ashkenaz and Poland. Among these were the well-known R. Saul Wahl of Poland, the grandson of the *Maharam* of Padua; and R. Eliezer Ashkenazi, the author of *Ma'asei haShem* (Venice, 1583), a student of R. Joseph Caro and R. Joseph Titatzek, who served as a rabbi in Egypt, Famagusta, Venice, Cremona, and finally settled in Cracow. The influence of Ashkenazi's book was considerable, as it brought the tradition of the East and of Italy regarding biblical commentary and homiletic literature, to Poland.

Direct communication routes to the east were also established in that generation. Questions were addressed to Isserles from Plevnah in Bulgaria and even from Turkey. One questioner was R. David ben Jacob, author of *Migdal David* (Salonica, 1550), whose son R. Judah was instrumental in introducing the customs of the kabbalists to Polish Jewry through his books *Tikkunei Shabbat* (Cracow, 1613) and *Tikkun Kri'at Shma She'al haMittah* (Prague, 1615). Polish sages also had both direct and indirect connections with the Land of Israel. This was true of Isserles and of Luria *(Maharshal)*—especially after the migration of his father-in-law R. Kalonymus and his student R. David Blumish to that land. Isserles even had connections (apparently through the *Maharam* of Padua) with R. Joseph Caro. There is evidence of other such ties as well.

In a 1984 article, Alexander Gutterman summarized the evidence produced regarding this subject.[14] He writes that although few Spanish Jews migrated to Poland either before or after their expulsion from Spain,

Sephardic Jews who had been active in Poland for a shorter or longer period brought the message of progress to the Jews of Poland. Polish Jewry of the 16th and 17th centuries was still sunken in the lethargy of the Middle Ages. Its spiritual world was the Talmud, *pilpul* and halakhah, the study of Torah, fulfillment of the commandments, and the fear of God. The spirit of humanism and the Renaissance had not penetrated the walls of the ghettos. Polish Jews were completely isolated from outside spiritual influences. They paid no heed to the thinking and ways of the gentiles; in their hearts they rejected these things. The appearance in Poland of Spanish Jews, most of whom were enlightened and wealthy . . . aroused the interest and curiosity of the Polish Jews (p. 76).

The picture I have limned differs completely from Gutterman's description of Polish Jewry and the limited spheres of interest of its scholars. What does Gutterman do with Isserles and his *Torat ha-Olah?* How does he explain the obvious interest Polish sages showed in all spheres of Jewish knowledge?[15] Moreover, Gutterman ignores the direct influence of Sephardic culture on the Jews of Poland; even if one doubts their openness to the ways of the gentiles, one cannot doubt their receptivity to all aspects and subjects of Jewish creative thinking. Indeed, it is relevant to query the extent to which sixteenth-century Polish and Ashkenazic Jewry had assimilated the products of the various types of Jewish creative thought in their own creative endeavors. While we cannot yet provide a conclusive authoritative answer based on verified facts, I should like to make three short remarks and examine one issue as an example.

1. The openness which I posit was not an ongoing phenomenon in the cultural milieu of Polish and Ashkenazic Jews. It was more like an episode. The degree of openness which characterized sages such as Moses Isserles was no longer a widespread phenomenon at the end of the 1620s; only seventy years after Isserles founded his yeshiva in Cracow (1550), we witness the renewed withdrawal of the Jews of Poland (and Ashkenaz) from outside ideas. Halakhah on the one hand, and kabbalah on the other, fill their entire existence.[16]

Obviously, in the absence of a continuing tradition it is hard to expect many to truly assimilate all the new elements in their world and to transform them into innovative factors in their own thinking. One can indeed learn from both books and sages, but only a few Polish scholars of that generation had either advantage, and the opportunity to learn from sages who, in turn, had learned from sages before them was extremely rare. Thus, there was no real crystallization of schools of thought to provide fertile ground for the development of great innovators who, by a dialectic process, are linked to their predecessors. He who delves into new areas requires a base from which to spring forward. Until now research has pointed to the tendency toward creative openness in sixteenth-century Polish and Ashkenazic Jewry; I believe, however, that their writings reflect more than a mere receptivity to new possibilities, and I have tried to show that this was so.

2. The creative output of that generation clearly displays a tendency to harmonize apparently contradictory views, in keeping with the talmudic epigram "Both these and these are the words of the living God." When this tendency dominates, differences between systems and approaches are necessarily blurred. This was the case with philosophy and kabbalah. "It is known," writes Isserles, "that the ways of the kabbalist are also the ways of the true, believing philosophers."[17] Similarly one finds attempts to reconcile opposing viewpoints in other areas of philosophical interest, both in general and in particular. One may suspect this harmonizing approach of superficiality; nevertheless, it deserves attention.

3. The literature of Ashkenazic Jews of that generation was formulated in ways which appear incompatible with philosophy. (They inherited this characteristic from their ancestors and passed it on to following generations.) The modes of expression of this literature are commentary (on the Bible, aggadah, etc.), and homiletics. It is not easy to lay bare innovative material in commentary or homiletics, both because any new concepts are deeply concealed, and because these literary forms are in themselves intricate and obscure. The writers' lack of literary skills is another complicating factor. "I am not one of those who speak easily and are masters of language, my mouth speaks with impediments [based on Ex. 4:10]; I am careful about the issue, not about the words," writes Isserles in response to Luria, who reproves him for his grammatical errors. Ashkenazic literature adopted very little of the systematic Sephardic form of discussion in philosophy, kabbalah, etc. Nor is linguistic sensitivity acquired in a flash. Nonetheless, innovations were introduced into traditional commentary and homiletics, and these literary genres differed in the sixteenth century from similar writings of previous generations. Without discussing this at any length, I should like to provide an example of the change, indeed the revolution, that occurred in Ashkenazic Jewry as a result of absorbing Sephardic traditions, by referring to one of the most widely discussed topics in ethics, namely, the problem of *teshuvah* (penitence).

The problem of *teshuvah* is dealt with in the homiletical writings of the sages of the fifteenth century (a) as a problem of practical halakhah, for example, determining what one must do when one wants to repent for one's sin, and (b) as a matter of principle. But, in fact, the difference between these two approaches was not great. The guiding principle was found in the system of ḥasidei Ashkenaz that included varying applications of the thinking of the *Roke'aḥ* (R. Eleazar ben Judah of Worms) and the concepts expressed in the *Yoreh Ḥata'im*. Some sages were more strict, others more lenient; but their rulings were all based on the view of ḥasidei Ashkenaz. A significant change occurs in the sixteenth century, even though it is not immediately felt. Isserles tells of one who rode in a carriage driven by a servant of whom he was very fond. The youth rode on the horses in front, while he sat behind, in the carriage. He held a rifle which he wanted to empty of its shells by shooting into the sky. When he breached the rifle "the devil entered the bullet," which accidently hit the young coachman and killed him. Isserles did not exact full penance as set forth in the *Roke'ah*, "for the act was hardly intentional," but the penance he imposed was still rather severe: "That he wander for one full year, spending no two nights in the same place" in addition to fasting and confession. In practice, Isserles was still following the rulings of the *Roke'ah*.

In a similar case, the *Maharam* of Lublin imposed severe acts of penance, as was his custom. This was the case of an individual known to have epilepsy who, while testing his gun by shooting at the gate, mistakenly killed someone entering the yard at the moment. He came seeking penance. In view of the fact that he was known to be ill and crippled and could not wander from town to town as is required of the complete penitent, that he lived among gentiles, and that he had children to support, the *Maharam* was relatively "lenient" and limited the penitent's exile to the immediate environs, that is, to the towns of the Ukraine. Twice a week he was to go on foot to another town, flagellate himself, and confess his sins. He was also forbidden to eat meat or drink wine except on the Sabbath and festivals, to sleep with pillows and quilts on weekdays, to change his clothes or wash his hair more than once a month, to attend feasts or shave. All this, and the *Maharam* believed he was being *lenient!*

The above also reflects the practice of other halakhic scholars. However, when we look at the theoretical discussions of these sages regarding penance, we discover a new phenomenon, namely, evidence of Sephardic moral writings which strongly oppose these sages. The aforementioned R. Abraham Horowitz, author of *Brit Avraham*, the first monograph written in Poland on the problem of penitence (first edition Lublin, 1577; second edition Cracow, 1602), no longer makes lists upon lists of acts of penance for murder, marital transgressions, etc. He is clearly attempting to deal with a different tradition, "And I saw many books on the subject of worshipping God, may He be blessed, such as *Sefer Ḥovot haLevavot* by Rabbenu Baḥya ibn Paquda of blessed memory, *Sefer haYashar* by Rabbenu Tam of blessed memory, *Sha'arei Teshuvah* and *Sha'arei Yirah* by Rabbenu Yonah of blessed memory, and many other respected works [which deal with the subject of penance]."

Missing from this passage is mention of R. Eleazar ben Judah of Worms, and when we examine the entire book, we find that this is not a chance oversight. It is significant that R. Abraham Horowitz relies primarily on Sephardic authors. He does not completely ignore the Ashkenazic traditions, and later on he does mention the *Roke'ah*, but the latter's system is not particularly emphasized. In contrast, he quotes long passages from works by R. Obadiah de Busal, Isaac Aboab, Bahya, R. Judah Kaletz, R. Jonah Gerondi, and others.

This is certainly a change, but it is not entirely one directional. In *Emek Berakhah* (Cracow, 1597), one of R. Abraham Horowitz's later works dealing with blessings, prayers, and festivals, he also deals with the subject of penitence, and there we find a clear return to the familiar Ashkenazic tradition. The motivation for this shift is instructive and also somewhat paradoxical. The return to the authentic Ashkenazic tradition is apparently to be attributed indirectly to the influence of R. Elijah de Vidas, the foremost exponent of kabbalistic moral literature, who gave his approval to the systems of the *Roke'ah*.[18] This process is typical of what was happening at the end of the period, which I have already referred to as the retreat of Ashkenazic Jewry into its own world. It finds fulfillment in its own traditions even as its soul rejoices in Lurianic kabbalah; and its writings alternated between the two for a long time. There was no significant cultural development that did not affect the life of Ashkenaz Jewry and, in turn, its cultural life affected other Jewish populations. But that is another topic.

I will sum up. The type of questions that are asked reflect the questioner, and the questioner reflects his generation. My very posing of the problem derives from our contemporary experience of a division between "east" and "west" (metaphorically speaking). However, none of the sages whose works I have examined rejected any tradition *a priori*, because of its geographical origins. The test of a tradition was the extent to which it was consistent with what the spiritual leaders of the generation believed to be the message of the Torah and the tradition of the sages, and this was true even of the generations ostensibly shrouded in the darkness of the Middle Ages. Tensions did exist in the world of the spirit and creativity; sharp polemics were a common occurrence. These were not, however, a result of external factors, but emerged from within, from the confrontation between opposing spiritual approaches in a vibrant dynamic world.

NOTES

1. For complete bibliographical details of the works cited in this article, see the original Hebrew version. For information about the rabbis of the fifteenth century, see Israel J. Yuval, *Scholars in Their Time: The Religious Leadership of German Jewry in the Late Middle Ages* (Jerusalem: Magnes, 1988; Hebrew). For rabbis of the sixteenth century and the issues dealt with by students of that period, see Jacob Elbaum, *Openness and Insularity: Late Sixteenth-Century Jewish Literature in Poland and Ashkenaz* (Jerusalem: Magnes, 1990; Hebrew).

2. These include the responsa of R. Jacob Moellin Segal (known as the *Ma-*

haril; 1355–1427 or later), the first printed edition appeared in Cremona, 1557; R. Jacob Weil (died 1453), first printed edition, Venice, 1523; R. Israel Isserlein (1390–1460), the greatest sage of fifteenth-century Ashkenaz; R. Israel Bruna (1424?–1480?), the student of Weil and Isserlein; R. Moses Mintz (1424/30–1479?), who moved to Posen in 1474 and was among those who brought the scholarship of Ashkenaz to Poland.

3. Most of this literature appears in manuscript form in various compilations, including the collection of R. Benjamin Katz of Regensburg (Oxford/Bodleian no. 784); *Hiddushim u-Pesakim* of R. Seligmann Bing (Ox/Bod no. 973); the collection in Ox/Bod no. 820; etc. One can obtain a general impression from two published books which belong to this genre, *Leket Yosher* and *Sefer Maharil*. Although these works are usually considered to be books of customs, they are actually collections of *pesakim*.

4. An example of this type of literature is *Nimmukei Menahem Merseburg*.

5. In an important article entitled "The Cultural Character of Ashkenaz Jewry and its Sages in the Fourteenth and Fifteenth Centuries," *Tarbiz* 42 (1973):113–47 (Hebrew), A. Kupfer argues that "it is possible to find clear signs of an intellectual awakening and an interest in philosophy in many circles of Ashkenaz Jewry in the period under consideration." Kupfer bases himself on contemporaneous correspondence and writings. Although Joseph Dan holds that this was simply a continued consideration of the problems concerning the unity of God that had long occupied hasidei Ashkenaz, there is no doubt that such a change occurred at this point with regard to writings outside the accepted corpus of works.

(Elbaum's Hebrew article, on which this English adaptation is based, includes extensive references to books of the period under consideration and refers to the scholarly analysis thereof in various Hebrew articles and monographs.)

6. One finds references to kabbalistic works in the writings of R. Avigdor Kara (died 1439), R. Yom Tov Lipmann Muelhausen (died 1421), R. Menahem Zioni, and others.

7. The attitude of the sages of that generation to the tradition of hasidei Ashkenaz requires elaboration. The latter's influence on biblical commentaries and on prayers is clear; however, there are also interesting manifestations of their influence in the realm of theosophy. In this connection, I will mention only *Adam Sihli* (Rational Man) by R. Simon ben Samuel (c. 1400; the book was also called *Hadrat Kodesh*) that contains, in addition to commentaries based on Sephardic kabbalah, "secrets" of hasidei Ashkenaz. The book (Thuengen, 1560) also exists in manuscript form and is mentioned in writings of the sages of the fifteenth century; it has not yet been a subject of scholarly bibliographical study.

8. One example is the only comprehensive book of sermons by a contemporary sage, namely, *Hatan Damim*, by R. Zalman Ronkel, printed in Prague in 1606. The book does not record the sermons verbatim but only provides their essence; nor does it include sermons on all portions of the Torah. The above description covers the works that have been published; other works in manuscript form still require a study.

9. S. Ettinger, "The Jewish Influence on Religious Fermentation in Eastern

Europe at the End of the Fifteenth Century," *Y. Baer Jubilee Volume* (Jerusalem: The Historical Society of Israel, 1961), 228–47 (Hebrew).

10. The latter book was devoted mainly to an explanation of the kabbalistic content in Baḥya. The author also makes reference to Recanati, to Zioni, and to kabbalistic works such as the *Bahir*, the *Zohar*, *Sha'arei Orah*, and *Ozar ha-Kavod*, which were in manuscript form. He shows a particular penchant for *Sefer Yezira*.

The siddur of R. Naftali Herz Trèves (Drifzan) was printed by the author's son, R. Eliezer, who added a preface with a philosophical nuance. Based on various indications, I believe that the commentary on *birkhot hashaḥar* and *pesukei dezimrah* were also written by the son. In the second preface (inserted before the commentaries of *tefillot hayotzer*), the author cites his sources: "The pillars of the kabbalah—Rokeaḥ, Ramban, Recanati, Baḥya, Zioni, Ginat Egoz . . . and other kabbalists whose names I do not know." In addition to those mentioned in this list, his sources included commentaries of a philosophical nature by R. Zeligmann Bing, R. Samuel ibn Tibbon, and fifteenth-century rabbis such as Johanan Luria, Israel Isserlein, etc. The combination of the traditions of ḥasidei Ashkenaz and the kabbalists can also be found in the supercommentary on the commentary of Baḥya.

11. *Sefer ha-Ikkarim* served as the subject of two commentaries: *Ohel Ya'akov* (Freibourg, 1584, and Cracow, 1597) by R. Jacob b. Samuel of Brisk, a scholar who made an important contribution to Yiddish literature; and *Etz Shatul* (Venice, 1618) by R. Gedalyah Lifshitz, the nephew of the *Maharam* of Lublin.

12. As examples, one may cite the commentary on *Tractate Avot* by R. Iḥiel Michal Moraptshik (*Minḥah Ḥadashah*, Cracow, 1576), a collection of "the works of the masters," including Maimonides, Abrabanel, R. Judah Limah, R. Moses Almosnino, and R. Solomon ben Isaac Halevi. In 1554, R. Samuel de Oceda published *Midrash Samuel*, a commentary enabling readers in Ashkenaz to become more familiar with the Sephardic commentaries on *Tractate Avot*. On the subject of midrashic commentary, one may point especially to *Matanot Kehunah* by R. Issaschar Ber ben Naphtali Katz (Cracow, 1587–1588), in which the influence of Sephardic midrashic commentary and kabbalistic literature is particularly evident.

13. Other works include *Zevaḥ Pesaḥ* by Abrabanel (Bistrich, 1592–1593); shortly thereafter an abridgement was composed by R. Jacob Heilborn, a sage of a noted Italian family who migrated to Poland. It was printed in Lublin in 1604 and received the imprimatur of the Council of Four Lands. Needless to say, kabbalistic books received much attention, for kabbalah was the most appealing topic of the time. Among such works printed were: *Zohar, Zohar Ḥadash Im Midrash ha-Ne'elam; Sha'arei Orah* with a commentary by Delacrut (Cracow, 1600); the works of R. Meir ben Gabbai—*Derekh Emunah* (1577), *Avodat haKodesh* (1577–1578), *Tola'at Ya'akov* (1581), all printed in Cracow. Kabbalistic ethical works were also printed for the first time in Poland—*Reshit Ḥokhmah* by R. Eliahu de Vidas (Cracow 1592–1593), and *Toza'ot Ḥayyim*, an abridgement of the above work. (Cracow, 1600), that was printed by R. Jacob b. Isaac Luzzato of Safed who wrote an aggadic commentary entitled *Kaftor vaFeraḥ* (Basel, 1581) and had some influence on Ashkenazic writers.

14. A. Gutterman, "Spanish Jews on Polish Soil," *Pe'amim* 18(1984):53–79 (Hebrew).

15. It appears that Gutterman adopted a characteristic "intellectual" approach which talks in generalities and cliches about the "lethargy of the Middle Ages," and ignored the indirect influences of Sephardic culture on the Jews of Poland. The evidence that I have cited does not support the conclusion that Polish Jewry was isolated from all outside cultural influences, and "paid no heed to the thinking and ways of the gentiles." Ashkenaz Jews did take note of non-Jewish philosophic thinking, but not in all its overt manifestations, and they did not reach the "exalted" level of Italian Jews (Gutterman's view) in which "Judaism and humanism were tempered with openness to the non-Jewish society."

16. R. Jair Hayyim Bacharach (1638–1702), author of *Havot Ya'ir*, writes: "In earlier generations, according to what I have heard, they would study, in their youth, *Sefer haAkedah, Ikkarim, Kuzari,* and the like, because their goal was to perfect their souls, that is, their faith in the rudiments of religion." However Bacharach does not wish to return to the past and continues: "The current generation does well in staying away from those studies, for we and our children should be content to believe what we are commanded to believe without searching." On a matter to which I will refer later, he writes: "The limited study of grammar is worthwhile for any rational being . . . but one should not spend time on all the small details and on the exceptions to the rules, for knowledge of these increases confusion and is of little practical use."

17. Isserles found support in R. Moses Butril whose words, "The wisdom of the kabbalah is the wisdom of philosophy, except that they speak in two different languages," he quotes in *Torat ha-Olah*.

18. This interesting point is elaborated upon in my article "R. Abraham Horowitz on Penitence," *Studies in Jewish Mysticism, Philosophy and Ethical Literature* (Jerusalem: Magnes, 1986), 537–67 (Hebrew), and in J. Elbaum, *The Heart's Repentance and Self-Flagellation: Studies in Paths of Repentance in the Writings of the Sages of Ashkenaz and Poland 1348–1648* (Jerusalem: Magnes, 1992; Hebrew).

ABOUT THE CONTRIBUTORS

YITZHAK F. BAER (1888–1979) was born in Germany, and in 1930 was appointed professor of history at The Hebrew University of Jerusalem. A founder of the Department of Jewish History, he was the great teacher of most of the historians in Israel. His most extensive studies were dedicated to the history of the Jews under Christian rule in the Iberian peninsula, and his two volume *History of the Jews in Christian Spain* is regarded as one of the finest examples of Jewish historiography. He was one of the founders and editors of the quarterly *Zion*, dedicated to research in Jewish history, in which most of his studies were published.

GERALD J. BLIDSTEIN is professor of Jewish Thought in the Department of History, Ben Gurion University of the Negev. His studies focus mainly on the history of halakhah in ancient times and in the Middle Ages, and on the beliefs and theology of the Sages.

ROBERT BONFIL is professor of Medieval Jewish History at The Hebrew University of Jerusalem. He has published numerous articles on Jewish history and religion in medieval Europe, often comparing Jewish and non-Jewish sources in order to arrive at a balanced, historically valid understanding of the period.

JOSEPH DAN is the Gershom Scholem Professor of Kabbalah in the Department of Jewish Thought, The Hebrew University of Jerusalem. He has published extensively in Hebrew and English concerning various aspects of ancient, medieval, and modern Jewish mysticism and literature.

JACOB ELBAUM is a professor in the Department of Hebrew Literature, The Hebrew University of Jerusalem. His studies deal with the world of the Sages of talmudic times and the works of late-medieval Hebrew writers, in the fields of ethics, homiletics, and kabbalah.

WARREN ZEV HARVEY is associate professor in Medieval Jewish Philosophy in the Department of Jewish Thought, The Hebrew University of Jerusalem. His numerous studies, in Hebrew and English, cover the main aspects of Jewish philosophy in Muslim and Christian Spain.

SARA O. HELLER WILENSKY is the Wolfson Professor Emerita of Jewish Philosophy at the University of Haifa. Her numerous studies cover the key developments in Jewish philosophy and mysticism in the High Middle Ages.

YORAM JACOBSON is senior lecturer in the Department of Jewish Philosophy at Tel Aviv University. His articles and books deal with various phases in the history of Jewish mysticism, up to and including the modern Hasidic movement.

JOSÉ MARÍA MILLÁS VALLICROSA (1897–1970) was a Spanish historian who studied the history of science, as well as literature and philosophy, in medieval Spain. He translated into Spanish several Hebrew texts and wrote numerous articles and books on these subjects.

MORDECHAI PACHTER is associate professor of Jewish Thought in the Department of History at the University of Haifa. His many published studies deal with the history and ideas of kabbalistic and ethical-kabbalistic literature between the sixteenth and nineteenth centuries.

ISRAEL J. YUVAL is senior lecturer of Medieval Jewish History at The Hebrew University of Jerusalem. His studies cover the history of culture and social structures of medieval Jewry, especially in German-speaking lands.

DATE DUE

ISBN 0-2

EAN

9 780275 947774

HARDCOVER BAR CODE

Printed
in USA